LASHING AND SECURING OF DECK CARGOES

Including

Packaged Timber, Vehicles On Ro-Ro Vessels,

And

ISO Containers In Non-Purpose Built Ships

With An Introduction To The
IMO Cargo Securing Manual

By

John R. Knott
BA, FCMS, FNI, MBACS, HCMM

LASHING AND SECURING DECK CARGOES

First edition published in 1985
Second edition published in 1994
Third edition published in 2002

ISBN 1 870077 18 0

The Nautical Institute, 202 Lambeth Road, London SE1 7LQ UK
Telephone + 44 (0)20 7928 1351

©The Nautical Institute 2002

Front cover: *Marmaris I* with a mixed deck cargo, photo courtesy of Foto Flite

Printed in England by O'Sullivan Printers, Southall, Middlesex UB2 5LF

Any wire cut to length will be found to be too short.
Murphy's 95th Law

Only the foolhardy believe that a heavy cargo unit's
inertia, alone, will restrain its movement during a sea voyage.
Anderson's Aphorism

Of the 1994 Edition:

Rules, regulations and wrinkles in the safe stowage of deck cargoes would be a satisfactory alternative title for this book, which deserves to be read by everyone involved in operating ships carrying this sort of cargo, those who lash cargo on board the ship, or those people who operate in the dark far away from the sea at factory premises....There is something here for lorry drivers - who are supposed to bear some responsibility for what goes on abaft their cabs. There is ammunition aplenty for lawyers who find themselves involved in coming to a rational explanation as to why 300 tonnes of timber standards, or half a dozen containers of deadly chemicals hurled themselves bodily into the sea one dark night.... The book is well illustrated, the principles and practice being clearly explained. (Michael Grey - Lloyd's List.)

John Knott has pulled together all the advice and guidance available on securing cargoes, and The Nautical Institute has published it in a bright and accessible format. It covers the whole business, from the simple question of the correct use of bulldog grips right through to the difficult task of calculating a full lashing scheme. No sort of lash-up, it is worth every penny, if only because it has no real competitors. (FAIRPLAY International Shipping Weekly.)

IMPORTANT CAUTION

THE SUGGESTIONS AND ADVICE GIVEN IN THIS BOOK
RELATE SOLELY AND ONLY TO THE LASHING AND
SECURING OF CARGO ON WATERBORNE TRANSPORT.

THE CONTENTS OF THIS BOOK SHOULD NOT BE APPLIED
TO ANY FORM OF LIFTING EQUIPMENT, CRANES, HOISTS,
SLINGS, AND THE LIKE, WHERE MUCH MORE STRINGENT
SAFETY RULES APPLY.

WHEN CONSULTING SOME RELEVANT IMO CODES AND RULES,
SOME RELATED EUROPEAN UNION STATUTORY REGULATIONS
AND/OR ISO PUBLICATIONS, CARE SHOULD BE TAKEN NOT TO
CONFUSE THEIR USE OF THE TERMS *LASHING* OR *SECURING* OR
LASHING AND SECURING WITH OTHER NATIONAL AND
INTERNATIONAL STANDARDS AND STATUTES DEALING WITH
LIFTING SAFETY REQUIREMENTS.

This Edition is dedicated to the masters,
officers and crews of the mercantile marine
of all nations as they go down to the sea in ships,
to do business in great waters.

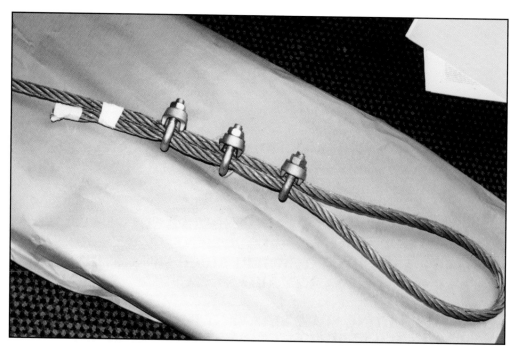

The correct way to apply bulldog-grips to make soft eyes (no thimbles) for cargo lashing purposes, only: bows (U-bars) on the back or static end, saddles (bridges) on the working part of the wire. Cut end whipped or taped before cutting. Loose end taped to working part of wire. Grips about 6 wire diameters apart, that is 96mm (roughly 3¾ ") for a 16mm diameter wire.
(For lifting purposes a minimum of 6 grips must be used.)

This is also acceptable for soft eyes. Grips correctly positioned and placed about 6 wire diameters apart, that is, 108mm (roughly 4¼ ") for an 18mm diameter wire. (Again, for lifting purposes, a minimum of 6 grips must be used.)

<u>Plate A</u>

ACKNOWLEDGEMENTS TO THE 1994 EDITION

In 1985 the Nautical Institute published the first edition of "Lashing & Securing of Deck Cargoes" as a monograph intended to provide seamen, riggers, and surveyors with practical, general and workable guidelines for dealing with an everyday marine problem. So far as it went the monograph proved useful and acceptable, but there were a number of requests to bring the text and advices in line with the then most recent recommendations and Codes of Practice, and to extend its scope to cover some specific items of deck cargo such as containers, packaged timber, and vehicles on ro-ro vessels. This turned a few handy pages into a book. Nevertheless, every effort has been made to keep things compact and easily accessible to the reader.

My acknowledgements are offered with thanks to the following:-

Julian Parker, Secretary, The Nautical Institute, for his support and enthusiasm.
Thomas Miller P. & I., of London, Managers' Agents for The United Kingdom Mutual Steam Ship Association (Bermuda) Ltd., for permission to use my earlier articles on containers and timber deck cargoes appearing originally in "Carefully to Carry", and for permission to use my latest test-bed results on bulldog-grip terminations which they financed.
The North of England Protecting & Indemnity Association Ltd., of Newcastle, for permission to use material mixed together from my earlier articles relating to hatch covers and to containers carried in non-purpose built vessels.
Bridon Ropes Ltd. (formerly British Ropes) of Doncaster, and the H.E.R. Group Ltd. of Aberdeen, for extracts from their fibre rope and wire rope data.
Coubro & Scrutton Ltd. (Securing Division), and International Lashing Systems, for the container securing component line drawings.
Dr. C. Corden, the Health & Safety Executive Research Laboratories, as reported by the Lifting Equipment Engineers Association, of Bishop's Stortford, in their Bulletin, December 1991.
Hoogovens Stevedoring Department for information relating to the measurement of roll angles.
Department of Transport Code of Practice - Safety of Loads On Vehicles : HMSO 1984, for some of their very clear drawings.
Swedish Transport Research Commission, Report 1986:6E - Securing Goods On Semi-Trailer : August 1986, for some of their excellent vehicle sketches and text.
Brian Gilbert - for turning my original sketches of wire-rope/bulldog-grip configurations in Chapter 3 into neat computer-generated drawings.
Chris McArthur - for assisting with some of the free-hand sketches in Chapter 1.
At Brookes, Bell & Co: the Partners for co-sponsoring the work of producing the book; Charles Bliault for so ably assisting with the most recent test-bed procedures; Peter McClelland for his knowledgeable input to Chapter 5 on curtain-sided trailers; Elizabeth Lloyd for typing the manuscript through several drafts and formatting the final version for the publishers; and to all my colleagues in the firm for putting up with me as the book finally got hammered into shape.

For any errors, omissions or shortcomings, the author takes full responsibility.

****

References For The First, Second and Third Editions

BS 3032: British Standards Institution 1958.

BS 3551: British Standards Institution 1962.

The Merchant Shipping (Load Line) Rules 1968: HMSO.

The Merchant Shipping (Load Line) (Deck Cargo) Regulations 1968: HMSO.

Department of Transport, Merchant Shipping Notice No.M.849, July 1978.

ISO 3075 - 1980.

BS 4942: British Standards Institution 1981.

BS 5073: British Standards Institution 1982.

Department of Transport, Merchant Shipping Notice No.M.1167, March 1985.

Department of Transport, Merchant Shipping Notice No.M.1279, June 1987.

ISO 2415 - Second Edition - 1987-04-15.

Department of Transport, Merchant Shipping Notice No.M.1346, August 1988.

Department of Transport, Merchant Shipping Notice No.M.1469, October 1991.

Code of Practice: Roll-on/Roll-off Ships - Stowage and Securing of Vehicles: HMSO 1991.

Code of Safe Practice for Ships Carrying Timber Deck Cargoes: IMO 1991.

International Convention For Safe Containers: IMO 1992.

Code of Safe Practice for Cargo Stowage and Securing (CSS): IMO 1992.

+ + + + + +

Publications Catalogue - IMO 2001-2002.

Amendments 1994/95 to the CSS 1992: IMO 1995, and the proposed Amendments to Annex 13 - 2001.

Guidelines for the Preparation of the Cargo Securing Manual: IMO 1997, and pending Amendments.

SOLAS 2000 Amendments - effective January & July 2002: IMO 2001.

SOLAS Consolidated Edition 2001: IMO 2001.

The Carriage of Cargoes Vol.1 - Instructions for the Guidance of Surveyors - MCA 1999.

ISO 9367-2:1994; BS EN 29367-2:1995; BS EN 818-2:1997.

Marine Guidance Notes issued by the UK Maritime & Coastguard Agency, including MSN 1708(M) (now superseded by MGN 107 (M)-The Merchant Shipping (Carriage of Cargoes) Regulations 1999 - and its attendant references and Appendices, including MGN 145 (M) and MGN 146 (M) of July 2000.

The Merchant Shipping (Load Line) Regulations 1998, as amended by the Merchant Shipping (Load Line) (Amendment) Regulations 2000 - MSN 1752 (M).

The INF Code - International Code for the Safe Carriage of Packaged Irradiated Nuclear Fuel, Plutonium and High-Level Radioactive Wastes on Board Ship - IMO 2001.

Code of Practice - Roll-on/Roll-off Ships - Stowage and Securing of Vehicles - 1997,and MGN 21 (M) and MGN 21 (M) both of 1998.

MSN 1705 (M) - Portable Tanks, Road Tank Vehicles (etc) for the Carriage By Sea of Liquid Dangerous Goods and Liquified Gases - MSA 1997.

Code of Safe Practice for Ships Carrying Timber Deck Cargoes - IMO 1991.

Cargo Securing Manual - Guidance Notes On Preparation - Lloyd's Register and other Classification Societies.

Various Components' Catalogues provided by Manufactures and Suppliers: (See Acknowledgements).

Draft & Part Published European Standards prEn 12195- Parts 1,2,3&4 with recent up-dates.

Code For Lifting Appliances in a Marine Environment - Lloyd's Register of Shipping - 1987.

Code of Safe Practice For The Safe Use of Lifting Equipment - L.E.E.A. - 2001.

Important Notes:

Readers should be alert to the likelihood of further Amendments to the CSS Code and the CSM Regulations following the publication of this Third Edition, and should act accordingly.

When the various European Standards relating to **lifting** and to **lashing & securing** aspects are all finally ratified, the members of the CEN - as listed hereunder - are bound to implement them and to withdraw any previous National Standards (or parts of National Standards) which are not compatible with them. To what extent this will conflict with the IMO CSS Code and the IMO Cargo Securing Manual Regulations remains to be seen.

CEN members, as of the date of publication of this book, are: Austria, Belgium, Czech Republic, Denmark, Finland, France, Germany, Greece, Iceland, Ireland, Italy, Luxemburg, Netherlands, Norway, Portugal, Spain, Sweden, Switzerland and the United Kingdom.

* *

Acknowledgements To This Third Edition

The acknowledgements to the 1994 edition still apply (although I retired from the Brookes Bell partnership in 1996) with the addition of my thanks to everyone who has used the book during the past seven years, especially to those readers who alerted me to a number of errors immediately following publication. I trust that any original errors have now been removed and new ones avoided.

Ships' officers are now swamped with paper work and their bookshelves overflow with Codes and Regulations. My sympathy goes out to them as they add to their daily burden the contents of the IMO Cargo Securing Manual. My hope is that this Third Edition of "Lashings" may ease the work-load and simplify the safe application of lashing procedures.

In assessing the most efficient way to up-date this Third Edition, my thanks to C. Julian Parker - long-time Secretary, to June Miller, Publications Manager, and Brian Bailey, Technical Secretary, all of The Nautical Institute - Julian for his well-considered comments, guidance and continuing support to push ahead with publication, notwithstanding the delay in the much-needed further amendments to the IMO CSS Code and the IMO Cargo Securing Manual Regulations; to June and Brian for their assessment in combining the previous and present texts; and to Jim Judd and Graham Draper who kindly computer-enhanced my drawings at Figs. X2, X3 & X4 of the **INTRODUCTION** and the single page line drawing of packaged timber in Chapter 4. I am also indebted to Julian for kindly agreeing to write the **Foreword** to this Third Edition.

On-going casualty experience has underlined the need for some additional comments on the carriage and securing of packaged timber deck cargoes in Chapter 4. In this connection, my thanks to the "Carefully to Carry" Committee, to "Fairplay International - Solutions" and to the International Institute of Marine Surveyors for permission to use and to modify the texts of articles of which I was the author and which they have published during the past six years. A new Addendum 5 provides a Table of Breaking Strengths and MSL's, and a new Addendum 6 illustrates a "short form" for calculating the approximate weight of cargo loaded/discharged, with particular reference to timber deck cargoes and stability factors.

In the event, quite extensive parts of the body of the original text have been amended, although most of the advice given earlier is as valid today as then. A detailed and most important **INTRODUCTION** ahead of Chapter 1 considers the implications and applications of the 1994/1995 Amendments to the IMO 1992 Code of Safe Practice for Cargo Stowage and Securing, and of the Cargo Securing Manual Regulations which became mandatory on 1st January 1998, together with later Amendments. Some of the implications of the new European Standards as they apply to the securing of cargoes on ship-borne vehicles are also assessed.

My gratitude to the manufacturers and suppliers who responded to my questionnaires over a period of more than five years, who provided equipment catalogues and did not withhold permission to reproduce parts thereof within the book: SpanSet Ltd., Coubro & Scrutton Ltd., Wood & Clark Ltd., the MacGregor-Conver Group, the Crosby Group Inc, Carl Stahl Ltd., and Roberts Forge-Lift Ltd. Solicitors and P & I Clubs unearthed colour prints of my relevant photographs lost and/or mislaid since 1994 but retained within original reports in their own archives.

To the individuals throughout the industry who provided support and much-valued information as I attempted to make sense, on behalf of ships' officers, of the arcane, frequently confusing, and ever-rising mounds of regulatory documentation relating to *lashing, securing,* and *lifting* requirements in a marine environment: Stuart Everitt, Technical Operations Manager, Carl Stahl Ltd; David Whittaker, Lloyd's Register of Shipping; Peter Rose, U.K.MCA; Mr.E. Wiese, Rudolph Seldis, Hamburg; Michael Bradney, Bradney Chain & Engineering Co. Ltd; Derrick Bailes, of the L.E.E.A; Stephen Read, of the BSI; Captain G. Scott-Morris of ICHCA; and specially to Charles Bliault, FCMS, Partner, Brookes Bell Jarrett Kirman, Mr. G. Cairns, Managing Director of Wood & Clark Ltd., and Captain Geoffrey Sowter, FNI, Marine & Industrial Consultant, whose access to so many technical committees prevented the formation of otherwise unbreachable log-jams in the exchange and flow of technical information.

Ex-colleagues and staff at the Brookes Bell Jarrett Kirman Partnership allowed me access to their archives and library, and the use of their reducing photocopying machines for the sizing of my drawings. Their overall assistance was invaluable Finally, my continuing thanks to my wife, Sylvia, without whose help and word-processor skills this Third Edition would never have seen the printers, and to Richard, our 13-year old son, whose computer literacy was called upon frequently to unscramble the tendencies of computers to go 'walk-about'.

John R. Knott - Liverpool - January 2002.

FOREWORD TO THE 1994 EDITION

It is essential that deck cargo is properly and effectively lashed and secured. This book by John Knott tells how.

The first edition was published as a monograph by The Nautical Institute in 1985, and included the basics in respect of lashing and securing. The 1994 book has been a long time in preparation, but it is my view all the work has been worth it! All aspects of the subject are covered, from the types of materials, equipment, and fittings which can be used variously for the securing of drums, through containers and timber, to large heavy-lift items, to the calculations which are involved. There is even an addendum of conversion factors. The text includes a mixture of good seamanship practice, extracts from relevant IMO Codes of Practice and legislation, with experience which John has gained during many years of work overseeing the proper securing of cargoes at the beginning of voyages, putting it right when things have gone slightly wrong, and investigating disasters after they have happened.

The understanding of a certain amount of mathematics and mechanics, and a spattering of physics, is very important if securing arrangements are to be set up correctly and efficiently; this publication takes the reader carefully through all the calculations, with diagrams where necessary. Such aspects as ship stability and roll period are also covered, and how they affect the vessel, her motion, and, of course, the cargo which is stowed on deck. To help with the understanding of the subject are many very detailed diagrams and sketches and numerous photographs which show how not to do it, as well as how lashing and securing should be done.

Bills of lading covering items of cargo which are carried on deck are usually claused "at shippers' risk". This, of course, does not mean that the master of the vessel need not see to it that the items involved are properly stowed and secured, bearing in mind the intended voyage, and kept so throughout that voyage to destination. On the contrary, the master must carefully carry the cargo. This book is more thorough and all-encompassing than any other work on the subject, and will become, I am sure, essential reading for all those involved - masters of deck cargo-carrying vessels, and those ashore, including shipowners, securing contractors, stevedores, and surveyors, and, not to forget, marine lawyers.

`Cost' is always on the mind of shippers and shipowners alike. If done properly and effectively, lashing and securing of deck cargo need not be extortionate. Things only become expensive when the work is not done correctly and things go wrong - ports of refuge can cost a lot!

Having worked with John Knott for a number of years, and having learned a great deal from him, it gives me great pleasure to write the foreword to this book, which will, I hope, in the long term, provide the shipping industry with the necessary information to reduce the risk of a shift or loss of deck cargo, and thereby reduce claims.

Charles Bliault - Liverpool - April 1994.

****

FOREWORD TO THIS THIRD EDITION

There are few activities which are more difficult to judge when sitting at a desk on dry land than trying to imagine the forces at work on a ship in a seaway. It is a fact that, in many companies operating on regular trades, the lashing and securing of deck cargoes can become a matter of trial and error. If deck cargo is lost overboard during one voyage, only then will extra lashings be provided to prevent a similar occurrence during subsequent voyages. Whilst trial and error may be one way at arriving at a solution, it is not a professional way to safeguard other people's property.

This is a book for seamen, surveyors, superintendents, riggers, contractors, supercargoes, maritime cargo operators, marine lawyers and arbitrators. All aspects are covered, including lashing materials, timber deck cargoes, general cargoes, vehicles on ro-ro vessels, ISO containers on non-purpose built ships, costings, conversion factors, safe welding procedures, and more.

There are various aspects which need to be addressed. For example, a new problem facing a master or loading superintendent, such as the opportunity to carry a power boat on top of a stack of containers. Alternatively, there is the situation where deck cargoes are being carried regularly, as in timber trades, where the lashings need to be fit for purpose, not too much which would be costly and not too little which would be inadequate.

Not all voyages are the same and the shipmaster can exercise some discretion in the course and speed steered to minimise motions and avoid green water on deck. There are other variables to consider. For instance, there is an environmental sensitivity of many deck cargoes particularly chemicals, and there can be extreme economic consequences if a critical section of plant is lost or damaged and fails to meet a just-in-time delivery.

Those responsible for cargo securing must have a fundamental knowledge of the breaking strain and extension of lashing systems under different loads. They must know how to provide tension to pick up this slack and they must be aware of the strength needed in deck fittings to hold the cargo in place adequately to withstand dynamic surge loadings. The distribution of weight on deck, the dunnage and chafing all add further complications to an already complex operation.

Lashing and Securing of Deck Cargoes by John Knott is the definitive guide on this subject. It is essential that all who are engaged in the transport of goods on deck understand the fundamental principles of ship movements and acceleration. These have to be applied to the mass and shape of the deck cargo according to its position on board. The book has that essential feel of good seamanship. The theoretical calculations start with the forces generated when a vessel moves in a seaway. This is the real world of seafaring and not the imaginary scenario so beloved of stevedores and charterers all anxious to save money based upon the static situation found in port. Wisdom also comes into it, as ships in heavy weather are exposed to wind and breaking seas which can significantly add to the forces needed to properly secure the deck cargo for a sea voyage. The book embraces these seamanlike precautions and is derived from the experienced awareness of a life-time's work advising shippers and shipowners on correct applications and attending court enquiries when accidents have occurred. Shipping is fortunate to have this valuable resource at its disposal. A comprehensive index rounds off the book

C. Julian Parker, Secretary, The Nautical Institute.
London, December 2001.

****

CONTENTS

Colour Plates J, K and L - at end of Chapter 6

Chapter 7 - Lashing Costs & Miscellaneous Information

Addenda

****

Preamble To The INTRODUCTION To The CSM Regulations

The IMO "Guidelines For The Preparation of the Cargo Securing Manual, 1997" (IMO-298E), are worded in very general terms permitting a rather broad interpretation by whichever Administration may attempt to apply them. Depending upon the type of vessel under consideration, the appropriate CSM will include the CSS Code and its Amendments and some or all of the various Codes of Safe Practice for particular cargoes. The responsibility for producing a CSM resides with the shipowner but, because the "Guidelines" booklet is insufficient in detail, the shipowner (or his appointed surveyor) will not know if his efforts have been successful until they are presented to, and possibly rejected by, the local Administration, even when prepared in line with Classification Society "Guides" literature, and even though an Administration officer is not required to visit the ship. In the U.K., an expanded text is available in Volume 1 - Instructions to Surveyors, MCA 1999, but even this leaves a lot to be desired by way of specific detail.

The IMO should, as a matter of urgency, prepare detailed guidelines with a full and acceptable format set out in clear, non-open-ended terms, capable of being followed and implemented without difficulty or ambiguity by shipowners technical staff and properly appointed non-Administration surveyors.

****

INTRODUCTION TO THE
IMO CARGO SECURING MANUAL

GENERAL

Regulations VI/5 and VII/6 of the 1974 SOLAS Convention require cargo units and cargo transport units to be loaded, stowed and secured throughout the voyage in accordance with a Cargo Securing Manual (CSM) approved by the Administration and drawn up to a standard at least equivalent to the guidelines developed by the International Maritime Organisation (IMO).

The guidelines, which originally were based on the provisions contained in various MSC/Circulars, have been expanded to take into account the provisions of the Code of Safe Practice for Cargo Stowage and Securing (CSS Code), the Amendments to that Code, the Code of Safe Practice for Ships Carrying Timber Deck Cargoes, and the Codes and Guidelines for Ro-Ro vessels, Grain Cargoes, Containers and Container vessels, and ships carrying Nuclear Waste and similar Radio-active products. Such individual publications are subject to amendments which need to be carried into the appropriate section of the Cargo Securing Manual as they occur.

Member Governments were invited to bring the Guidelines to the attention of all parties concerned, with the aim of having Cargo Securing Manuals prepared and on board all vessels, other than dedicated bulk solid, bulk liquid, and gas-carrying vessels, not later than 31st December 1997. Hence, as from 1st January 1998, it is a mandatory Regulation for all vessels, other than exempted vessels, to have on board an approved and up-to-date Cargo Securing Manual. Some Administrations may exempt certain cargo-carrying ships of less than 500 gross tons and certain very specialised ships, but such exemption should not be assumed in the absence of a formal exemption certificate.

It is a mandatory requirement for masters and ships' officers to be conversant with the CSM, to understand its application for the vessel in which they are serving, and to be capable of deploying correctly the hardware which goes with it. All securing of cargo units shall be completed before the ship leaves the berth. The CSM and its associated hardware are subject to Port State Control inspection. Violation of the CSM requirements may give rise to vessel detention and/or prosecution of the master and owners.

COMMENTS

The CSS Code and CSM Regulations and their Amendments contain much sound and well-tried advice, and should not be treated lightly. There are, however, a number of anomalies, and in some instances the applied text is difficult to reconcile with safe practice and sound seamanship. It is hoped that these shortcomings may be rectified by future Amendments. In the meantime, the following suggestions may be found useful by ships' officers, loading superintendents, supercargoes, surveyors, and the like, and will be referred to at various places in the main text of the book.

A. Lashing Strength Calculations.

The CSM's I have seen include the Chapter 3, 1994/1995 and 1997 Amendments, to the CSS Code, wherein Section 7 deals with the **Advanced Calculation Method** for strength of securing elements. For professional consultants involved with the forward planning and securing of specific deck cargoes, such method may be appropriate - despite its very obvious shortcomings. For the ship's officer, supercargo or surveyor, however, faced with a deck cargo comprising one or more widely different items, a workable rule-of-thumb will be acceptable, and is provided for at Section 6 of the CSS Code Amendments. And here arises the first of several anomalies.

The Rule-Of-Thumb Method given in Section 6 of the current CSS Code Amendments indicates that the MSL (Maximum Securing Load) values of the securing devices on each side of a cargo unit (port as well as starboard) should equal the weight of the unit, and a proposed amendment to Table 1 in Section 4 now provides MSL's as hereunder:

Table 1 -Determination of MSL from breaking strength

Material	MSL
Shackles, rings, deckeyes, turnbuckles of mild steel	50% of breaking strength
Fibre rope	33% of breaking strength
Wire rope (single use)	80% of breaking strength
Web lashing	50% of breaking strength (was 70%)
Wire rope (re-useable)	30% of breaking strength
Steel band (single use)	70% of breaking strength
Chains	50% of breaking strength

"For particular securing devices (e.g. fibre straps with tensioners or special equipment for securing containers), a permissible working load may be prescribed and marked by authority. This should be taken as the MSL. When the components of a lashing device are connected in series (for example, a wire to a shackle to a deckeye), the minimum MSL in the series shall apply to that device."

Say that a cargo unit of 18 tonnes mass is to be secured using only shackles, web lashings, chains and turnbuckles - all MSL's of 50% breaking strength (BS). The unit will require 18 tonnef MSL on each side, namely, 36 tonnef total MSL (72 tonnef BS for these items), representing a **total lashing breaking strength to cargo mass** ratio of 72/18 = **4.**

Secure the same cargo unit with steel band, only. Total MSL required will still be 36 tonnef (72 tonnef BS) but the MSL of steel band is nominated as 70% of its breaking strength - so this gives a total lashing breaking strength of (36x100)/70 = 51.42 tonnef, representing a **a total lashing breaking strength** to **cargo mass** ratio of 51.42/18 = **2.86.**

Do the calculation using wire rope, re-useable, and the answer is (36x100)/30 = 120 tonnef: ratio 120/18 = **6.67.** For wire rope, single use, the answer is (36x100)/80 = 45 tonnef: ratio 45/18 = **2.5**, and for fibre rope the ratio is **6**. And these ratios (or multipliers) remain constant for equal cargo mass. (If you do the same calculations using, say, 27 tonnes and 264 tonnes cargo mass, you will finish up with the same **4, 2.86, 6.67, 2.5 & 6** ratios (or multipliers). If a component was assigned a 66⅔% MSL the result would be a ratio of **3** - the *three-times rule* multiplier.

What the CSS Code is doing here is changing the seaman's commonly-held approach and understanding of the term 'rule-of-thumb' - a single multiplier easy to use and general in application - by inserting, at an intermediate stage, a step in the calculation otherwise entirely foreign to the concept of the 'rule-of-thumb', ie, the MSL percentages, to produce a range of rule-of-thumb multipliers. I consider this to be confusing and irrational. If five different types of components each have identical breaking strengths (or nominal break loads - NBL's) independent of their make-up, their size, shape or durability, why apply a different rule-of-thumb multiplier when it should be the equivalence of the **breaking strength** which is the critical governing aspect?

Just to labour the point. If the cargo mass to be secured was 18 tonnes, and we use the five results obtained by using Sections 4 & 6 of the Code, the total lashing breaking strength required in each instance would be:- 72 tonnef, or 51.48 tonnef, or 120.06 tonnef or 45 tonnef or 108 tonnef - and to me that seems plain daft!

If you have followed the foregoing assessment, and I hope you will test its arithmetic rather than take it on trust, you will appreciate that one way of partly rationalising this 'enigma' is to create an additional column on the right-hand side of the MSL Table 1, as shown hereunder:-

Table 1a -Determination of MSL from breaking strength, including Rule-of-Thumb multipliers.

Material	MSL	R.O.T. MULTIPLIER
Shackles, rings, deckeyes, turnbuckles of mild steel	50% of breaking strength	4.00
Fibre rope	33% of breaking strength	6.06
Wire rope (single use)	80% of breaking strength	2.50
Web lashing	50% of breaking strength (was 70%)	4.00
Wire rope re-useable)	30% of breaking strength	6.67
Steel band (single use)	70% of breaking strength	2.86
Chains	50% of breaking strength	4.00
(Compare with overall general component)	*(66⅔% of breaking strength)*	*(3.00)*

By looking at this Table 1a - and in respect of any cargo mass - you can use the multipliers without going through all the calculations required by the Sections 4 & 6 route and, more importantly, you will be able to see clearly the extent to which the MSL multipliers degrade or upgrade the generally accepted *three-times-rule* - not on the basis of strength of components - but on type. I have seen the arguments in favour of these variable rule-of-thumb multipliers, but I am not convinced that they are anything other than unnecessarily confusing.

In the First and Second Editions of "Lashing and Securing of Deck Cargoes" I advocated the *three-times-rule* - and I do so again in this Third Edition - where the **total breaking strength** to **cargo mass** ratio is **3** when GM's are not large and roll periods are 13 seconds or more. I see no reason to change that recommendation *with all the safety and sound seamanship provisions that go with it elsewhere herein*. In the instance of the 18 tonne cargo unit given above, the lashings total breaking strength would be 54 tonnef when the three-times-rule is applied. Simply 18x3=54 tonnef total BS, that is:-

Cargo Mass x Rule Number = Lashings Total Breaking Strength.

B. Tables 3 and 4.
Section 7 of the CSS Code Amendments provides Tables 2, 3 & 4 to the application of the **Advanced Calculation Method.** Now, while I advocate the *three-times-rule* rule-of-thumb as adequate, I always recommended a little extra where GM's are large and roll-periods are less than 13 seconds, and Tables 3 and 4, as shown reproduced on the following page, provide a measured way of applying that extra strength.

Table 3 - Correction factors for length and speed

Length (m) Speed (kn)	50	60	70	80	90	100	120	140	160	180	200
9	1.20	1.09	1.00	0.92	0.85	0.79	0.70	0.63	0.57	0.53	0.49
12	1.34	1.22	1.12	1.03	0.96	0.90	0.79	0.72	0.65	0.60	0.56
15	1.49	1.36	1.24	1.15	1.07	1.00	0.89	0.80	0.73	0.68	0.63
18	1.64	1.49	1.37	1.27	1.18	1.10	0.98	0.89	0.82	0.76	0.71
21	1.78	1.62	1.49	1.38	1.29	1.21	1.08	0.98	0.90	0.83	0.78
24	1.93	1,76	1.62	1.50	1.40	1.31	1.17	1.07	0.98	0.91	0.85

Table 4 - Correction factors for B/GM < 13

B/GM	7	8	9	10	11	12	13 or above
on deck, high	1.56	1.40	1.27	1.19	1.11	1.05	1.00
on deck, low	1.42	1.30	1.21	1.14	1.09	1.04	1.00
'tween deck	1.26	1.19	1.14	1.09	1.06	1.03	1.00
lower hold	1.15	1.12	1.09	1.06	1.04	1.02	1.00

NOTE: The datum point in Table 3 is length of ship 100m, speed of ship 15 knots and, in Table 4, B/GM = 13.

Again, however, a word of caution. I would firmly recommend ships' officers to ignore in Table 3 any correction factor less than 1, and I have shaded them above. For all those values less than 1 let the rule-of-thumb calculation stand on its own. **Only apply Table 3 factors when the values are greater than 1.** This way you will never compromise the safety of the *three-times-rule* or any other rule-of-thumb you may care to use.

Table 4 is a useful aid, the application of which I would encourage when using rules-of-thumb although, personally, I am not happy with the B/GM approach. Dividing metres into metres produces a dimensionless ratio which must not be confused with rolling period, a phenomenon which is expressed in the "time" dimension of seconds. Table 4 may appear to be easy to apply but, in my opinion, the *correction factor* would have been more in line with well-used general principles if the Table had been headed *"Correction factors for Rolling Period < 13 seconds"* and the tabular results adjusted accordingly, rather than produce yet another change in principle.

C. Safety Factor (Section 5 of the current CSS Amendments says, and I quote):

"**5   Safety Factor**

Within the assessment of a securing arrangement by a calculated balance of forces and moments, the calculated strength (CS) of securing devices should be reduced against MSL, using a safety factor of 1.5, as follows:

$$CS = \frac{MSL}{1.5}$$

The reasons for this reduction are the possibility of uneven distribution of forces among the devices, strength reduction due to poor assembly and others.
Notwithstanding the introduction of such safety factor, care should be taken to use securing elements of similar material and length in order to provide a uniform elastic behaviour within the arrangement."

e, including myself, were puzzled by that expression CS=MSL/1.5 appearing where it did because the phrase *calculated strength* appeared to have no direct relationship to the 2, 3 & 4 preceding it, nor did it sit easily with any attempt to apply it to Section 6 which More than 100 circulars were sent out on a world-wide basis - including to the IMO, the United Kingdom MCA, some Classification Societies, and many other interests and organisations - requesting some enlightenment on the question. Several replies were received by fax, by e-mail, by telephone and by direct conversation, including most helpful communications from the IMO in London and Bremen; and latterly from the U.K. MCA. The Classification Societies, and other certifying authorities responsible for approving CSM's issued to date all kept their heads down.

It can now be stated with some authority that Section 5 (other than the third paragraph thereof) and its CS=MSL/1.5 expression **does not relate to, nor should any attempt ever be made to apply it to, Section 6 or any other rule-of-thumb,** other than the admonition in the third paragraph relating to securing elements of similar material and length.

Section 5 and its CS=MSL/1.5 are wrongly placed in the text. They relate to the **Advanced Calculation Method** illustrated in Section 7. To make sense of Section 5 there is currently a proposed amendment to Annex 13 indicating that the expression should be re-sited under paragraph **7.2.1.** In Section 7 *calculated strength* is used within a set calculation method, and it is in that sense and in that context that *calculated strength (CS)* should be applied. So, unless you are involved with a full **Advanced Calculation Method,** just ignore CS=MSL/1.5. Also, it appears that the phrase in English - *calculated strength* - is a slight mistranslation from the original German text where the phrase used is *calculation strength* in keeping with the Section 7 heading - **Advanced Calculation Method** which is, itself, also under review. Readers should be alert to the likely soon promulgation of formal Amendments to these aspects and act accordingly.

D. The CSS Code

I here show **Figure 2** from page 29 of the CSS Code, a figure which is also shown on pages 23 and 25. Such illustrations are reproduced in the Cargo Securing Manuals I have sighted without amendment, and also in other publications dedicated to the safe carriage of cargo. I do not agree that the securing method there illustrated is "safe" or reasonable, and I would like to know who gave to it the IMO accreditation of "preferred method"?

"**8.2** Lashings attached to items without securing points should pass around the item, or a rigid part thereof, and both ends of the lashing should be secured to the same side of the unit (figure 2)."

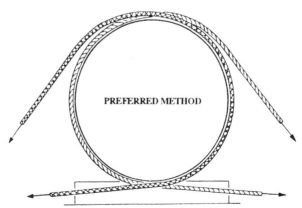

PREFERRED METHOD

Figure 2 - *Principle of securing heavy items having no suitable securing points.*

On the next two pages I illustrate - at Fig. X1 how the Code's drawing is interpreted by some of its users; at Fig.X2 how those lashings would look when applied to a cylinder in that fashion; at Fig.X3 the consequential result of just one such lashing failing; and at Fig.X4 an alternative and, I believe, a better method of using those lashings.

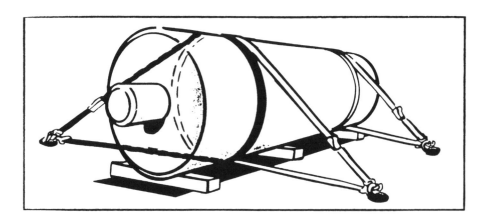

Fig. X1 - From the Swedish Club's publication "Securing of Cargo for Sea Transportation" 1996.

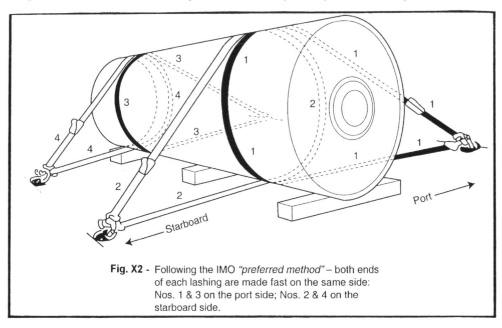

Fig. X2 - Following the IMO *"preferred method"* – both ends of each lashing are made fast on the same side: Nos. 1 & 3 on the port side; Nos. 2 & 4 on the starboard side.

Line drawings computer-enhanced: Jim Judd & Graham Draper

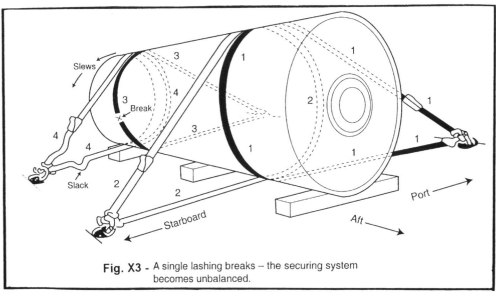

Fig. X3 - A single lashing breaks – the securing system becomes unbalanced.

In Fig.X3, for example, I indicate that lashing No.3 has broken. Lashing No.4 then goes slack and there is nothing to check the forward end of the cylinder (in my sketch) from swinging and slewing to starboard (in my sketch); and that slewing effect will be added to by the pull exerted by the port side/aft end lashing No.1. In effect, once a single lashing component fails the securing system becomes unbalanced and the cargo item becomes susceptible to loss overboard.

An alternative and more efficient method is shown in Fig.X4. Shaped timber wedge chocks nailed securely to each side of each transverse bearer, in contact with the round of the cylinder, should be considered an essential feature to resist any tendency to roll. The lashings pass circumferentially around the cylinder and cross over the upper surface/under the lower surface in pairs. From this it follows that even if one lashing component fails the securing system remains in balance, still secured against slewing and with no tendency for the other lashings to go slack or to operate to defeat the system. I should add that, depending upon the length and weight of the cylinder, I would probably apply a pair of similar lashings at mid-length.

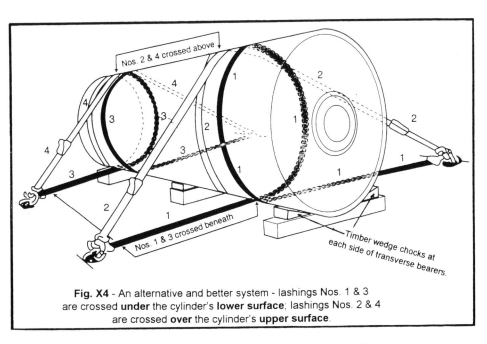

Fig. X4 - An alternative and better system - lashings Nos. 1 & 3 are crossed **under** the cylinder's **lower surface**; lashings Nos. 2 & 4 are crossed **over** the cylinder's **upper surface**.

Line drawing computer-enhanced: Jim Judd & Graham Draper

The proposed amendment to Annex 13 will, I believe, attempt to exclude the application of the Fig.X4 method on the grounds, apparently, that the frictional forces involved cannot be evaluated, an assessment which fails to consider adequately the need for a "balanced system" and the fact that a numerical assessment of the frictional forces is here not only unnecessary, it is irrelevant in the context of securing such cargo where the application of an adequate rule-of-thumb and a sensible disposition of the correct strength lashing components - webbing, wire, chain or strapping - is the critical requirement.

The principle of the system indicated in Fig.X4 was advocated and illustrated in this book's First and Second Editions, and is recommended again in this Third Edition in Chapter 3, Fig. 3.44.

It is difficult to comprehend how the method of securing cylinders - as illustrated in the IMO Code of Safe Practice - could have been proposed and accepted as a "preferred method" when such method is critically faulty, with a built-in failure factor. The irony of the situation resides in the fact that many approving authorities continue to reproduce the IMO "preferred method" without any cautionary comments.

Worse still, because the "preferred method" forms part of the CSS Code it is carried through automatically into the statutory obligations required by the Cargo Securing Manual and, currently, is likely to be included as the "preferred method" in the European Standard CEN prEN 12195-1 unless urgent steps are taken to amend it.

E. Containers On Deck

Page 17 of the CSS Code, as carried through to the CSM, illustrates at **Method B** a system of foot-chocking Containers on the weather-deck of a non-purpose-built vessel, as shown hereunder.

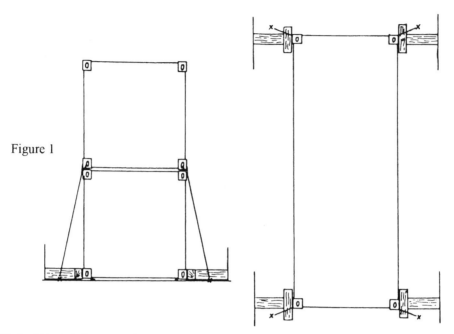

Figure 1

Method B - *Medium-weight containers: weight of top container may be more than 70% of that of bottom container - (figure 1)*

The associated text on the Code's facing page 16 says, and I quote: *"2.2 Containers should be secured using one of the three methods recommended in figure 1 or methods equivalent thereto."* In my view, Method **B** as illustrated on the Code's page 17 may suffice in calm weather, but in adverse sea conditions such chocks will be shocked loose or washed away leaving bottom corner castings without restraint. This is not theory - it is a fact - and lack of adequate foot-chocking has contributed to several instances of stack failures of deck-stowed Containers in non-purpose-built ships. Timber foot chocks require very positive securing arrangements, some examples of which are illustrated in Chapter 6 of this book.

F. The Code of Safe Practice For Ships Carrying Timber Deck Cargoes, 1991.

This Code is also carried bodily into the Cargo Securing Manual, and hereunder I have reproduced Figures 12 & 13 from Appendix A.

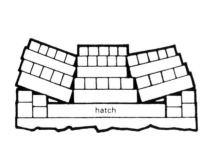

Figure 12

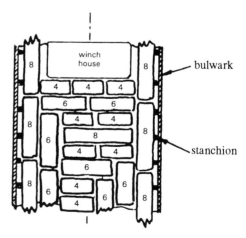

Figure 13

Figure 13 is congruent with its respective text, but Figure 12 is in conflict with paragraph **2.8** of Appendix A, and no master or stevedore superintendent would contemplate attempting to stow four tiers of packaged timber canted steeply inboard as illustrated in Figure 12. This Figure 12 was not part of the 1974 Timber Code, and appears to have got into the 1991 Code by default.

Figure 13 clearly illustrates - and sensibly so - that outboard wing packages **must** be stowed fore-and-aft. Chapter 4 of the Code also makes it clear that each package shall be secured by **at least** two transverse lashings which shall be spaced not more than 3m apart for heights not exceeding 4m, and not more than 1.5m apart for heights above 4m. When packages in the outer wing stow are of lengths less than 3.6m the spacing of the lashings should be reduced as necessary.

However, if non-adjacent tiers are stowed **athwartships** to the far outer wings - as illustrated in Figure 12 - the intent of Chapter 4 is frustrated, because the ends of no more than the odd random package will be "caught" by any lashing. The result, when the vessel is rolling in the seaway, is that **athwartship** packages stowed to the far outer wings literally "pop out" of the stow and go overboard with consequential collapse of otherwise tight securing arrangements and the loss of other packages. In my view, Figure 12 should be removed from the Code by a suitable amendment. More on Timber Deck Cargoes in Chapter 4 and colour plates **H** and **L** of this book.

G. Breaking Strengths

How do you define *breaking strength*? Is it when the component reaches its first yield point or its second yield point; when it first starts to crack or when one or more of its parts physically separates? There are probably more than a dozen acceptable definitions for *breaking strength*, all of them valid in their own contexts. Within the CSS Code and the CSM Regulations the phrase is currently not specifically defined. However, as I understand it within the context of those two documents, the phrase *breaking strength* shall mean *the point at which the component, material or element can no longer support or sustain the load*. What follows hereunder may prove to be very boring to read but, if you can wade your way through it, some of the practical problems of applying the requirements of the CSM may be made a little less complex, pending some possible amendments by the IMO.

For the statutory requirements relating to **lifting gear** manufacturers are required to state the **safe working load (SWL)** or **working load limit (WLL)** of the component and its relation to the **proof load** as defined by whatever Standard the component is supposed to meet; but, because *breaking strength* can mean different things in different contexts, manufacturers of **lifting gear** are not generally required to state the *breaking strength,* although they must work to it. For instance, in some Grades of shackles and chains and the like, the **SWL/WLL** may vary from one-sixth to one-third of the *nominal breaking strength*, with the **proof load** usually twice the **SWL,** but in the manufacturers'/suppliers' catalogues the *breaking strength* will not necessarily be stated - only the **SWL** or **WLL** and the **proof load.**

The ISO 2415 Standard for Grade 6 shackles, for instance (excluding anchor shackles and other special applications) may be thought of as the 1:2:4 standard, where if *minimum ultimate strength* equals 100%, then **SWL** is 25% and **proof load** is 50% of that *minimum ultimate strength*. On the other hand, BS 3032 for Grade 6 shackles (recently superseded, but most commonly seen in component catalogues) and other current ISO Standards most often encountered, work to a scale of 1:2:5, where if *minimum breaking force* equals 100%, then SWL is 20% and **manufacturing proof load** will be 40%. The CEN/EU Standard for Grade 6 shackles will also be 1:2:5, and possibly is, by the time this Edition is published. In the new Addendum 5 at the end of this book, I have used the 1:2:5 principle in the Tables of applicable MSL's for shackles.

Notice that **proof load** is twice the **SWL** in each instance, even though the SWL/Breaking Strength ratio is not the same in each instance. The proof load-twice-the-SWL tends to be the general rule whatever the SWL/Breaking Strength ratio, but there are variations and it can be confusing.(Grade 8 chain, for instance, complies with the 1:2½:4 standard, where if *breaking force* is 100%, then **SWL/WLL** is 25% and **proof load** is 62½% of *breaking force*, respectively.). Similar considerations relate to lifting rings, and the like. Are you with me?

The point of all the foregoing is that many standards quoted relate to high tensile or higher tensile steel components for **lifting** purposes and on which the SWL or WLL must be permanently stamped. The CSS Code, on the other hand, defines the values of Maximum Securing Loads (MSL) of such **mild steel** components for **securing** purposes as 50% of breaking strength (see Table 1 at page **xvi**, earlier herein). The 1997 Amendments to the CSM require such components *inter alia* to have "***Identification marking**", "***Strength test result or ultimate tensile strength result**" and "***Maximum Securing Load (MSL)**", all to be supplied by the manufacturer/supplier with information as to individual uses, and/strengths/MSL values to be given in kN - kiloNewtons. (To convert kN to tonnes force (tonnef) - multiply by 0.1019761, or for a rough value, divide by 10). (See, also, Tables of Conversion Factors at Addendum 1 of this book.)

The CSS Code 1994/95 Amendments say: *"**Maximum securing load** is to securing devices as **safe working load** is to lifting tackle."* And Appendix 1 of the 1997 Amendments to the CSM says: *"**Maximum securing load (MSL)** is a term used to define the allowable load capacity for a device used to secure cargo to a ship. **Safe working load (SWL)** may be substituted for MSL for securing purposes, provided this is equal to or exceeds the strength defined by MSL."* This latter definition is included in the proposed amendment to Annex 13 of the CSS Code. (Are you still with me?)

There are difficulties likely to result from this mix of terms. Firstly, imagine that the components available on board or in a distant port are of the stamp-marked approved *lifting* type, and say that the MSL required for the cargo item requires *securing* components of 10 tonnes breaking strength, ie, 5 tonnes MSL, but you don't know the breaking strength of the *lifting* components. The CSM says you must use the SWL (or WLL) as the MSL, but a *lifting* component with a 5 tonnes SWL will likely have a proof load of 10 tonnes and a breaking strength of 4 or 5 times the SWL - 20 or 25 tonnes - twice or more times the breaking strength required by the 5 tonnes MSL, but that is what you will have to use if you follow the CSM. In effect, you will be using for *securing purposes* a component at least twice as large, in terms of breaking strength, as you require.

Secondly, say you **know** the breaking strengths of the *lifting* components available. Could you take, for instance, a shackle stamp-marked SWL 2 tonnes as equivalent to a 5 tonnes MSL? I cannot see any reason why not were it not for yet another difficulty.

A *lifting* component of 10 tonnes breaking strength, stamp-marked for 2 tonnes SWL, will most likely have a proof load of 4 or 5 tonnes; so if you use that component to half its breaking strength of 5 tonnes you will equal or exceed the proof load, in which circumstance it would be foolhardy and highly unsafe to return that component to any use involving *lifting*!

Over the past five years I have corresponded world-wide with manufacturers/suppliers to the marine industry of chains, shackles, turnbuckles, and the like. Currently, they do not apply **MSL identification** direct to their components. They are equally averse to identifying SWL or WLL in kN. It seems they prefer to keep to "tonnes" in the sense of "tonnef" or "tonnes force", and only in relation to SWL's, WLL's and Proof Loads. All this makes me query the validity of the Cargo Securing Manuals issued and/or approved to date by the various National Administrations, and the other Approved Certifying organisations. If the components are not identifiable by at least their MSL's, they are not complying with the CSM Regulations.

To overcome this problem I have suggested in the relevant quarters that all aspects could be safely met by attaching, with suitable wire, small coloured metal tags stamped with the MSL of the component, much as is currently required for components approved for the securing of Timber Deck Cargoes. (See Figs. X5, X6 and X7, below, for instance.) Responses received from the industry to date would give positive support to this proposal.

Fig. X5   *Photos: Charles Bliault*   **Fig. X6**

Timber deck cargo approved lashing gear with metal tags stamped
with the correct working load and wired to the respective components.

A similar tagging system could be used safely to correctly identify the MSL's of lashing gear components.

Fig. X7

My advice to ships' officers and others trying to apply the requirements of the CSM is this: If the chains, shackles, rings, and the like, available to you are not clearly identified as to their MSL's (and remember, they should be so identified) use the stamped SWL as required by the CSM, thereby using a component which may have a breaking strength two-times greater than is needed, but you will have complied with the letter of the Regulations. Alternatively - and this is what I would do:- multiply the stamped SWL value by 4 (4, rather than 5, just to be on the safe side) to obtain the breaking strength, and apply the percentages given in Table 1 to obtain the MSL - **and then remove that component from any possibility of use for lifting purposes.** This will, I believe, have fulfilled the spirit of the Regulation without resorting to the use of massively oversized lashing components.

If anyone using this book and reading this **INTRODUCTION** finds that any vessel actually has such components "marked" and "identified" within the terms of the CSM, I would be most pleased to be informed, together with the name(s) and address(es) of the manufacturers/suppliers, and similarly for the Approving Authority involved. It would be nice to know that someone, somewhere, is attempting to comply with the Code and the Regulations.

H. The Advanced Calculation Method
I referred to this aspect, in passing, at items **B** & **C**, earlier herein. I have always considered the published method to be flawed, and there is currently in circulation a proposed Amendment to Section 7 of the CSS Code covering this Advanced Calculation Method. In my view, the proposed Amendment is unlikely to make its application any easier or reasonable, and ships' officers and others should take time to read pages 12 and 13 of the 1994/1995 CSS Code Amendments, of which I here quote only selected parts:-

*"5. The principal way of calculating forces within the securing elements of a complex securing arrangement should necessarily include the consideration of the following - load-elongation behaviour (elasticity), geometric arrangement (angles, lengths), pre-tension - of each individual securing element. This approach would require a large volume of information and a complex, iterative calculation. **The results would still be doubtful due to uncertain parameters.** "*(My emphasis).

And: *"6. It should be borne in mind that meeting or missing the balance calculation just by a tiny change of one or the other parameters indicates to be near the goal anyway. There is no clear-cut borderline between safety and non-safety. **If in doubt the arrangement should be improved.** "* (Again, my emphasis).

Quite simply, the advanced calculation method is an impractical mess which seamen will do well to avoid. Even if you have the time (the money) and the energy to collect the data, and the time and know-how to put it into a computer (always supposing one is available for you to use) you are unlikely to obtain a result any more reliable than the *"three-times-rule"* applied in a balanced and sensible manner, as proposed earlier and later in this book.

I. Summary
It is clear that the IMO needs to take a much closer look at several parts of the CSS Code and the CSM Regulations, including those referred to in the foregoing paragraphs of this **INTRODUCTION**. Ships' officers have difficulties enough without attempting to rationalise the anomalies and inconsistencies within documents supposedly designed for safety purposes. It is to be hoped that suitable amendments will be formulated and published in the not too distant future, so be ready to note and adopt their contents if they provide the necessary corrections.

In closing this **INTRODUCTION** I record my thanks to Charles Bliault, Ex.C., FCMS, Partner with Brookes Bell Jarrett Kirman, for his continued assistance in tidying my thoughts and presentation in connection with the MSL Table 1 Enigma, although this should not be taken as implying that he agrees with all I have to say on the subject.

John R. Knott - Liverpool - January 2002

LASHING AND SECURING OF DECK CARGOES

CHAPTER 1

Deck Cargoes - General

What Is A Deck Cargo?

The phrase "deck cargoes" refers to items and/or commodities carried on the weather-deck and/or hatch covers of a ship and thereon exposed to sun, wind, rain, snow, ice and sea, so that the packaging must be fully resistant to, or the commodities themselves not be denatured by, such exposure. The intention is to retain the cargo on deck and to deliver it in sound state to the port of destination. Items of deck cargo are not automatically at "shippers' risk", and responsibility for loading, stowing and securing - and any subsequent damage or loss which may arise - does not automatically lie with such shippers. Where damage and loss occur to cargo shipped on deck at anyone's risk and expense, the shipowners, the master and his officers, and the charterers, must be in a position to demonstrate there was no negligence or lack of due diligence on their part.

Deck cargoes, because of their very location and the means by which they are secured, will be subjected to velocity and acceleration stresses greater, in most instances, than cargo stowed below decks. More often than not, there is no shell plating, framing or bulkhead to stow against and secure to, and isolated structures may offer little protection against the force of waves shipped over decks and hatches. Even in ro-ro vessels, many areas above the actual 'Hold' space can reasonably be considered as "on deck" even though not fully exposed to the onslaught of wind and sea. The combined effects of wind, sea and swell can be disastrous. When two or more wave forms add up algebraically a high wave preceded by a deep trough may occur; this may be referred to as an "episodic wave": a random large wave - noticeably of greater height than its precursors or successors - which occurs when one or more wave trains fall into phase with another so that a wave, or waves, of large amplitude is/are produced giving rise to sudden steep and violent rolling and/or pitching of the ship. These are popularly - and incorrectly - referred to as "freak" waves. They are not "freak", however, because they can, and do, occur anywhere at any time in the open sea. The risk is widespread and prevalent. The stowage, lashing, and securing of cargoes therefore require special attention as to method and to detail if unnecessary risks are to be avoided.

The International Maritime Organisation (IMO) publishes a range of relevant Conventions and Codes of Safe Practice; the Swedish Transport Research Commission publishes excellent guide lines for the securing of goods on semi-trailers; the P & I Clubs circulate up-to-date loss prevention literature, and the United Kingdom Maritime & Coastguard Agency (MCA), all provide rules and recommendations for securing general items of deck cargo, as well as specific recommendations as to the stowage and securing of containers, timber, and vehicles on ro-ro vessels. In some instances such recommendations - and the general intent thereof - are carried through from the International Load Line Rules, the Department of Transport earlier edition of "Instructions to Surveyors", and the IMO Codes of Safe Practice.

Causes Of Losses

Unfortunately, despite all the loss-prevention literature available, there is a continuing incidence of the collapse and/or loss overboard of deck cargo items. Losses continue of large vehicles, rail cars, cased machinery, steel pipes, structural steelwork, packaged timber, freight containers, hazardous chemicals, boats, launches, etc.

When investigated fully, the causes of such losses fall into the following random categories which are neither exhaustive as to number nor mutually exclusive in occurrence:-

1. Severe adverse weather conditions.

2. Lack of appreciation of the various forces involved.

3. Ignorance of the relevant rules and guiding recommendations.

4. Cost limitation pressures to the detriment of known safety requirements.

5. Insufficient time and/or personnel to complete the necessary work before the vessel leaves port.

6. Dunnage not utilised in an effective manner.

7. Inadequate strength, balance and/or number of lashings.

8. Wire attachment eyes and loops made up wrongly, including incorrect methods of using bulldog-grips.

9. Lack of strength continuity between the various securing components.

10. Taking lashing materials around unprotected sharp edges.

11. Incorrect/unbalanced stowage and inadequate weight distribution.

12. The perversity of shore-based labour when required to do the job properly.

13. Securing arrangements, both supplied and approved, not fully utilised on the voyage under consideration. This last is particularly true of ISO freight containers and timber cargoes carried on the weather-deck, and of large commercial vehicles carried in ro-ro vessels.

It is significant that very heavy, ungainly, and top-heavy items are adequately secured and arrive safely at the discharge port whilst, on the other hand, geometrically regular items disappear overboard with worrying frequency. The intent of this Chapter is to provide a few hints which may prove helpful in reducing the overboard losses of deck cargo items in general. Later chapters deal with specific cargoes such as packaged timber, vehicles on ro-ro vessels, and ISO containers.

All interests involved in the lashing and securing of deck cargoes should bear in mind that high expense in the purchase of lashing materials is no substitute for a simple design and a few basic calculations before lashing operations commence. Other than in ro-ro and purpose-built container operations where standardisation of gear and rapid loading and turn-round times pose different problems, ship masters should be encouraged - on completion of lashing operations - to make notes of the materials used, to produce a representative sketch of the lashing system, to insist upon being provided with the test/proof certificates of all lashing components involved, and to take illustrative photographs of the entire operation. These, at least, will be of great assistance to the vessel's interest in the event of related future litigation.

General Guidelines

It is intended that this book will be found useful on an international basis, and so the relevant IMO Codes and Regulations, ISO Standards, and European Standards will be referred to, albeit with necessary cautions and alternatives as indicated in general terms in the **INTRODUCTION** given ahead of this Chapter and which should be read in some detail before using the suggestions which follow. In other instances, however, the clearest guidelines may be found in earlier maritime codes and regulations which have been withdrawn in part or in whole, and I have not hesitated to adapt some of the wording and principles therefrom where the promotion of common-sense and good seamanship practice prevail.

For instance, The Merchant Shipping (Load Lines) (Deck Cargo) Regulations 1968 set out some of the general ideas to be followed when securing deck cargoes. The list of requirements is not exhaustive but provides a realistic base from which to work, and reads, inter alia:-

"2. **Deck cargo shall be so distributed and stowed -**
  (1)   **as to avoid excessive loading having regard to the strength of the deck and integral supporting structure of the ship;**
  (2)   **as to ensure that the ship will retain adequate stability at all stages of the voyage having regard in particular to -**
    (a)   **the vertical distribution of the deck cargo;**
    (b)   **wind moments which may normally be expected on the voyage;**
    (c)   **losses of weight in the ship, including in particular those due to the consumption of fuel and stores; and**
    (d)   **possible increases of weight of the ship or deck cargo, including in particular those due to the absorption of water and to icing;**
  (3)   **as not to impair the weathertight or watertight integrity of any part of the ship or its fittings or appliances, and as to ensure the proper protection of ventilators and air pipes;**
  (4)   **that its height above the deck or any other part of the ship on which it stands will not interfere with the navigation or working of the ship;**
  (5)   **that it will not interfere with or obstruct access to the ship's steering arrangements, including emergency steering arrangements;**
  (6)   **that it will not interfere with or obstruct safe and efficient access by the crew to or between their quarters and any machinery space or other part of the ship used in the working of the ship, and will not in particular obstruct any opening giving access to those positions or impede its being readily secured weathertight.**"

Also, the Department of Transport, Merchant Shipping Notice No.M.1167, March 1985, is of interest, and relates to statutory duties:-

"(7) The Merchant Shipping (Load Lines) (Deck Cargo) Regulations 1968 relate to the safe stowage of deck cargoes and the provision of safe access for the crew. Failure to observe the requirements under these Regulations renders a master liable to proceedings under the Merchant Shipping (Load Lines) Act 1967."

It is not unreasonable to allow for the fact that the MCA and similar National Administrations will instigate such proceedings where breaches of the Load Line Rules occur.

Co-Efficients Of Friction
Metal on Steel, Timber on Steel - Dunnage

If all deck cargo items could be welded to or structurally attached to the weather-deck using components of acceptable strength this would remove the necessity to consider co-efficients of friction between the base of the cargo and the deck or dunnage on which it rests. In many instances, of course, such base securing measures are effected - cargo winches, large heavy machinery cargo items, and freight containers are cases in point - and reinforce the principle that if all movement of the cargo relative to the deck of the ship can be restrained it is more than likely that the cargo will remain on board despite severe adverse weather conditions. Such is the large range of deck cargoes which do not lend themselves to such securing, however, that an appreciation of the sliding effect brings us naturally to consideration of co-efficients of friction.

The value for the co-efficient of friction between various metals and steel - as may be the situation with some items - is recorded in numerous text books, and may be taken as ranging from 0.1 to 0.3, for our purposes. Co-efficients of friction are normally expressed in terms of the natural tangent of the angle at which movement between the two surfaces will first occur in the absence of velocity or acceleration factors. As 0.1 is the natural tangent of 5.7°, and 0.3 is 16.7°, movement between two unrestricted metal surfaces can be expected to occur at angles between 5° and 16°. As this angle is likely to occur with fairly rapid frequency when a ship is rolling in a seaway, means to increase the frictional co-efficient have conventionally taken the form of timber dunnage. Conventionally, 0.4 (21.8°) is accepted as the co-efficient of friction between a steel deck and rubber vehicle tyres; whilst 0.2 (11.3°) is accepted as the co-efficient of friction between a vehicle trailer frame and the trestle (or horse) on which it rests.

The values given for the co-efficient of friction between dry timber and dry steel vary from 0.3 (17°) to 0.7 (35°); but, prior to this book's earlier editions, there appeared to be no published data relating to the co-efficient of friction between timber dunnage and the painted surface of steel decks or steel hatch covers - which was not very satisfactory from a deck stowage calculation point of view. Accordingly, with the kind co-operation of, and aboard one of the vessels belonging to, the United Arab Shipping Company, carefully controlled experiments were carried out in Liverpool under the author's supervision. The material used was 9" x 3" x 8ft sawn pine deals, some of which had earlier been allowed to float in water; others had been stored in covered conditions so as to conform to normal atmospheric moisture content.

The experiments were carried out on hinge-opening, hydraulic-powered, precision-controlled steel MacGregor hatch covers in clean painted condition free of any unusual roughness and/or obstruction.

The series of tests used dry timber on dry covers; wet timber on dry covers; dry timber on wet covers; and, lastly, wet timber on wet covers. The lowest value - 0.51 (27°) - occurred with wet timbers on wet covers; the highest value occurred with wet timber on dry covers - 0.645 (33°). The average of all results was 0.58415 (30°). On the basis of such results the lowest value of 0.51 (27°) should be accepted as relating to the most common condition likely to be found on the weather-deck of a sea-going ship, i.e. wet timber on wet decks.

With inclination, only, and without any effects likely to be introduced by velocity and/or acceleration stresses due to rolling, **timber dunnage alone will start to slide of its own accord at angles of inclination of 27° and greater**; thereafter, sliding will continue at progressively smaller angles. It follows that, when the vessel is rolling and timber dunnage is unsecured, it will begin to slide at angles of inclination considerably less than 27°. (*Note: A value of 0.4 (rather than 0.5) is assigned in the latest proposed amendment to the CSS Code, erring on the side of safety.*)

From such results it follows that the normal practice of utilising timber dunnage and of keeping downward-leading lashings as short and as tight as possible should be continued and encouraged. A near vertical lashing is of great benefit in resisting the cargo item's tendency to tip; a near horizontal lashing will greatly resist sliding forces. There is no substitute for commonsense and experience, but guard against becoming blasé. Do not overload lashing terminals and/or shackles. Think in terms of the effective strength of a lashing - its "holding power". Equate the "slip-load" of a properly made-up bulldog-gripped eye, grommet or loop in a wire with the nominal breaking strength/breaking-load (NBL) of a shackle, a bottle-screw or a chain, if those values are known. A lashing system is no stronger than its weakest part.

Dunnage - Spread The Load

Point-loading and uneven distribution of cargo weight can, and frequently does, cause unnecessary damage to decks and hatch covers. Unless the weather-deck has been specially strengthened, it is unlikely to have a maximum permissible weight-loading of more than 3 tonnes/m^2. Similarly, unless hatch covers have been specially strengthened, it is unlikely they will have a maximum permissible weight-loading of more than 1.8 tonnes/m^2. The ship's capacity plan and/or general arrangement plan should always be consulted. If the information is not there, try the ship's stability booklet. In the event that specific values are not available on board the ship, allow no more than 2½ tonnes/m^2 for weather-deck areas; and no more than 0.75 tonnes/m^2 for hatch covers in small vessels, or 1.30 tonnes/m^2 in vessels over 100m in length.

The adverse effects of point-loading are not always fully appreciated. On the one hand, a 6-tonne machine with a flat-bed area of 3m^2 will exert a down-load of 2 tonnes/m^2 - Fig.1.01

Fig.1.01   *The 6-tonne weight is exerting a down-loading of 2 tonnes/m^2.*

(Adapted from CROSBY Group Inc.)

On the other hand, a lady of 60kg weight in evening-shoes with heel areas 50mm^2 (0.00005m^2) will exert a point-loading of 1200 tonnes/m^2 if, when dancing, she stands on your toe with all her weight on one heel - Fig.1.02. Which is why our ladies are often more dangerous than machines!

Fig.1.02   *The heel of the lady's shoe is exerting a point-loading of 1200 tonnes/m^2.*

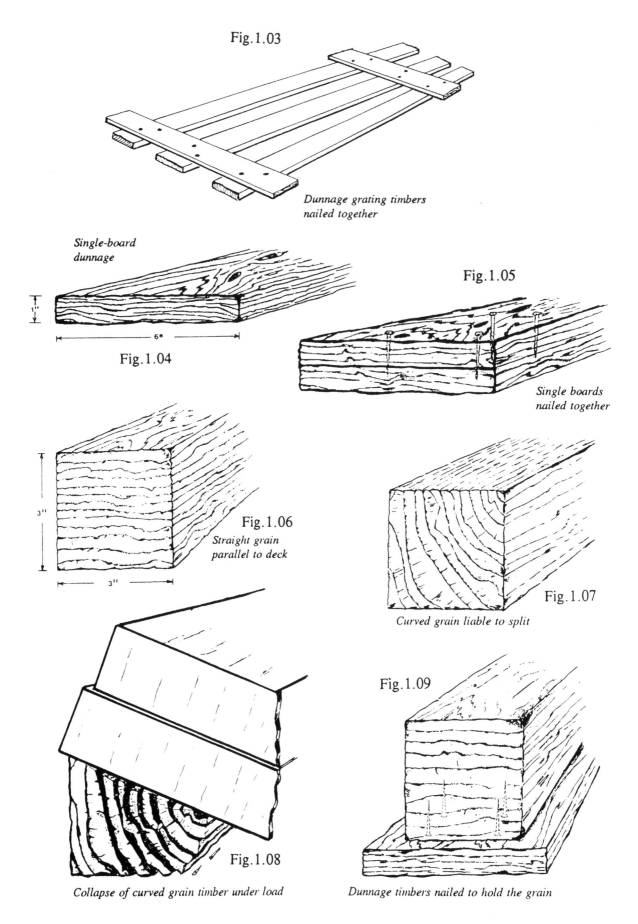

Fig.1.03

Dunnage grating timbers
nailed together

Single-board
dunnage

1"

6"

Fig.1.04

Fig.1.05

Single boards
nailed together

3"

3"

Fig.1.06
Straight grain
parallel to deck

Fig.1.07

Curved grain liable to split

Fig.1.09

Fig.1.08

Collapse of curved grain timber under load

Dunnage timbers nailed to hold the grain

When exceptionally heavy weights are to be carried, it may be necessary to shore-up the weather-deck from below; but, again, care must be taken to spread the load on the 'tween deck so as not to overload that plating or its associated hatch covers. In the not so dense range of cargoes, units of 20 to 40 tonnes weight are common today, and stacking of unit weights is widespread. If a piece of machinery weighing, say, 30 tonnes with a base area of $6m^2$ is placed direct on the weather-deck the point-loading will be $30/6 = 5$ tonnes/m^2. If, however, the deck plating has a maximum permissible loading of 2½ tonnes/m^2 then the **minimum** area over which that 30-tonne load must be spread is $30/2.5 = 12m^2$. Good dunnage must be used to spread the load - Fig.1.03.

Again, it is not always prudent to weight the deck or hatch covers to their maximum permissible loading. Some reasonable allowance should be made to err on the safe side given that heavy seas may be shipped on board and/or ice may accrue, so it is always good practice to add 5% to the weight to be loaded before working out the dunnage area. For the 30-tonne weight, for instance, 31½ tonnes would be used and the dunnage area would go from $12m^2$ to $12.6m^2$.

Dunnage timber is often no more than 6" x 1" (150 x 25mm) rough planking - Fig.1.04; but where weighty cargo items are involved dunnage should not be less than 50mm (2") thickness x 150mm (6") width, and preferably 75mm (3") x 225mm (9"). It is acceptable, however, to use two dunnage planks nailed together securely to make-up the thickness - Fig.1.05. A dunnage width greater than 150mm is always acceptable - 225mm (9") to 305mm (12"), for instance; but where the thickness goes to 75mm (3") care must be taken to choose straight-grained timbers of as great a width as possible, and to ensure that they are laid with the grain horizontal and parallel with the deck - Fig.1.06.

Incidents have occurred where what appeared to have been soundly-dunnaged and well-secured deck cargo items broke adrift and were lost overboard due to a sequence of events commencing with the collapse of 3" x 3" dunnage timbers along the curved grain used on its edge - Figs.1.07 and 1.08 - followed by consequential slackness in otherwise adequate lashing arrangements, followed by increasingly accelerated cargo movement and finally breakage of the lashings.

It is because of the random nature of grain configurations in the thicker dunnage timbers that the author prefers to see thicknesses made-up of planks nailed together. A 2"-thick dunnage timber can be made-up using 1"-thick planks, and a 3"-thick dunnage timber can be made-up using 2" and 1"-thick timber planks, all securely nailed together. To a large degree, this will correct the tendency for separation in timber with a badly-aligned grain. (See Fig.1.09, for instance.)

Given the same problems, but with only hatch covers available to take the cargo, a very carefully-constructed grating system would be required if the maximum permissible loading on the hatch covers was no more than 1.75 tonnes/m^2. Naturally, similar considerations apply on 'tween deck plating and 'tween deck hatch covers, and also on tank-top plating, although, in the latter instance, maximum permissible loading will be considerably greater than that allowed for weather-deck areas and hatch covers. Also remember that it will be as important to install good lower-level foot lashings as it will be to install downward-leading lashings if load-spreading dunnage is to remain fully effective.

Bear in mind, also, that steel girders - or similar - welded and/or bracketed to the deck plating may provide a more efficient method of load-spreading in the presence of very heavy cargo items. In later Chapters, more on dunnage construction, hatch covers, and the correct way to stow and secure Containers on non-purpose built ships. See, also, the **INTRODUCTON** to the Cargo Securing Manual preceding this Chapter.

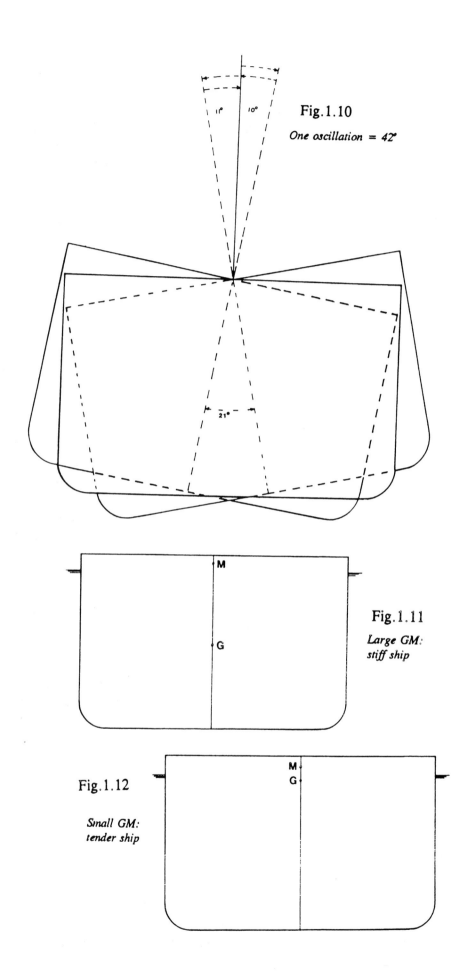

Fig.1.10

One oscillation = 42°

Fig.1.11

*Large GM:
stiff ship*

Fig.1.12

*Small GM:
tender ship*

Rolling Periods

It is not the purpose of this book to deal with ship stability aspects, so far as those aspects may be avoided. However, it is worth repeating a few established and relevant stability facts. For instance, the roll period of a ship is the time taken to make one complete transverse oscillation; that is, from the upright position to starboard inclination, from starboard inclination back to upright and through to port inclination, thence back to upright. Hence, if the roll period is 15 seconds and if the roll to starboard is 10° and the roll to port is 11°, the total "sweep" within the 15-second roll period will be 10 + 10 + 11 + 11 = 42° - Fig.1.10.

When a ship rolls the axis about which the rolling takes place cannot generally be accurately determined, but it is accepted as being near to the longitudinal axis passing through the ship's centre of gravity. The time period of the roll is generally independent of the roll angle, provided that the roll angle is not large. Thus, a vessel with a 15-second roll period will take 15 seconds to make one full transverse oscillation when the roll angle (to port and to starboard) is anything from say 2° to 30°. The crux, from a cargo lashing viewpoint, lies in realising that a roll angle of 2° and a roll period of 15 seconds involves a "sweep" of no more than 8°, where a roll angle of 20° and a roll period of 15 seconds involves a "sweep" of 80° (ten times greater) **in the same time**. The first will be barely noticeable; the second will be violent and will involve large acceleration stresses particularly when returning to the upright.

A "stiff" ship is one with a large GM (metacentric height); difficult to incline and returns rapidly to the upright and beyond, sometimes with whiplash effect. This imposes excessive acceleration stresses on cargo lashings - Fig.1.11. A "tender" ship is one with a small GM; easy to incline and returns slowly to the upright, sometimes even sluggishly - Fig.1.12. Although acceleration stresses are small the inclined angles may attain 30°, and the simple gravitational effects of such angles and slow returns may impose equally excessive stresses on cargo lashings. Seamen try to avoid the extremes of either condition; and it is worthwhile working on the assumption that, if deck cargo is to remain safely in place during adverse weather conditions, the lashing arrangements should be sufficient to sustain 30° roll angles associated with 13-second roll periods.

Reference should be made, however, to **Table 3** and **Table 4** of the Cargo Securing Manual (CSM) where correction factors for length, speed, and *B/GM* are provided, and on which comments may be found in the **INTRODUCTION** to the CSM preceding this Chapter, and also later herein..

The beam of a vessel, her GM, and her rolling period are closely related. A Table of Rolling Periods is usually to be found affixed to the chart-room or wheelhouse bulkhead or in the vessel's stability booklet. In their absence, useful approximate values may be found in Brown's Nautical Almanac. For seamen who wish to make their own assessments the following formula is useful:-

$$T = \frac{2\pi K}{\sqrt{g.GM}}$$

where   T = one complete oscillation in seconds;
        K = radius of gyration (when known).

It is seldom in day-to-day practice that the radius of gyration will be known, bearing in mind that it varies with every weight taken into and out of the ship; so an easier approximation is arrived at by simplifying the equation as shown on the following page with its applied examples:-

$$T = \frac{C \times B}{\sqrt{GM}} \quad \text{and} \quad GM = \left(\frac{C \times B}{T}\right)^2$$

where B = the ship's beam to outside of hull;
C = a constant.

For vessels up to 70m in length the IMO inclining and rolling tests found the best results were obtained when using C as

0.88 where ship is empty or in ballast condition.
0.78 when all liquids on board amount to 20% of total deadweight.
0.75 when all liquids on board amount to 10% of total deadweight.
0.73 when all liquids on board amount to 5% of total deadweight.

However, **for all larger ships** Lloyd's Register of Shipping and the 1991 HMSO Code of Practice for Roll-on/Roll-off Ships **use C = 0.7.**

Examples

a. A bulk carrier of length 142m and beam 21m has a fluid GM of 1.41m. What is the likely rolling period?

$$T = \frac{C \times B}{\sqrt{GM}} = \frac{0.7 \times 21}{\sqrt{1.41}} = 12.4 \text{ seconds}$$

b. A coaster of length 67m and beam 12m has a fluid GM of 1.35m when in ballast condition. What is the likely rolling period?

$$T = \frac{C \times B}{\sqrt{GM}} = \frac{0.88 \times 12}{\sqrt{1.35}} = 9.1 \text{ seconds}$$

c. An SD22-type 'tween decker of length 150m and beam 28m has a rolling period of 13 seconds. What is her approximate fluid GM?

$$GM = \left(\frac{C \times B}{T}\right)^2 = \left(\frac{0.7 \times 28}{13}\right)^2 = 2.27 \text{m}$$

d. A fully-loaded single-hold coaster of 56m length and beam 11m has a rolling period of 18 seconds when liquids make up 5% of deadweight. What is her approximate fluid GM?

$$GM = \left(\frac{C \times B}{T}\right)^2 = \left(\frac{0.73 \times 11}{18}\right)^2 = 1.89 \text{m}$$

The foregoing are only approximations; but if the fluid GM can be calculated accurately from basic stability data and using the correct principles, the formulae will provide an acceptable roll period. Similarly, if the roll period in reasonably calm weather conditions can be timed accurately with a stop-watch, the formulae will provide an acceptable fluid GM. **Remember, severe loading on deck cargo securing arrangements may well arise where roll periods of less than 13 seconds occur. When such roll periods cannot be avoided, the holding power of the lashings must be increased.** (See the application of the CSM Tables 3 & 4 later in this Chapter.)

With reference to the tests and results reported for vessels up to 70m length, IMO also says:-

"It must be noted that the greater the distance of masses from the rolling axis, the greater the rolling coefficient will be.

Therefore it can be expected that:

> *the rolling coefficient for an unloaded ship, i.e. for a hollow body, will be higher than that for a loaded ship;*

> *the rolling coefficient for a ship carrying a great amount of bunkers and ballast - both groups are usually located in the double bottom, i.e. far away from the rolling axis - will be higher than that of the same ship having an empty double bottom.*

The above recommended rolling coefficients were determined by tests with vessels in port and with their consumable liquids at normal working levels; thus the influences exerted by the vicinity of the quay, the limited depth of water and the free surfaces of liquids in service tanks are covered.

Experiments have shown that the results of the rolling test method get increasingly less reliable the nearer they approach GM-values of 0.20 m and below.

For the following reasons, it is not generally recommended that results be obtained from rolling oscillations taken in a seaway:

> *1   exact coefficients for tests in open waters are not available;*

> *2   the rolling periods observed may not be free oscillations but forced oscillations due to seaway;*

> *3   frequently, oscillations are either irregular or only regular for too short an interval of time to allow accurate measurements to be observed;*

> *4   specialized recording equipment is necessary.*

However, sometimes it may be desirable to use the vessel's period of roll as a means of approximately judging the stability at sea. If this is done, care should be taken to discard readings which depart appreciably from the majority of other observations. Forced oscillations corresponding to the sea period and differing from the natural period at which the vessel seems to move should be disregarded. In order to obtain satisfactory results, it may be necessary to select intervals when the sea action is least violent, and it may be necessary to discard a considerable number of observations.

In view of the foregoing circumstances, it needs to be recognized that the determination of the stability by means of the rolling test in disturbed waters should only be regarded as a very approximate estimation." (See, also, the IMO Code of Safe Practice for Cargo Stowage and Securing, 1992, its later Amendments and the general requirements of the Cargo Securing Manual.)

Roll Angles

As a matter of general interest, and in relation to the strength of cargo lashings in particular, the Stevedoring Department of Messrs. Hoogovens, steel exporters, instituted a series of controlled roll angle measurement tests in 1989/1990 on board 25000 DWT bulk carriers engaged on North Atlantic crossings. The cargo generally comprised steel coils in the holds, with the inevitable short roll period - typically about 7 to 8 seconds - associated with such cargoes. Comparisons were made between the angles indicated by the bridge inclinometer and the angles shown by a gyro-stabilised heel indicator. The results were quite dramatic, a few of which are reproduced in précis hereunder.

1.   When the bridge inclinometer showed 30° or more, the gyro heel indicator did not exceed 13.1°.

2.   The bridge inclinometer tended to exaggerate the true heel angle by a factor of as much as 1.5.

3.   Inclinometer angles of 45° were, in fact, no greater than 21°.

The two graphs following are part of the Hoogovens presentation, and are here reproduced with due acknowledgement to that Company.

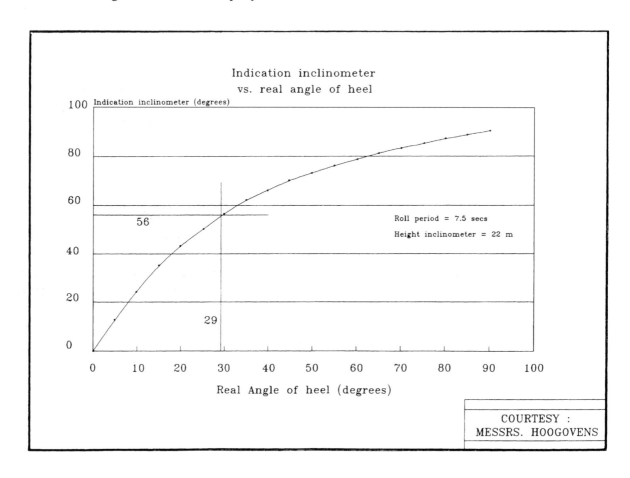

Hoogovens analysed the data and concluded that the excessive difference between the indicated angles was due firstly to the fact that the bridge inclinometer was situated at a very high distance from the ship's centre of rotation - typically about 22 metres - and additionally to the very short roll period - typically 7 to 8 seconds; two factors which did not impinge upon the accurate responses of the gyroscopic heel indicator.

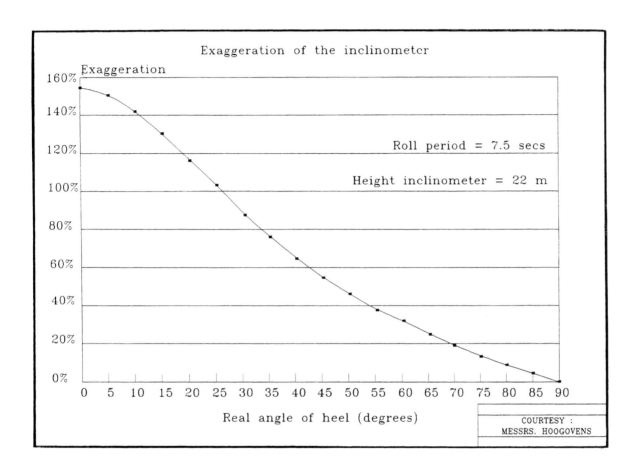

The Hoogovens Stevedoring Department presented their paper "Innovation in Lashing and Stowage of Coiled Steel in Transatlantic Shipping" with a most informative slide back-up.

In the February 1994 edition of "SEAWAYS" Captain Michael Robinson of the Sydney Institute of Technology presented a paper entitled "Inclinometer Problems" which - although not referring to the Hoogovens investigation - briefly but clearly sets out the physical reasons for the Hoogovens results. The Nautical Institute - and the author of this book - would be most interested to hear of any similar research undertaken in relation to roll/heel angles in seagoing ships. Bearing in mind that the Hoogovens' tests involved roll periods of 7 to 8 seconds, similar tests involving, say, 10 to 20 second roll periods would prove of worthwhile practical value.

RANGING
The Six Spatial Movements of a Ship
Alongside a Wharf and/or at Sea

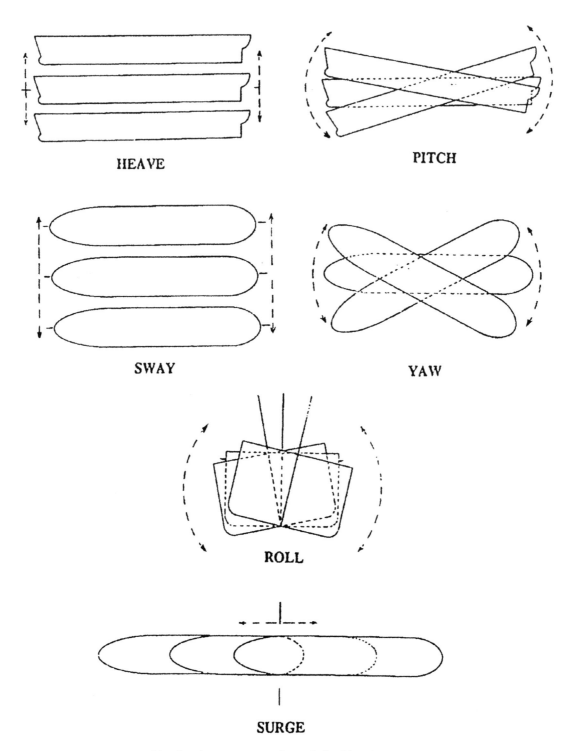

HEAVE

PITCH

SWAY

YAW

ROLL

SURGE

Line drawings computer-enhanced: David Anderson

Rule-Of-Thumb For Lashing Strength

The seaman's basic rule-of-thumb for securing cargoes with a tendency to move during a moderate weather voyage is simply that the sum of the minimum breaking-loads of **all** the lashings should be not less than twice the static weight of the item of cargo to be secured. That is, a single item of 10 tonnes weight requires the lashings used to have a total breaking-load of not less than 20 tonnes - on the positive assumption that the lashings are all positioned in a balanced, efficient, and non-abrasive manner. This rule may be adequate, or even too much, below decks - though not necessarily so in all instances - **but it will not be adequate on the weather-deck in instances where calm seas and a fair weather passage cannot be guaranteed.**

In circumstances where, for **any time** during a voyage, winds of Force 6 and upwards together with associated wave heights are more likely to be encountered, the increased stresses arising therefrom are those here considered, allowing for 30° roll angles with not less than 13 second roll periods. (See, also, Tables 3 & 4 on page 18, taken from the CSM, and my earlier comments in the **INTRODUCTION** preceding this Chapter.)

In such cases, the sailor's rule-of-thumb - the *"3-times rule"* - tends to be that the sum of the **safe working load** of all the lashings shall equal the static weight of the cargo item to be secured; **the safe working load** being arrived at **by dividing by 3** the minimum breaking-load/slip-load/holding power of the lashings. In other words, if the breaking-load/slip-load/holding power of **all** the lashings is 30 tonnes, then they can safely hold an item whose static weight is 10 tonnes - **again on the assumption that all securing arrangements are deployed in a balanced, efficient, and non-abrasive manner.** The author is not aware of any failures of lashings/securing arrangements or loss of deck cargo where this *"3-times rule"* has been applied in a sensible manner.

It is derived from the earlier International Load Line Rules within which framework the United Kingdom Department of Transport, in earlier Instructions to Surveyors, gave the following guidance, inter alia:-

> **"When severe weather conditions (ie sea state conditions equal to or worse than those associated with Beaufort Scale 6) are likely to be experienced in service the following principles should be observed in the design of the deck cargo securing arrangements:**

> | (iv) | Lashings used to secure cargo or vehicles should have a breaking load of at least 3 times the design load, the design load being the total weight of the cargo or cargo plus vehicle subjected to acceleration of: |
> |---|---|
> | | **0.7 `g' athwartships,** |
> | | **1.0 `g' vertically and** |
> | | **0.3 `g' longitudinally,** |
> | | relative to the principal axis of the ship. |

(See Addendum 1 for Conversion Factors.)

> **"When sea state conditions worse than those associated with Beaufort Scale 6 are unlikely to be experienced in service, a lesser standard of securing such items of cargo might be acceptable to approval by the Chief Ship Surveyor.**

> **"The equipment and fittings used to secure the deck cargoes should be regularly maintained and inspected."**

To condense those recommendations into a form simple to apply, reference should be made to the boxed paragraph on the previous page. Put into practical and approximate terms, and using the phrase **"holding power"** to indicate "breaking-load/slip-load/holding power", this means:-

a)   The holding power of all lashings holding the cargo item vertically downward to the deck should be **equivalent - at least - to three times the ordinary static weight of the cargo item in tonnes,** i.e. a 10-tonne cargo item requires total lashings having a holding-down potential of 30 tonnes.

b)   The holding power of all lashings preventing the cargo item moving to port and to starboard should be equivalent to seven-tenths of the holding-down potential of (a), above: i.e. a 10-tonne item requires lashings with holding power preventing transverse movement of 21 tonnes.

c)   The holding power of all lashings preventing the cargo moving forward or aft should be equivalent to three-tenths of the holding-down potential of (a), above: i.e. a 10-tonne item requires lashings with holding power preventing longitudinal movement of 9 tonnes.

The current Amendments to the CSS Code and the CSM Regulations change the emphases of the foregoing paragraphs to those discussed in the **INTRODUCTION** to the **IMO Cargo Securing Manual** preceding this Chapter.

The CSM "rule-of-thumb" varies as the MSL's of the different lashing components, as listed in its *(Table 1)* - shown below on this page - giving rise to five different answers to the one problem. For the most part, vertical acceleration appears to have been replaced by a 1g transverse acceleration, except, that is, in the instance of containers of radioactive wastes, and the like, when accelerations shall be considered to be 1.5g longitudinally, 1.5g transversely, 1.0g vertically up, and 2.0g vertically down - in accordance with the values prescribed in the INF Code 2000 Edition (Safe Carriage of Packaged Irradiated Nuclear Fuel, etc).To date, the IMO have not offered an explanation as to why a tonne of radio active waste should be considered to " weigh" twice as much as, say, a tonne of tetraethyl lead or some other equally noxious substance.

In the CSM, the *SWL* and the *MSL* can supposedly mean the same thing - but only in the unlikely event that the *SWL* is the same as or better than the *MSL* and only where securing of deck cargoes is involved. (Again, see the **INTRODUCTION** to the CSM preceding this Chapter.) The CSM criteria for *MSL's* are shown hereunder.

(Table 1 -Determination of MSL from breaking strength)(*Including the latest proposed amendment*)

Material	MSL
Shackles, rings, deckeyes, turnbuckles of mild steel	50% of breaking strength
Fibre rope	33% of breaking strength
Wire rope (single use)	80% of breaking strength
Web lashing	*50% of breaking strength* (Was 70%)
Wire rope re-useable)	30% of breaking strength
Steel band (single use)	70% of breaking strength
Chains	50% of breaking strength

"For particular securing devices (e.g. fibre straps with tensioners or special equipment for securing containers), a permissible working load may be prescribed and marked by authority. This should be taken as the MSL"
"When the components of a lashing device are connected in series (for example, a wire to a shackle to a deckeye), the minimum MSL in the series shall apply to that device."

Unfortunately, the wire rope configurations of soft-eyes, loops, and grommets, made up using bulldog grips, most common in the securing of deck cargoes and as detailed in Chapter 3 later herein, are not considered currently in the CSM Table or elsewhere in the CSM, and only briefly in passing in the the CSS Code. Some formal Amendment is required in that direction

The anomalies arising from the CSM treatment of breaking strength, maximum securing load (MSL), safe working load (SWL), Working Load Limit (WLL), calculated strength (CS). safety factor, and rule-of-thumb, are dealt with in the **INTRODUCTION** to the CSM preceding this Chapter, and are referred to elsewhere in passing.

In the absence of acceptable explanations and/or satisfactory amendments to the CSM Regulations, I recommend that the **3-times rule** explained earlier herein, together with the supporting text which follows in later Chapters, be adopted as the most simple and efficient deployment of deck cargo lashing components. **And, just to be on the safe side of the CSS Code/INF Code/CSM Regulations, and pending clarification of the point, it would seem necessary to double the 3-times rule holding-power when carrying containers of nuclear fuel and radio active waste, or similar, as deck cargo.**

Fig.1.13, below, illustrates how down-angled lashings referred to at a), b) and c) on page 16, can be used to take account of all three directional forces.

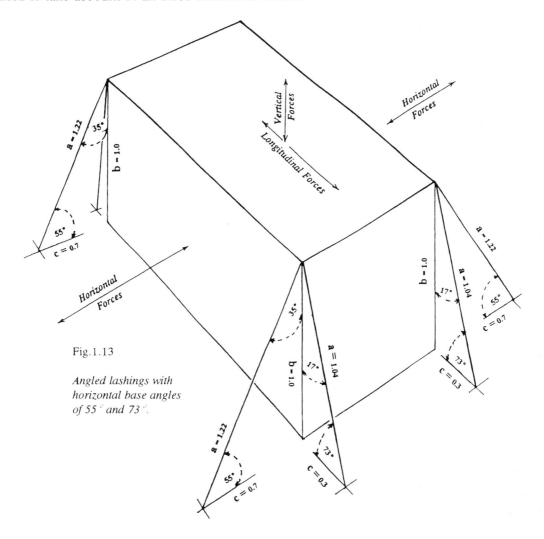

Fig.1.13

Angled lashings with horizontal base angles of 55° and 73°.

Simply, a transverse down-angled lashing with an upper peak angle of 35° and a base angle of 55° will form the triangle of forces: 1.22, 1 and 0.7. Similarly, a fore-and-aft down-angled lashing with an upper peak angle of 17° and a base angle of 73° will form the triangle of forces: 1.04, 1 and 0.3. Figs.1.14, 1.15 and 1.16 on page 19 illustrate similar considerations for 45° angles.

There is an awareness that some difficulty was encountered with the arithmetical examples given in the earlier edition. This was due to lack of adequate step-by-step exposition of the text, a shortcoming which hopefully is corrected hereunder. **The basic practical concept is that the real lashing which you use is more likely than not to be the hypotenuse of a triangle.**

In the instance of Fig.1.13, if the holding power of the transverse lashing - (a = 1.22) - is 5.5 tonnes, then its holding-down ability (b) will be 5.5(1/1.22) equals 4.5 tonnes. Its ability to resist transverse forces (c) will be 0.7 (5.5 x 1/1.22) equals 3.16 tonnes - but only for that specific lashing angle. No other triangle will give the same simple proportions, and the 55°/35° triangle is here used merely for illustration purposes to show what a vertical hold of value 1 with a transverse hold of value 0.7 looks like for a specific lashing holding power. Its helpfulness lies in the fact that if you can get your lashing angles to those approximate values then the apportionment of holding ability is easy without the use of trigonometry.

In general terms, the vertical holding-down ability of downward-angled lashings is related directly to the trigonometrical sine of the base angle; the transverse holding ability of downward-angled lashings is related directly to the trigonometrical cosine of the base angle; all on the assumption that the angle between vertical and horizontal components at the deck is 90°. On page 19, for instance:-

Fig.1.17   The transverse lashing is fully horizontal, so the base angle is 0°. Where the base angle is 0°, the cosine is 1 and the sine is 0, so the full holding power of the lashing is operating in the transverse horizontal mode, with no holding power in any other plane.

Fig.1.18   The transverse lashing is, say, 30° to the horizontal. The cosine of 30° is 0.87, the sine of 30° is 0.5; so 87% of the holding power of the lashing is operating to restrain transverse horizontal movement and half of the lashing's holding power will be operating to restrain vertical movement. (That is not a contradiction in terms.)

Fig.1.19   The transverse lashing is, say, 60° to the horizontal. The cosine of 60° is 0.5 and the sine of 60° is 0.87; so half the holding power of the lashing is operating to restrain transverse horizontal movement and 87% of the lashing's holding power will then be operating to restrain vertical movement. (Again, that is not a contradiction in terms.)

Similarly for lashings operating to restrain fore-and-aft movement. In the instance of Fig.1.13, if the holding power of the fore-and-aft lashing - (a = 1.04) - is 5.5 tonnes, then its holding-down ability (b) will be 5.5(1/1.04) equals 5.3 tonnes; its ability to resist fore-and-aft forces (c) will be 0.3 (5.5 x 1/1.04) equals 1.59 tonnes - but only for that specific lashing angle. No other triangle will give the same simple proportions, and the 73°/17° triangle is here used merely for illustration purposes to show what a vertical hold of value 1, with a horizontal hold of value 0.3, looks like for a specific holding power. Its helpfulness resides, again, in the fact that if you can get your lashing angles to those approximate values then the apportionment of holding ability is easy without the use of trigonometry. And an appreciation of the use of roughly 30°/60° lashing angles is always helpful. For instance, a horizontal foot of 4m with a vertical height of 2½m will give a base angle of 32°. A horizontal foot of 2½m with a vertical height of 4m will give a base angle of 58°. It's not an exact science!

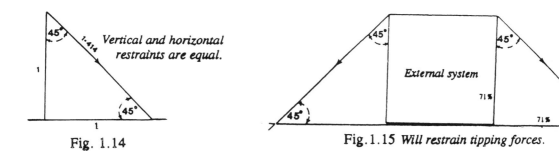

Vertical and horizontal restraints are equal.

Fig. 1.14

External system

71%

71%

Fig. 1.15 Will restrain tipping forces.

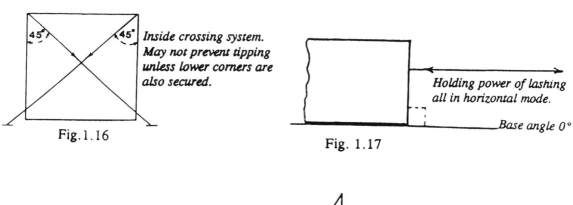

Inside crossing system. May not prevent tipping unless lower corners are also secured.

Fig. 1.16

Holding power of lashing all in horizontal mode.

Base angle 0°

Fig. 1.17

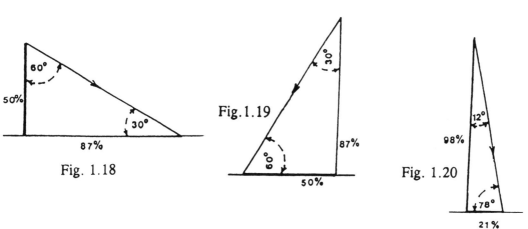

50%

60°

30°

87%

Fig. 1.18

Fig. 1.19

30°

60°

87%

50%

12°

98%

78°

21%

Fig. 1.20

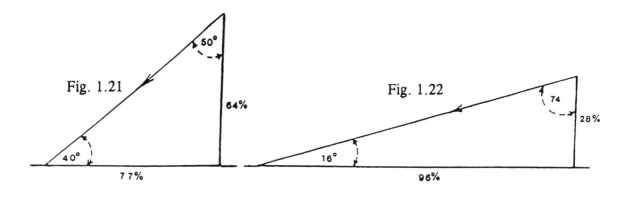

Fig. 1.21

50°

64%

40°

77%

Fig. 1.22

74

28%

16°

96%

Again, in more general terms, the fore-and-aft holding ability of downward-angled lashings is directly related to the trigonometrical cosine of the base angle; so that Figs.1.17, 1.18 and 1.19 on page 19 apply equally to fore-and-aft restraints, and to the whole range of angles between 0° and 90°. Figs.1.20, 1.21 and 1.22 provide some more examples, any and all of which may be applied to the arrangement shown at Fig.1.13 for a regular-shaped cargo item.

On the assumption, for instance, that the holding power/slip load of a lashing made up using turnbuckles, shackles and wires with bulldog-grips is 5.5 tonnes then, calculated for every 5° of base angle, a Table of values can be produced as hereunder, in which "holding power" means "slip-load" as explained in Chapter 3.

TABLE 1 - Vertical, Transverse & Fore-and-Aft Restraints

When Lashing Holding Power/Slip Load = 5.5 Tonnes

Base Angle Degrees	Peak Angle Degrees	Holding Power/ Slip Load Tonnes	Vertical Restraint Tonnes	Transverse and Fore-and-Aft Restraint Tonnes
0	90	5.5	0.00	5.50
5	85	5.5	0.48	5.48
10	80	5.5	0.96	5.42
15	75	5.5	1.42	5.31
20	70	5.5	1.88	5.17
25	65	5.5	2.32	4.98
30	60	5.5	2.75	4.76
35	55	5.5	3.15	4.50
40	50	5.5	3.54	4.21
45	45	5.5	3.89	3.89
50	40	5.5	4.21	3.54
55	35	5.5	4.50	3.15
60	30	5.5	4.76	2.75
65	25	5.5	4.98	2.32
70	20	5.5	5.17	1.88
75	15	5.5	5.31	1.42

From Table 1, it can be seen that only at base and peak angles of 45° will the vertical restraint be the same as the transverse or fore-and-aft restraint. Figs.1.14, 1.15 and 1.16 on page 19 illustrate this fact. (See Chapter 3, for Tables using other holding powers/slip loads.)

The *three times rule* is a general, easily-workable, guide; but a little extra is always welcome when roll periods fall below 13 seconds associated with large GM's. In this connection *(Table 3)* - **Correction factors for length and speed,** and *(Table 4)* - **Correction factors for B/GM <13**, from the CSS Code and the Cargo Securing Manual are worth consulting and applying to the rules-of-thumb although, in my opinion, a factor of less than 1.00 in *(Table 3)* should **never** be applied. As a matter of mathematical theory a correction factor of 0.85 may apply to a vessel of length 200m doing 24 knots in bad weather conditions, but reducing the holding power of the deck lashings by 15% - as would be indicated by *(Table 3)* - is not an action compatible with safe practice and sound seamanship. (See my comments in the **INTRODUCTION** to the CSM preceding this Chapter.) I would recommend that ships' officers ignore in *(Table 3)* any correction value less than 1 (those values which I have shaded-in below) when applying the **length/speed** corrections to any rule-of-thumb.

(Table 3) *Correction factors for length and speed*

Length (m) Speed (kn)	50	60	70	80	90	100	120	140	160	180	200
9	1.20	1.09	1.00	0.92	0.85	0.79	0.70	0.63	0.57	0.53	0.49
12	1.34	1.22	1.12	1.03	0.96	0.90	0.79	0.72	0.65	0.60	0.56
15	1.49	1.36	1.24	1.15	1.07	1.00	0.89	0.80	0.73	0.68	0.63
18	1.64	1.49	1.37	1.27	1.18	1.10	0.98	0.89	0.82	0.76	0.71
21	1.78	1.62	1.49	1.38	1.29	1.21	1.08	0.98	0.90	0.83	0.78
24	1.93	1.76	1.62	1.50	1.40	1.31	1.17	1.07	0.98	0.91	0.85

(Table 4) *Correction factors for B/GM < 13*

B/GM	7	8	9	10	11	12	13 or above
on deck, high	1.56	1.40	1.27	1.19	1.11	1.05	1.00
on deck, low	1.42	1.30	1.21	1.14	1.09	1.04	1.00
'tween deck	1.26	1.19	1.14	1.09	1.06	1.03	1.00
lower hold	1.15	1.12	1.09	1.06	1.04	1.02	1.00

I certainly encourage the application of *(Table 4)* to any rule-of-thumb calculations, although I am not entirely happy with the B/GM approach because dividing metres into metres produces a dimensionless result which must not be confused with rolling period. The *(Table 4)* values may appear to be easy to apply but, in my opinion, the *correction factor* would have made more sense if the Table had been headed *"Correction factors for Rolling Period < 13 seconds"* and the tabular results adjusted accordingly. The Code/CSM add the following cautions:-

"In the case of marked roll resonance with amplitudes above ±30°, the given figures of transverse acceleration *(that's in Table 2 - not quoted here)* may be exceeded. Effective measures should be taken to avoid this condition. *(The measures to be taken are not indicated, but certainly a change of heading and a reduction in speed would seem to be the least risky and quickest to put into effect.)*

"In the case of heading into the seas at high speed with marked slamming shocks, the given figures of longitudinal and vertical acceleration *(Table 2, again)* may be exceeded. An appropriate reduction of speed should be considered. *(Indeed.)*

"In the case of running before large stern or quartering seas with a stability which does not amply exceed the accepted minimum requirements, large roll amplitudes must be expected with transverse accelerations greater than the figures given. An appropriate change of heading should considered." *(This means a vessel with a very small GM - a 'tender' ship. Changing headings under these conditions can be a very dangerous business if the vessel falls into the trough of a beam sea. On the other hand, a single 'pooping' sea under these circumstances can cause immense damage to both ship and deck cargo.)*

I appreciate that *(Tables 3 & 4)* in the CSM are related principally to the **Advanced Calculation Method** set out in Section 7 of the CSS Amendments. Those two Tables, however, provide very worthwhile guidance to upgrading other less rigorous assessments. I consider it safe to say that a sensible and balanced application of the *3-times rule* as explained earlier in this Chapter, together with the lashing principles explained in later Chapters and a cautious use of the Code/CSM *(Tables 3 & 4)*, will provide adequate securing of deck cargo in a properly-handled vessel. There is no substitute for good seamanship.

Section 5 of the CSS Code Amendments as carried forward into the CSM's that I have sighted, places that Section after Section 4 and before Section 6 - such that the expression CS=MSL/1.5 appears to be irrelevant to the surrounding text. It is, and requires amendment! Readers should refer to the **INTRODUCTION** to the CSM preceding this Chapter and ignore the CS=MSL/1.5 expression when using any rule-of-thumb method for lashing deployment calculations.

Keep the lashings as short as possible. Long lashings are difficult to tighten and difficult to keep taut. Don't fall into the trap of believing that because the cargo item is "heavy" it will stay where you put it with only minimal securing - it won't. No matter what theoretical physics may tend to show to the contrary, and no matter the extent to which vertical accelerations may be downgraded in the CSM in some instances - **Remember: The cargo item will lift before it shifts! So tie it down well.**

Sea Waves and Swell Waves

To the "wave" aspect touched upon in the second paragraph of this Chapter the following additional comments may prove helpful, because there is a physical distinction between "sea" and "swell".

The system of waves raised by the local wind blowing at the time of observation is usually referred to as "sea". Wave forms not raised by the local wind blowing at the time of observation, but due either to winds blowing at a distant point, or to winds that have passed, or to winds that have ceased to blow, are known collectively as "swell". Usually, one component of the swell dominates the rest, but occasionally two component wave motions crossing at an angle may be observed. These are referred to as "cross swells". Sea and swell may both be present at the same time, and the sea may be - and frequently is - from a different direction and have a different period and height to the swell, or both sea and swell may be from the same direction.

There exists a considerable range of literature dealing with wave formation, height, period, frequency, etc., from which it can be seen that when two or more wave forms add up algebraically a high wave preceded by a deep trough may occur; this may be referred to as an "episodic wave". The term "episodic wave" means a random large wave - noticeably of greater height than its precursors or successors - which occurs when one or more wave trains combine momentarily with another (known correctly as "falling into phase") so that a wave, or waves, of large amplitude are produced. These are popularly - and incorrectly - referred to as "freak" waves; they are not "freak", because they can, and do, occur at any time in the open sea and along exposed coastlines.

The Journal of The Royal Institute of Navigation supports the growing knowledge of wave propagation, and parts of the paper by Dr. Laurence Draper of the National Institute of Oceanography, appearing in Vol.24, July 1971, are of particular interest:-

"Perhaps the most surprising thing about sea waves is that they come in a vast range of shapes and sizes. The casual observer on a ship in waters not exposed to an ocean, for example the southern North Sea, may rightly think that the waves he can see have all been generated by the same wind blowing over some particular stretch of water for a fixed length of time. It then seems almost

logical to deduce that all the waves ought to be of the same height, length and shape. Unfortunately this is not the case, the energy of sea waves is locked in wave components spread over a wide range of wave periods, each of which travels at a speed dictated by its period. Considering the very simple case of a sea with only two wave components, when a crest of one component overtakes the other a higher wave will ensue. As a result of this process, high waves come in groups; during the time in which the components gradually get into phase the wave height builds up giving a train of waves of increasing height, which then decreases as the faster component travels away, until when they are out of phase the sea is temporarily fairly calm. This is the reason why it is commonly said that every seventh wave is the highest, although whether it is every fourth or every fourteenth depends on the relative speeds of the components."

Dr. Draper, in considering the difficulty of ascribing meaningful numbers to wave height, continues by saying: "**However, there is one parameter, named significant wave height, and defined as the average height of the highest one-third of all the waves, which is a useful one to have. It is a meaningful parameter to the theoreticians, and it has the additional virtue that on average it is very close to the value which an experienced seaman would give if asked to estimate the wave height. It has been shown by both theory and measurement that if the sea is watched for the duration of about 60 waves, typically about ten minutes, the height of the highest wave which appears is about 1.6 times the significant height....**" And continues: "**An important characteristic of individual waves is their lack of longevity; once again, it is simply because the really big wave is the result of a chance superimposition of many components overtaking each other at one point in space and time. Before long, perhaps two or three wave periods and over a distance of less than a mile, the height of any large individual wave has decreased and it is no longer distinguishable from any other wave.**"

In his paper "Wave Climatology of the U.S. Continental Shelf" Dr. Draper says: "**The quietest open water areas, with respect to waves, are to the south-east of the British Isles; here, the differences in wave heights are more noticeable than the differences in wind speed might suggest. This is because these areas of lower wind speeds are also the areas of more restricted fetches and, more importantly, shallower water. The latter is effective in removing wave energy by friction on the sea bed so that, compared with the deeper oceanic water, the wave spectrum cannot grow fully, especially at the longer-period end. This effect manifests itself (in the shallow waters) mainly in the greater apparent steepness of the waves (because the longer-period waves are absent), resulting in short wave-length steep choppy seas.**"

The Admiralty Manual of Seamanship, Vol.III, provides a concise explanation of sea and swell waves, and says *inter alia:-* "**4. In the most general terms, the fact that a wave attains its maximum height when passing near the centre of a group accounts for the familiar periodic appearance of an extra large wave. The combination of two or more wave patterns similarly results in a fairly regular recurrence of groups of large and small waves, with occasional periods of comparative calm. The number of waves in each group and the interval between successive appearances of extra high groups vary with the type of sea.**"

The following page, hereof, reproduces a copy of the Beaufort Wind Scale with probable mean wave heights for deep sea criteria. For instance, in the open sea, a WNW'ly wind of force 7 is likely to be accompanied by sea waves of from 4m to 5.5m (13ft to 22ft) in height. Such heights may be suddenly and randomly increased where swell waves are also present. Where heavy swell waves are involved the heights and troughs may be twice or more the average value before just as suddenly decreasing again to a more average value. **So make sure that deck cargo is well-dunnaged, properly lashed, and thoroughly secured before you start the voyage - because you may not get a second chance.** (See colour Plate C between Chapters 2 and 3.)

BEAUFORT WIND SCALE

(For an effective height of 10 m above sea level)

Beaufort Number	Descriptive Term	Mean wind speed equivalent		Deep Sea Criterion	Probable mean wave height* in metres
		Knots	m/sec		
0	Calm	<1	0–0·2	Sea like a mirror	—
1	Light air	1–3	0·3–1·5	Ripples with the appearance of scales are formed, but without foam crests	0·1 (0·1)
2	Light breeze	4–6	1·6–3·3	Small wavelets, still short but more pronounced; crests have a glassy appearance and do not break	0·2 (0·3)
3	Gentle breeze	7–10	3·4–5·4	Large wavelets; crests begin to break; foam of glassy appearance; perhaps scattered white horses	0·6 (1)
4	Moderate breeze	11–16	5·5–7·9	Small waves, becoming longer; fairly frequent white horses	1 (1·5)
5	Fresh breeze	17–21	8·0–10·7	Moderate waves, taking a more pronounced long form; many white horses are formed (chance of some spray)	2 (2·5)
6	Strong breeze	22–27	10·8–13·8	Large waves begin to form; the white foam crests are extensive everywhere (probably some spray)	3 (4)
7	Near gale	28–33	13·9–17·1	Sea heaps up and white foam from breaking waves begins to be blown in streaks along the direction of the wind	4 (5·5)
8	Gale	34–40	17·2–20·7	Moderately high waves of greater length; edges of crests begin to break into spindrift; foam is blown in well-marked streaks along the direction of the wind	5·5 (7·5)
9	Strong gale	41–47	20·8–24·4	High waves; dense streaks of foam along the direction of the wind; crests of waves begin to topple, tumble and roll over; spray may affect visibility	7 (10)
10	Storm	48–55	24·5–28·4	Very high waves with long overhanging crests; the resulting foam, in great patches, is blown in dense white streaks along the direction of the wind; on the whole, the surface of the sea takes a white appearance; the tumbling of the sea becomes heavy and shock-like; visibility affected	9 (12·5)
11	Violent storm	56–63	28·5–32·6	Exceptionally high waves (small and medium sized ships might be for a time lost to view behind the waves); the sea is completely covered with long white patches of foam lying along the direction of the wind; everywhere the edges of the wave crests are blown into froth; visibility affected	11·5 (16)
12	Hurricane	64 and over	32·7 and over	The air is filled with foam and spray; sea completely white with driving spray; visibility seriously affected	14 (—)

* This table is only intended as a guide to show roughly what may be expected in the open sea, remote from land. It should never be used in the reverse way, ie, for logging or reporting the state of the sea. In enclosed waters, or when near land, with an off-shore wind, wave heights will be smaller and the waves steeper. Figures in brackets indicate the probable maximum height of waves.

SOURCE: The Mariner's Handbook - 6th Edition - HMSO 1989

*Light to Medium
Overcentre Buckle*

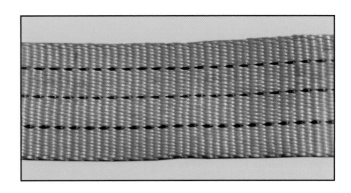

3-tonne NBL stitch-coded webbing

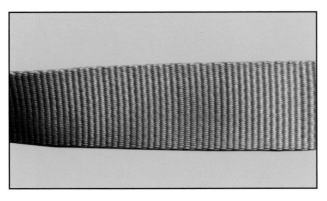

Blue, non-coded, webbing (probably 4-tonne NBL)

Heavy-duty Hand Ratchet

ERGO**ABS**

*Hand Ratchet & Webbing
10-tonne NBL*

*"SuperLash 98"
13.6 tonne NBL*

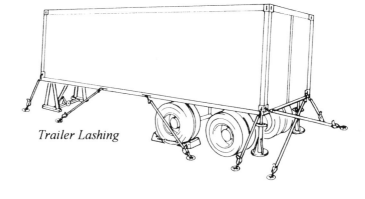

Trailer Lashing

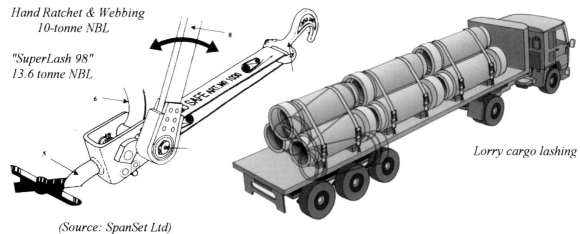

Lorry cargo lashing

(Source: SpanSet Ltd)

Plate B

Deck Cargoes adrift after heavy weather

Plate C

Closed-eye/bolted-jaw rigging screw

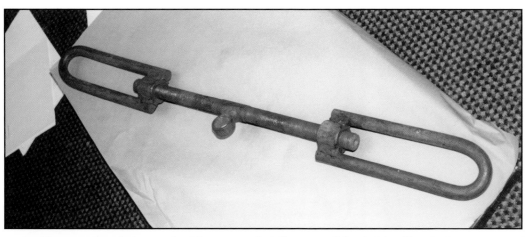

Before attaching to wire, chain, or shackle, ensure that the eyes of the turnbuckle, rigging-screw, or bottle-screw, are wound out to their fully-extended position. (Here, a good example of a well-made, fabricated, hamburger turnbuckle - break-load in excess of 12 tonnes.)

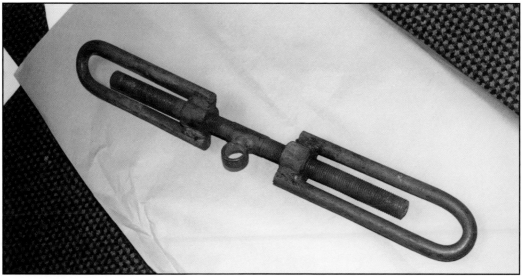

If lashing is commenced with the turnbuckle fully extended, as in the middle view above, it allows the full length of the thread to be wound inward - as here shown - first to tighten the lashings, and then to take-up any slack which may develop during the voyage.

Plate D

Before cutting the wire, whip or tape on both sides of the cut point.

Cut cleanly through the wire.

Taping at cut ends holds the strands together.

Plate E

CHAPTER 2

Lashing Materials

All sizes and characteristics of materials considered herein are given in good faith as being representative of the manufacturers' data available; occasional slight national variations are unlikely to be of adverse significance. The recommendations given in this Chapter exclude consideration of timber deck cargoes, containers and ro-ro vessels except where mentioned in passing. Importantly, see also the section on "breaking strengths" included in the **INTRODUCTION to the CSM** preceding Chapter 1.

Wires - Sizes and Strengths

For efficient lashing purposes wire ropes should be round-strand, flexible, and not so great in diameter as to make their use cumbersome. The most common of such general-purpose wires is 16mm diameter (2" circumference) of 6 x 12 construction galvanised round-strand with fibre core, having a certificated minimum breaking strength of 7.75 tonnef (tonnes force). This is usually termed the "nominal breaking load" (NBL); that is, the force **calculated** at which the wire will break on the theoretical basis of its materials, construction, and size. The "actual breaking load" can only be found by physically testing the wire to destruction. In new wire that value is almost always greater than the "nominal" (NBL) value. Although it is common practice to speak and write of breaking loads in terms of tonnes weight, they should more correctly be referred to as tonnes force - or tonnef, for short - and the correct "tonnef" will be used from here onwards.

Inexpensive wire for its size, 16mm will turn easily around thimbles and lashing points, can be spliced or bulldog-gripped without difficulty, and does not become tiresome to use. Part of the results of tests undertaken by the Health & Safety Executive Research Laboratories, and completed in March 1991, indicated that - so far as bulldog-grips are concerned - wire-cored ropes gave better results than those constructed with fibre cores; ordinary lay ropes gave better results than Lang's lay ropes; and non-galvanised wire ropes gave better results than galvanised ropes.(See Addendum 2 : L.E.E.A. Bulletin, December 1991.) Other wires of different construction, sizes or strengths may, however, be necessary for particular lashing purposes; but throughout the examples given in this book only standard marine galvanised fibre-cored flexible steel wire ropes are considered, and the following Table 2 provides some limited characteristics.

The NBL's given in Table 2 are generally the lowest values for the types of rope specified. Where special construction/special steels are employed, the manufacturers' literature should be consulted. Table 2 on the following page illustrates the fact that, size for size, the 6 x 19 construction provides the greatest NBL. Its use should be encouraged despite the fact that it is more expensive than, and not quite as flexible as, the more commonly used 6 x 12 construction. Figs.2.01, 2.02 and 2.03 on page 27 show the constructions. The measurement of wire size must be made carefully using a calliper. The correct diameter is found in the circle which encloses all the strands of the rope, as shown in Fig.2.04, i.e. the greatest diameter.

Note: The IMO Cargo Securing Manual requires the MSL for wire rope used once, only, to be allowed as 80% of breaking strength; and the MSL for wire ropes used more than once to be allowed as 30% of breaking strength. In such contexts "breaking strength" should be considered to be the same as NBL, above, **unless a test certificate for the actual wire being used indicates a different value.** For guidance on the safe application and use of bulldog-grips in the making-up of eyes and grommets see Chapter 3, hereof.

TABLE 2 - Galvanised Flexible Steel Wire Ropes - Nominal Breaking Loads

Diameter (mm)	Construction Strands x Wires	Approx. Weight kg/100m	Nominal Breaking Load - Tonnef
8	6 x 12	16	1.94
8	6 x 19	21	2.85
8	6 x 24	20	2.60
12	6 x 12	36	4.35
12	6 x 19	46	6.42
12	6 x 24	45	5.85
16	6 x 12	64	7.75
16	6 x 19	87	11.40
16	6 x 24	79	10.40
18	6 x 12	80	9.80
18	6 x 19	111	14.40
18	6 x 24	100	13.20
20	6 x 12	100	12.10
20	6 x 19	136	17.80
20	6 x 24	124	16.20
22	6 x 12	120	14.60
22	6 x 19	165	21.60
22	6 x 24	150	19.70

(1 tonnef = 9.80665kN - see Addendum 1 - Conversion Factors)

In the 16mm size, for instance, the 6 x 19 is 47% stronger than the 6 x 12. In time, labour and bulldog-grips it costs the same to rig a 6 x 19 lashing as it does to rig a 6 x 12, and labour costs and time tend to be the largest items of expenditure in a lashing job. In many instances, the use of 6 x 19 wire in place of 6 x 12 wire will reduce the number of lashings required by as much as one-third; i.e. 8 lashings instead of 12, for instance, where a 20-tonne item is involved. Bearing in mind the realities of supplying ships with lashing wire, however, it is almost certain that the cheapest 16mm of 6 x 12 (7.75 tonnef NBL) will be most frequently used, except in pre-planned circumstances where alternative wire sizes may be specified. That having been said, 18mm of 6 x 24 (13.20 tonnef NBL) is not uncommon and due consideration is given to that size of wire later herein, although illustrative calculations will mostly be restricted to 16mm wire of 6 x 12 construction using NBL's from Table 2, above.

Stretch

The stretch or extension in length of a wire rope under load consists of

a. **Permanent constructional stretch**, which is due to the settling and compacting of the wires in the strands, settling-in of the strands themselves, and the compression of the central core. This stretch is not recoverable - it remains; and most of it occurs during the early part of the rope's working life. For new wire ropes, the permanent constructional stretch within acceptable limits, expressed as a percentage of the rope length under load will be

6-strand ropes - **fibre core** - 0.50% under light load to 1.00% under heavy load.
6 -strand ropes - **steel core** - 0.25% under light load to 0.50% under heavy load.

(**Note:** Wire ropes of different construction, say 8-strand with fibre core, will achieve 0.75% to 1.00% permanent stretch under load.)

 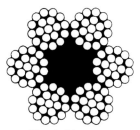 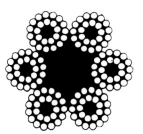

Fig.2.01 *6 x 12*
(12/Fibre) FC

Fig.2.02 *6 x 19*
(12/6/1/Fibre) FC

Fig.2.03 *6 x 24*
(15/9/Fibre) FC

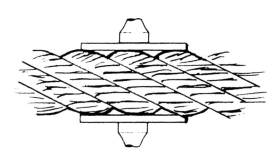

Fig.2.04 *Correct method by which to measure the diameter of wire rope*

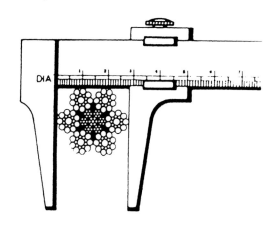

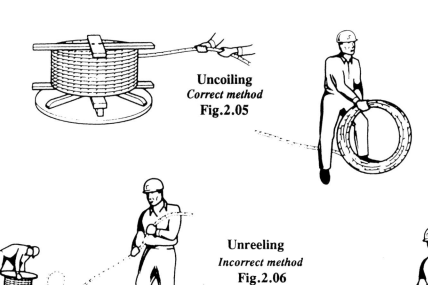

Uncoiling
Correct method
Fig.2.05

Unreeling
Incorrect method
Fig.2.06

SOURCE: HER Group

b. **Elastic stretch**, which is the ability of the individual wires to elongate under load due to their elastic properties. Providing the rope is not subjected to loads beyond its elastic limit, the rope will return to its original length after removal of the load - original, that is, from whatever point in permanent stretch had been attained earlier. The formula for calculating the elastic stretch requires the knowledge of four aspects, namely: the load on the rope, the working length of the rope, the cross-sectional area of the rope, and its modulus of elasticity.

$$\text{Elastic stretch in mm} = \frac{WL}{AE}$$

Where W is the load on the rope in kgf
L is the length of the rope under load in mm
A is the metallic cross-sectional area of the rope in mm^2
E is the modulus of elasticity of the rope in kgf/mm^2

(*SOURCE: H.E.R. Group.*)

By plotting the results of a representative number of calculations a quick approximate rule-of-thumb can be devised, as follows:

For 16mm dia. wire rope - Elastic stretch under load, expressed as a percentage of the length of the wire under load, will be:-

Wire

6 x 12	=	Load (in tonnef)/6	=	% stretch
6 x 19	=	Load (in tonnef)/10	=	% stretch
6 x 24	=	Load (in tonnef)/8	=	% stretch

Examples: What will be the approximate elastic stretch of a) 16mm (6 x 12) wire under a 2 tonnef load; b) 16mm wire (6 x 19) under a 10 tonnef load; c) 16mm wire (6 x 24) under a 7 tonnef load?

a.	=	2/6	=	0.3% elastic stretch
b.	=	10/10	=	1.0% elastic stretch
c.	=	7/8	=	0.875% elastic stretch

For 18mm dia. wire rope - Elastic stretch under load, expressed as a percentage of the length of the wire under load, will be:-

Wire

6 x 12	=	Load (in tonnef)/7.7	=	% stretch
6 x 19	=	Load (in tonnef)/13.0	=	% stretch
6 x 24	=	Load (in tonnef)/10.4	=	% stretch

Examples: What will be the approximate elastic stretch of d) 18mm (6 x 12) wire under a 5 tonnef load; e) 18mm wire (6 x 19) under a 10 tonnef load; f) 18mm wire (6 x 24) under a 2 tonnef load?

d.	=	5/7.7	=	0.65% elastic stretch
e.	=	10/13.0	=	0.77% elastic stretch
f.	=	2/10.4	=	0.19% elastic stretch

For reasons which will become clear in Chapter 3, the loads on lashing wires which are of first importance are 1½ and 2 tonnes, ½NBL and 0.7NBL and, based on the foregoing approximate rules-of-thumb, some of those values can be set out as in Table 3, below.

TABLE 3 - Approximate Non-Permanent Elastic Stretch

Wire Construction	NBL (tonnef)	% Stretch in 16mm dia.			
		@ .7NBL	@ .5NBL	@ 2 tonnef	@ 1½ tonnef
6 x 12	7.75	0.90	0.65	0.33	0.25
6 x 19	11.40	0.78	0.57	0.20	0.15
6 x 24	10.40	0.91	0.65	0.25	0.19

Wire Construction	NBL (tonnef)	% Stretch in 18mm dia.			
		@ .7NBL	@ .5NBL	@ 2 tonnef	@ 1½ tonnef
6 x 12	9.80	0.90	0.64	0.26	0.19
6 x 19	14.40	0.78	0.55	0.15	0.12
6 x 24	13.20	0.89	0.63	0.19	0.14

Table 3 illustrates something which experienced seamen have mainly thought to be the case, namely, that given elastic stretch, alone, lashing wires under normal loadings short of breaking point are unlikely to extend by more than 1% of the working length of the wire. With new wire straight off the coil, however, some increment to Table 3 must be allowed for permanent constructional stretch referred to earlier. For instance, a new unused 16mm 6 x 12 wire subjected to a load equal to 0.5NBL would first go through a permanent stretch of roughly 0.75% and then through an elastic stretch of 0.65%, making a total of 1.4%.

Chains
The use of chain alone for the securing of general deck cargoes is not widespread. Where chain lashing are used they tend to be supplied in rather precise lengths already fitted with terminal points and tightening devices. The advantage of using chain resides, in some circumstances, in the fact that, under the normal loads for which it is designed, it will not stretch. Thus, if all chain lashings are set tight before the voyage and the cargo neither settles nor moves, there is no normal loading circumstance which will cause the chain to lose its tautness. Hence, its widespread use in the securing of freight containers and vehicle trailers.

In general, however, chain for non-specific uses tends to be awkward to handle, tiresome to rig, difficult to cut to length, and it does not render easily. For general purposes it is used most effectively in relatively short lengths in conjunction with, and as part of, lashings otherwise composed of wire, webbing or tightening devices. Figs.2.07, 2.08, 2.09 and 2.10 provide illustrations of some chain types and arrangements. Table 4 gives approximate data relevant to strengths and sizes of the chain Grade most likely to be met with in cargo securing applications. The identification of Grade 8 (BS EN 818-2:1997) by that number may be changed by the pending EU Standard (EN 12195-3, for instance) but the approximate values in Tables 4 will be near enough (±0.04 tonnef) to comply with those Standards where deck cargo securing is involved and Lashing

Capacity (LC) means and is the same as Maximum Securing Load (MSL) in accordance with the CSS Code - **not, repeat, not the same as SWL!**

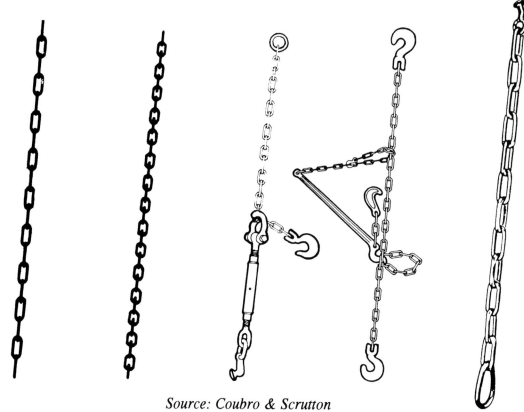

Source: Coubro & Scrutton

Fig. 2.07
Long link chain

Fig.2.08
Short link chain

Fig.2.10
Chain with tensioners.

Fig.2.09
Chain with ring lug one end, oval link the other.

TABLE 4 - Chain Strengths - Grade 8 - Short Link (EN 12195-3)

Dia. of Bar Forming Link	Link Type	Break-Load Tonnef	Proof-Load Tonnef	Lashing Capacity/ (MSL) Tonnef
9mm	Short	10.40	6.53	5.20
10mm	Short	12.84	8.00	6.42
11mm	Short	15.70	9.85	7.85
13mm	Short	21.62	13.56	10.81
16mm	Short	32.84	20.60	16.42
18mm	Short	41.50	26.04	20.75
20mm	Short	51.30	32.18	25.65
22mm	Short	62.00	38.90	31.00

Note: In these instances Proof-Load is roughly two-thirds of Break-Load and Lashing Capacity/MSL is 50% of Break-Load in keeping with the requirements of the CSS Code/CSM Regulations but, if used to those values, it would not then be safe to use that chain for *lifting* purposes where the required SWL/WLL will be no more than 20% or 25% of Break-Load. And other Grades may have much lower strength values.

It is important to remember that within the CSM Regulations manufacturers/suppliers of lashing chains now have a mandatory duty to provide the user vessel with details of breaking strengths, MSL's and MSL identification; so Table 4 should only be used in the absence of other more precise data and when you know the chain you have is of the Table 4 Grade. In the absence of MSL identification, but with **any** chain **marked** with its SWL/WLL, or of which its SWL/WLL **is known for certain**, it would be reasonable to multiply the SWL/WLL x 4 and then divide by 2 to obtain the approximate Lashing Capacity/MSL of the chain.(See **INTRODUCTION to the CSM** earlier herein.)

The CSS Code/CSM Regulations apply the MSL of the various securing materials as a prime governing factor; and there are circumstances where chains, shackles, turnbuckles and wires may be used together and/or in part, so that relative strengths must be balanced, like-with-like. If chain is selected because it has a break-load of, say, 20 tonnef (MSL 10 tonnef), there is little point - on strength or economic grounds, that is - in joining it to a single run of 16mm wire with bulldog-gripped soft eyes which have a 5½ tonnef slip-load, attached by means of shackles which have a break-load of 15 tonnes (MSL 7.5 tonnef). The system will be no stronger than its weakest component, namely, the 16mm wire soft eye slip-load of 5½ tonnef. However, if one length of chain and one shackle are used to connect more than one wire at one point, then clearly some increased balanced assessments are equally necessary. These aspects are dealt with more fully in Chapter 3 and onwards.

Webbing Slings
The use of webbing slings and webbing lashings for cargo securing purposes is now widespread. Operational results differ widely. There are people who would use nothing else; there are others who avoid using webbing under any circumstance. The material's merit lies somewhere between those two extremes, depending largely upon using the correct webbing for the job. There are instances where webbing is ideal for securing deck cargoes; there are other instances where its use should be treated with caution.

Large-bore pipes of reinforced plastic and/or with contact-sensitive outer coatings, large cylinders lacking securing lugs, and bronze propellers, for instance, make webbing an ideal securing medium; its relatively broad flat surfaces and reduced cutting nature allow it to be turned around in short spans and tightened - using its appropriate hand-ratchets - against the cargo item's surfaces to produce a firm, efficient, and acceptable securing component. On the other hand, large high-standing crated items and/or high-standing heavy machinery, where relatively long spans may be involved, generally require wire or chain lashings either in whole or in part, because it is difficult to apply rigid tension to long drifts of webbing on its own, although some of the "superlash" systems now available can overcome this problem most effectively,

Webbing is frequently used in conjunction with, and as part of, lashings formed of chain and, less commonly, of wire. See Figs.2.11 and 2.12. Fig.2.13 shows the method of tensioning and releasing a ratchet hand tensioner on webbing.

Webbing is mostly manufactured from impregnated woven polyester fibre, and therefore has stretch characteristics greater than wire rope. It is supplied in reels and may easily be cut and fashioned to any required length. For cargo lashing purposes it is not required to be colour-coded as to NBL, and can be supplied in NBL's of from 3 tonnef to 14 tonnef. **Webbing should not be used without clearly confirming its nature, breaking load, and applicability - all from the manufacturers' literature**.(See colour Plate B at the end of this Chapter.)

Fig.2.11 *Webbing with 5-tonne MBL and various end attachments.*

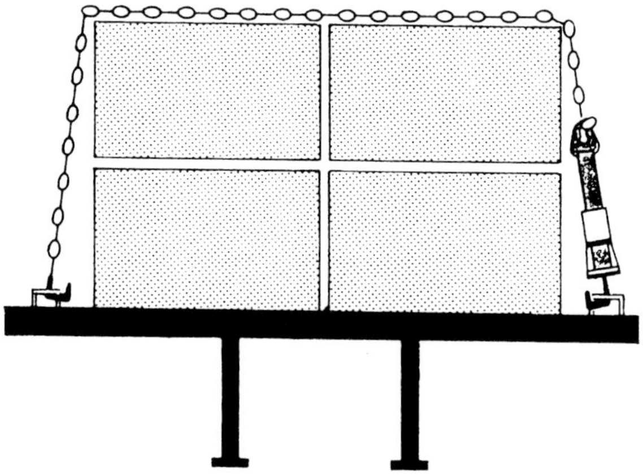

Fig.2.12 *One method of using webbing and chain lashings*

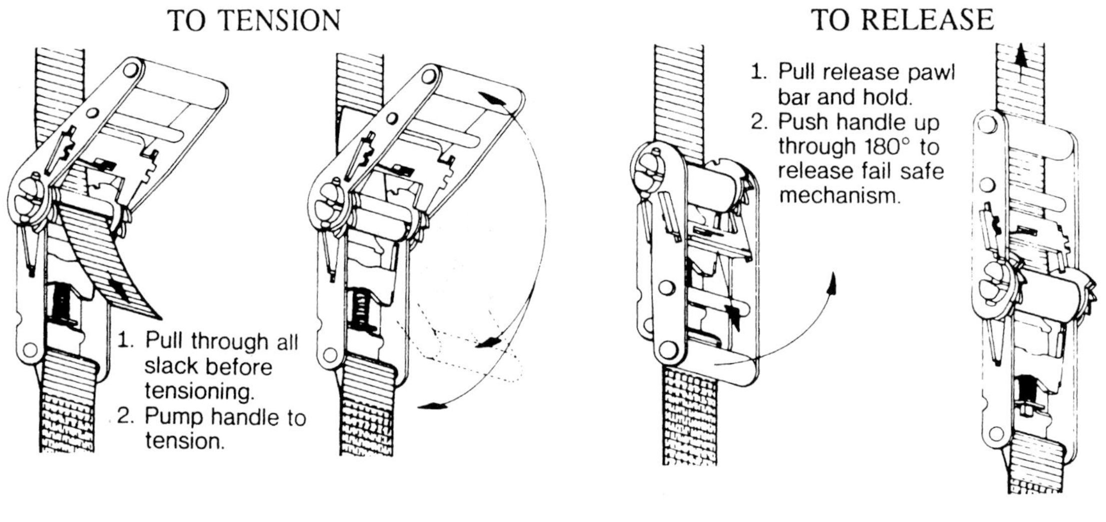

Fig.2.13

TO TENSION

1. Pull through all slack before tensioning.
2. Pump handle to tension.

TO RELEASE

1. Pull release pawl bar and hold.
2. Push handle up through 180° to release fail safe mechanism.

(SOURCE: Spanset Limited)

Some time prior to the publication of the 1994 edition, the author, in arrangement with the United Arab Shipping Company, carried out a number of tests on webbing and tensioners at a manufacturer's premises on Merseyside, the aggregate results of which are indicated below:-

i) Under relatively low and relatively high acceleration loading, a single run of new webbing, without a ratchet or tensioner but with a machine-stitched loop in each end, will fracture at loads in excess of the manufacturers' marketed breaking load.

ii) Similarly, a continuous loop, with machine-stitched connections, will fracture at loads **in excess of twice** the manufacturers' marketed breaking load.

iii) Ratchet hand tensioners of 10000lb (4.536 tonnes) nominal breaking load failed at loads minimally in excess of such values but generally at loads below 5 tonnes.

iv) Ratchet spanner tensioners of the heavy-duty type and 15-tonnef nominal breaking load were not tested. It is assumed that they, and their associated 12 tonnef break-load webbing, will perform at values not less than the manufacturers' marketed break-loads.

v) When a loop (or bight) of webbing is used with a hand tensioner in the loop, a failure of the webbing at the ratchet barrel or a failure of the ratchet standing pawl will occur at loads near the manufacturers' marketed breaking load for the tensioner (i.e. 4.536 tonnes - see iii, above) rather than at twice the breaking load of the webbing as would be expected from ii, above. The manufacturers take note of this and recommend the following simple formula:-

$$\frac{\text{Cargo Weight (tonnes)} \times 2^*}{4.536} = \text{minimum number of webbing lashings required}$$

Note: * This would comply with the CSS Code/CSM Regs 50% amendment for web lashings' MSL. In my view, this is acceptable for below-decks securing, but the 2* should be `3' for weather-deck stowages when following the *three-times-rule* as dealt with earlier herein.

Additionally, the following points should be borne in mind:-

a) Unsupported length of webbing should be kept as short as possible.

b) Always use protective sleeves between webbing and abrasion points/areas.

c) Tension on a hand ratchet is achieved easily up to 0.45 tonnes; thereafter with some difficulty up to a maximum of 0.60 tonnes. **A spanner or bar must never be used to tighten a ratchet hand tensioner. A recoil could seriously injure the user**.

d) Keep webbing away from acids and alkalis, and ensure that webbing is never used to secure drums or packages of corrosive materials or chemicals whose adverse effect is unknown.

e) Inspect all webbing frequently and, if re-used, ensure that all lengths are free of defects or degradation.

f) For securing ISO freight containers use only those webbing systems designed for such purpose.

Rope - Natural and Synthetic Fibres and Composites
Ropes of up to 25mm dia. (3" circ.) are handy to use, but are more likely to be found on below-decks cargo. For weather-deck cargoes the use of fibre ropes should be restricted to light loads of limited volume in areas partly sheltered by the ship's structure; they should never be used to secure acids, alkalis, or substances likely to have corrosive characteristics.

It is not simply a matter of intrinsic strength; rather, the difficulty is in maintaining the tautness of fibre rope lashings as they become subjected to load stresses and/or the wetting and drying-out effects inherent in the exposed situation. The use of turnbuckles with fibre ropes should be avoided; they may quite easily overload the rope lashings and create the very failure conditions you wish to avoid. Tautening of rope lashings is best achieved by the use of bowsing ropes and frappings. (See Figs.2.14 and 2.15.) Table 5A gives some indication of sizes, materials and strengths for hawser-laid 3-strand ropes. Table 5B provides additional strength data on larger ropes.

TABLE 5A - Hawser-Laid 3-Strand Ropes - Break-Loads: SWL's

Material Fibre	Dia./Circ. mm/ins.		Break-Load Tonnef	SWL* Tonnes
Manila	8	1	0.54	0.09
"	16	2	2.03	0.34
"	20	2½	3.25	0.54
"	24	3	4.57	0.76
Sisal	8	1	0.48	0.08
"	16	2	1.80	0.30
"	20	2½	2.85	0.47
"	24	3	4.07	0.68
Polyprop'	8	1	0.96	0.16
"	16	2	3.50	0.60
"	20	2½	5.40	0.90
"	24	3	7.60	1.26
Polyester	8	1	1.02	0.17
"	16	2	4.10	0.70
"	20	2½	6.30	1.05
"	24	3	9.10	1.51
Nylon	8	1	1.35	0.23
"	16	2	5.30	0.90
"	20	2½	8.30	1.40
"	24	3	12.00	2.00
Nylon Braid	8	1	1.45	0.24
"	16	2	5.50	0.90
"	20	2½	9.00	1.50
"	24	3	12.7	2.10

*Note: The SWL's here listed are based on a safety factor of 6, in keeping with statutory requirements for lifting gear, and the like. The IMO uses MSL = 33% of breaking strength for cargo securing purposes. Hence, a sisal rope of 2.85 break-load will have a statutory SWL of 0.47 tonnef and an IMO cargo securing MSL of 0.94 tonnef!

It should be realised that both knotting and splicing weaken cordage by an amount dependent on the termination chosen. However, a rope containing both knots and splices, or a succession of different knots, will not be weakened cumulatively as a result. It will be weakened by the amount caused by the least efficient knot or splice used.

TABLE 5B - Break-Loads in kN (9.81kN = 1 tonnef) *Source: Rope Properties - Vol.B - British Ropes*

Size No.	Nom. Dia. (mm)	Nylon BS4928 *Part 2*	Poly-ester BS4928 *Part 2*	Poly-ethylene BS4928 *Part 2*	Poly-propylene BS4928 *Part 1*	Manila BS2052	Sisal BS2052	Braid-line —	Thor —
—	4	3·14	2·90	1·96	—	—	—	—	—
—	5	4·90	3·92	—	—	—	—	—	—
—	6	7·35	5·54	3·92	5·39	—	—	9·3	—
—	7	10·0	7·55	—	—	3·63	3·24	—	—
—	8	13·2	10·0	6·86	9·41	5·35	4·74	14·2	—
—	9	16·7	12·5	—	—	—	—	—	—
—	10	20·4	15·6	10·7	13·9	6·91	6·23	26·7	—
—	12	29·4	22·3	15·1	19·9	10·4	9·36	31·2	—
—	14	40·2	31·2	20·5	27·3	14·2	12·5	42·4	—
—	16	52·0	40·2	27·5	34·3	19·9	17·7	53·9	—
—	18	66·0	50·0	34·0	43·6	23·9	21·0	77·5	—
—	20	81·0	62·0	42·0	52·6	31·9	28·0	—	—
—	21	—	—	—	—	—	—	93·2	—
—	22	98·0	75·0	50·0	63·7	37·8	33·4	—	—
3	24	118	89·0	60·0	73·5	44·8	39·9	124·5	—
3½	28	155	120	79·0	99·0	59·8	53·3	176·5	—
4	32	196	154	102	125	77·5	67·2	215·7	—
4½	36	244	190	128	158	94·6	85·3	264·8	—
5	40	294	235	153	190	117	102	353·0	304
5½	44	351	279	185	229	140	125	411·9	412
6	48	412	329	220	267	164	145	490·3	490
6½	52	479	384	257	309	192	169	588·4	530
7	56	549	439	296	353	220	194	676·6	652
7½	60	626	489	336	404	249	222	764·9	—
—	62	—	—	—	—	—	—	—	775
8	64	706	568	379	457	284	252	882·6	794
—	68	—	—	—	—	—	—	—	992
—	70	—	—	—	—	—	—	—	1 010
9	72	882	707	476	574	351	320	1 069	—
10	80	1 080	867	—	706	426	379	1 353	—
11	88	1 280	1 040	—	847	505	459	1 638	—
12	96	1 510	1 230	—	1 000	588	525	1 912	—
13	104	1 780	1 430	—	1 130	686	613	2 275	—
14	112	2 060	1 650	—	1 320	794	706	2 618	—
15	120	2 350	1 880	—	1 520	912	814	2 991	—
16	128	2 670	2 140	—	1 720	1 040	922	3 334	—
17	136	3 000	2 400	—	1 910	1 180	1 040	—	—
—	140	—	—	—	—	1 320	1 170	—	—
18	144	3 350	2 690	—	2 150	—	—	4 119	—
19	152	3 730	2 980	—	2 400	—	—	—	—
20	160	4 120	3 300	—	2 650	—	—	—	—
21	168	4 530	3 630	—	2 940	—	—	5 590	—
22	176	4 960	3 970	—	3 190	—	—	—	—
23	184	5 410	4 330	—	3 480	—	—	—	—
24	192	5 880	4 710	—	3 780	—	—	7 453	—
27	216	—	—	—	—	—	—	9 610	—
30	240	—	—	—	—	—	—	11 768	—
33	264	—	—	—	—	—	—	14 122	—
36	288	—	—	—	—	—	—	16 867	—

The British Standard shown in the column heading relates to sizes of up to 96 mm diameter (No. 12) for man-made fibres, and up to 144 mm diameter for natural fibre ropes. The data given for sizes larger than these has been agreed by the Cordage Manufacturers' Institute and agreement for its inclusion in British and International Standards will be sought. This information must be regarded as being provisional and may be subject to slight alteration.

Nylon fibre absorbs between 8% and 9% of water; the overall effect, when under load, is to reduce its effective strength by about 15%. Premature failure of nylon rope occurs under limited cyclic loading up to 70% of its effective strength. Therefore, nylon rope is not recommended for deck cargo securing purposes.

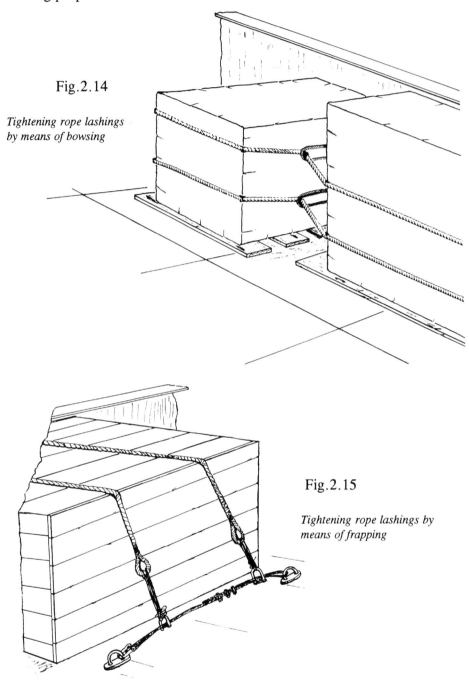

Fig.2.14

Tightening rope lashings by means of bowsing

Fig.2.15

Tightening rope lashings by means of frapping

Knots - Weakening of Fibre Ropes

All the jointing and attachment knots traditionally used for natural fibres may be employed with man-made fibre cordage. However, it must be borne in mind that with polyethylene, and to some extent, polypropylene, knots can slip under load and the use of 'stopper knots' is advocated. Such slippage is due to the waxy nature of the cordage polymer, and not to the rope construction employed.

Similarly, knots, once tied and loaded, are frequently difficult, if not impossible, to untie. This difficulty arises from the extension of the cordage under load which locks the knot once the load is removed, and is quite different in mechanism from the swelling of the natural fibres when wet which produces a similar effect.

It must be realised that both knotting and splicing weaken cordage by an amount dependent on the termination chosen. However, a rope containing both knots and splices, or a succession of different knots, will not be weakened cumulatively as a result. It will be weakened by the amount caused by the least efficient knot or splice used.

For example, a nylon rope containing an eye-splice and a bow-line will not be weakened by 19 + 42 = 61% (the values of percentage strength loss shown in Table 6, below), but instead it would be expected to lose 42% - the effect of the least efficient termination.

Table 6 shows the effect of commonly-encountered knots on the strength of ropes of the various fibres. The results have been established from numerous tests on new ropes in the size range 6 - 14mm diameter. Some reduction in these values might be expected from ropes larger in circumference or in a worn condition and accordingly the information must be regarded as being of an advisory nature.

Under no circumstances should knots be used in items of lifting equipment such as rope slings.

TABLE 6 - Knot Efficiency of Cordage

			Polypropylene		
Material	Nylon	Polyester	Fibrefilm	Staple	Sisal
Reef Knot	37	45	44	43	53
Overhand Knot	40	43	47	39	50
Bow-Line	58	56	57	64	63
Sheet Bend	53	49	49	41	50
Double Sheet Bend	57	42	54	45	50
Clove Hitch	55	52	65	51	81
Eye-Splice	81	89	86	86	90
Timber Hitch	55	65	61	57	94
Double Figure-of-Eight	74	Not Tested	Not Tested		

The figures in the vertical columns represent percentage of NBL remaining. Hence, to find percentage weakening subtract the relevant number from 100. For instance: by how much is a sisal rope weakened by using a reef knot? Answer: 100 - 53 = 47% NBL reduction. (*SOURCE: Rope Properties - Vol.B - British Ropes Ltd.*)

Composites
Composite rope - frequently referred to as "lashing rope" - is made up of wire fibres and sisal or polypropylene fibres interwoven, giving to the flexibility of sisal and polypropylene some of the strength of steel. It is most frequently supplied in coils of 10mm dia. rope. The breaking load should be considered as about 0.8 tonnes for sisal-based, and 1.8 tonnes for polypropylene-based, composite ropes. **Use it with caution and with those strength values in mind**. (See Chapter 7 and Addendum 5 for more details on small diameter wire ropes, turnbuckles and rigging screws.)

Shackles and Turnbuckles

Shackles come in several shapes, sizes, and strengths of material. The two shapes most commonly used for general cargo lashing purposes are the D-shackle and the Bow-shackle - each with eyed screw-pin. Figs.2.16 and 2.17, together with Tables 7A, 7B, 7C and 7D, give some of the data relating to such shackles. See, also, Addendum 5 at the end of this book for breaking strength and MSL details.

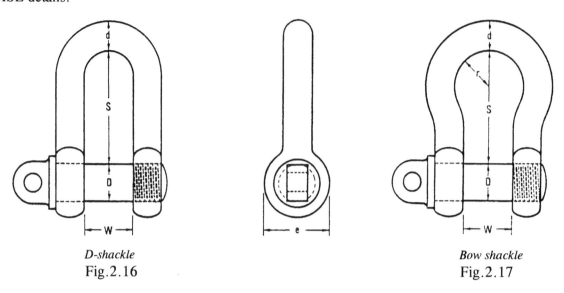

D-shackle
Fig.2.16

Bow shackle
Fig.2.17

Source: Ward & Clark Ltd.

TABLE 7A - Small D-Shackles

S.W.L. tons cwt.	Tonnes	d in	d mm	D in	D mm	w in	w mm	s in	s mm
6	0·30	1/4	6	3/8	10	3/8	10	7/8	22
12	0·60	3/8	10	1/2	13	5/8	16	1 3/8	35
1 0	1·01	1/2	13	5/8	16	7/8	22	1 7/8	48
1 15	1·77	5/8	16	3/4	19	1	25	2 1/4	57
2 10	2·54	3/4	19	7/8	22	1 1/4	32	2 3/4	70
3 10	3·53	7/8	22	1	25	1 3/8	35	3 1/4	83
4 10	4·57	1	25	1 1/8	29	1 1/2	38	3 5/8	92
5 10	5·58	1 1/8	29	1 1/4	32	1 3/4	44	4 1/8	105
7 0	7·11	1 1/4	32	1 3/8	35	1 7/8	48	4 1/2	114
8 0	8·12	1 3/8	35	1 1/2	38	2 1/8	54	5	127
10 15	10·92	1 1/2	38	1 3/4	44	2 3/8	60	5 1/2	140
13 0	13·20	1 5/8	41	1 7/8	48	2 1/2	64	5 7/8	149
14 15	14·98	1 3/4	44	2	51	2 3/4	70	6 3/8	162
16 15	17·02	1 7/8	48	2 1/8	54	2 7/8	73	6 3/4	171
19 0	19·30	2	51	2 1/4	57	3	76	7 1/4	184
20 0	20·32	2 1/8	54	2 3/8	60	3 1/4	83	7 3/4	197
25 0	25·40	2 3/8	60	2 3/4	70	3 5/8	92	8 5/8	219
30 0	30·48	2 1/2	64	2 7/8	73	3 7/8	98	9	229
35 0	35·26	2 3/4	70	3 1/8	79	4 1/4	108	10	254
40 0	40·64	2 7/8	73	3 1/4	83	4 3/8	111	10 3/8	264
50 0	50·80	3 1/4	83	3 3/4	95	5	127	11 3/4	298
65 0	66·04	3 5/8	92	4 1/4	108	5 1/2	140	13 1/8	333
80 0	81·28	4	102	4 5/8	117	6 1/8	156	14 1/2	368

N.B. Proof load = 2 x safe working load. (W.)   *Source: Taylor Pallister & Co. Ltd.*

TABLE 7B - Large D-Shackles

tons	cwt	Tonnes	d (in)	d (mm)	D (in)	D (mm)	w (in)	w (mm)	s (in)	s (mm)
	5	0·25	1/4	6	3/8	10	1/2	13	1	25
	10	0·51	3/8	10	1/2	13	3/4	19	1 1/2	38
	15	0·76	1/2	13	5/8	16	1 1/8	29	2 1/8	54
1	10	1·52	5/8	16	3/4	19	1 1/4	32	2 1/2	64
2	0	2·03	3/4	19	7/8	22	1 1/2	38	2 7/8	73
3	0	3·05	7/8	22	1	25	1 3/4	44	3 1/4	83
3	15	3·81	1	25	1 1/8	29	2	51	3 3/4	95
5	0	5·08	1 1/8	29	1 1/4	32	2 1/8	54	4 1/8	105
6	0	6·10	1 1/4	32	1 3/8	35	2 3/8	60	4 1/2	114
7	0	7·11	1 3/8	35	1 1/2	38	2 5/8	67	5	127
9	10	9·65	1 1/2	38	1 3/4	44	2 3/4	70	5 3/8	137
11	5	11·43	1 5/8	41	1 7/8	48	3	76	5 3/4	146
13	0	13·21	1 3/4	44	2	51	3 1/4	83	6 1/8	156
14	5	14·48	1 7/8	48	2 1/8	54	3 5/8	92	7	178
16	5	16·51	2	51	2 1/4	57	3 7/8	98	7 3/8	187
18	0	18·29	2 1/8	54	2 3/8	60	4 1/8	105	7 3/4	197
20	0	20·32	2 1/4	57	2 1/2	64	4 1/4	108	8 1/4	210
25	0	25·40	2 1/2	64	2 7/8	73	4 3/4	121	9 1/4	235
30	0	30·48	2 3/4	70	3 1/8	79	5 1/4	133	10 1/4	260
35	0	35·56	3	76	3 3/8	86	5 1/2	146	11	279
40	0	40·64	3 1/8	79	3 1/2	89	5 7/8	149	11 1/2	292
50	0	50·80	3 1/2	89	4	102	6 3/4	171	13	330
65	0	66·04	4	102	4 1/2	114	7 1/2	191	14 3/4	375
80	0	81·28	4 1/2	114	5	127	8 5/8	219	16 1/2	419

TABLE 7C - Small Bow-Shackles

Source: Taylor Pallister & Co. Ltd.

tons	cwt	Tonnes	d (in)	d (mm)	D (in)	D (mm)	w (in)	w (mm)	2r (in)	2r (mm)	s (in)	s (mm)
	4	0·20	1/4	6	3/8	10	1/2	13	5/8	16	1	25
	10	0·50	3/8	10	1/2	13	5/8	16	7/8	22	1 1/2	38
1	0	1·01	1/2	13	5/8	16	7/8	22	1 1/8	29	2	51
1	10	1·52	5/8	16	3/4	19	1 1/8	29	1 1/2	38	2 1/2	64
2	0	2·03	3/4	19	7/8	22	1 3/8	35	1 3/4	44	3	76
3	0	3·04	7/8	22	1	25	1 1/2	38	2	51	3 1/2	89
4	0	4·06	1	25	1 1/8	29	1 3/4	44	2 3/8	60	4	102
5	0	5·08	1 1/8	29	1 1/4	32	2	51	2 5/8	67	4 1/2	114
6	5	6·35	1 1/4	32	1 3/8	35	2 1/4	57	3	76	5	127
7	10	7·62	1 3/8	35	1 1/2	38	2 3/8	60	3 1/4	83	5 1/2	140
9	5	9·39	1 1/2	38	1 3/4	44	2 5/8	67	3 1/2	89	6	152
10	10	10·66	1 5/8	41	1 7/8	48	2 7/8	73	3 7/8	98	6 1/2	165
12	10	12·70	1 3/4	44	2	51	3 1/8	79	4 1/8	105	7	178
14	5	14·48	1 7/8	48	2 1/8	54	3 3/8	86	4 1/2	114	7 1/2	191
16	10	16·76	2	51	2 1/4	57	3 5/8	92	4 3/4	121	8	203
18	10	18·80	2 1/8	54	2 3/8	60	3 3/4	95	5	127	8 1/2	216
20	0	20·32	2 1/4	57	2 1/2	64	4 1/8	105	5 3/8	137	9	229
25	0	25·40	2 1/2	64	2 3/4	70	4 1/2	114	6	152	10	254
30	0	30·48	2 3/4	70	3 1/8	79	5	127	6 5/8	168	11	279
35	0	35·56	3	76	3 3/8	86	5 3/8	137	7 1/4	184	12	305
40	0	40·64	3 1/8	79	3 1/2	89	5 5/8	143	7 1/2	191	12 1/2	318
50	0	50·80	3 1/2	89	3 7/8	98	6 1/4	159	8 3/8	213	14	356
65	0	66·04	4	102	4 1/2	114	7 1/4	184	9 5/8	244	16	406
80	0	81·28	4 1/2	114	5	127	8 1/8	206	10 1/4	273	18	457

N.B. Proof load = 2 x safe working load.

TABLE 7D - Large Bow-Shackles

Source: Taylor Pallister & Co. Ltd.

S.W.L.		d		D		w		2r		s	
tons cwt.	Tonnes	in	mm	in	mm	in	mm	in	mm	in	mm
3	0·15	¼	6	⅜	10	½	13	¾	19	1⅛	29
9	0·45	⅜	10	½	13	⅝	16	1	25	1⅝	41
15	0·76	½	13	⅝	16	⅞	22	1¼	32	2⅛	54
1 5	1·27	⅝	16	¾	19	1⅛	29	1⅝	41	2¾	70
2 0	2·03	¾	19	⅞	22	1⅜	35	2	51	3⅜	86
2 15	2·79	⅞	22	1	25	1⅝	41	2¼	57	3⅞	98
3 15	3·81	1	25	1⅛	29	1¾	44	2½	64	4¼	108
4 15	4·82	1⅛	29	1¼	32	2	51	2⅞	73	4⅞	124
5 15	5·84	1¼	32	1⅜	35	2¼	57	3¼	83	5⅜	137
7 5	7·36	1⅜	35	1½	38	2½	64	3½	89	6	152
8 10	8·63	1½	38	1¾	44	2¾	70	3⅞	98	6⅝	168
9 10	9·65	1⅝	41	1⅞	48	3	76	4⅜	111	7⅜	187
11 10	11·68	1¾	44	2	51	3⅜	86	4¾	121	8⅛	206
13 0	13·21	1⅞	48	2⅛	54	3⅝	92	5⅛	130	8¾	222
15 0	15·24	2	51	2¼	57	3⅞	98	5½	140	9⅜	238
18 10	18·80	2¼	57	2½	64	4⅛	105	6	152	10⅛	257
20 0	20·32	2⅜	60	2⅝	67	4⅜	111	6⅜	162	10¾	273
25 0	25·40	2⅝	67	2⅞	73	4¾	121	7	178	11⅞	302
30 0	30·48	2⅞	73	3⅛	79	5¼	133	7¾	197	13	330
35 0	35·56	3⅛	79	3⅜	86	5¾	146	8⅜	213	14⅛	359
40 0	40·64	3⅜	86	3⅝	92	6¼	159	9	229	15¼	387
50 0	50·80	3¾	95	4	102	6¾	171	10	254	16⅞	429
65 0	66·04	4¼	108	4⅝	117	7¾	197	11¼	286	19	483
80 0	81·28	4⅝	117	5	127	8½	216	12⅛	308	21	533

N.B. Proof load = 2 x safe working load.

Those Tables are for Grade 6 shackles, comply with the current ISO Standards, and will comply with the CEN/EU Standard 1:2:5 where, if the *minimum breaking force* equals 100%, then **SWL/WLL** is 20% and **proof load** is 40% of that breaking force. Note, again, that proof load equals twice the SWL/WLL. Naturally, it is correct to think of, and use, shackles in terms of their statutory SWL/WLL whenever lifting gear, cranes, hoists, and the like are involved, but the IMO, through the 1994/1995 Amendments to the Code of Safe Practice for Cargo Stowage and Securing carried through into the Cargo Securing Manual, now recommends a MSL of 50% of breaking strength for shackles, as well as chains, etc, to secure cargo.

According to one of the definitions given in the CSM: *"Maximum Securing Load" (MSL) is a term used to define the allowable load capacity for a device used to secure cargo to a ship. "Safe Working Load" (SWL) may be substituted for MSL for securing purposes, provided this is equal to or exceeds the strength defined by MSL. "*

It seems to follow that most, if not all, shackles, chains, rigging-screws, eye-plates, and the like, which have been stamped with statutory SWL's, will fall short of the CSM parameters for MSL's, size for size. A large bow shackle from Table 7D, above, with a stamped SWL of 3.81 tonnes (25mm pin diameter) for instance, will presumably be considered **not** to have a MSL of any greater value; yet its breaking strength will be 19.05 tonnef (SWLx5); and if no more than the breaking strength were known to the users they would be quite within the CSM requirements to treat that shackle as having a MSL of 9.53 tonnef (50% of 19.05).

A certain degree of chaos is bound to occur if a strict application of the letter of the CSM is adopted in practice. Reference should here be made again to the section on breaking strengths in the **INTRODUCTION** preceding Chapter 1. My view, is that where a shackle is supplied without a clear MSL identification tag, or similar, but on which the SWL/WLL is stamped, it is reasonable to calculate the MSL by multiplying the SWL/WLL by 4 (rather than 5 - just to be on the safe side) and divide the result by 2, that is, MSL = (SWLx4)/2. In other words, **use the proof load as the MSL!** In the instance of the 25mm pin diameter shackle, where only the SWL of 3.81 tonnef was known, I would consider it appropriate to use (and certainly I would do so) that shackle as having a MSL of 7.62 tonnef - **and then remove that shackle from any possibility of it being used for any lifting purpose: - tag it as having a MSL=7.62 tonnef.**

TABLE 8A - Bottle-Screws - Closed-Body - Sizes and Average Strengths

B	A	C		Proof-Load	SWL
mm	mm	Closed	Open	Tonnef	Tonnes
16	229	368	565	1.52	0.76
19	229	394	584	2.29	1.15
22	305	470	730	3.31	1.66
25	356	546	851	4.32	2.16
29	356	546	851	5.59	2.80
32	381	600	918	7.63	3.82
38	406	657	987	10.42	5.21

It can be seen that bottle-screws, like shackles, have a safe working load which, generally, is half the proof-load. Again the break-load is likely to be about five times the SWL, so using proof load x 2 would provide a reasonable and safe MSL in the absence of MSL formal identification.

Screw-size for screw-size, some open-sided rigging-screws and skeleton straining-screws may have lower strengths than solid bottle-screws. Recent tests on "hamburger" type turnbuckles, however, indicated strengths at least as good as - if not better than - those in Table 8A, when the diameter of the threaded bar is the governing factor. Generally speaking, a well-made hamburger turnbuckle with 28mm diameter screws will only start to deform at loads in excess of 12 tonnef, indicating a MSL of about 6 tonnef. Nevertheless, the suppliers/manufacturers should be asked to provide the relevant tested and certificated breaking strengths and proof-loads, as for Table 8B, hereunder, together with their MSL's.

TABLE 8B - Hamburger Turnbuckles   *Source: International Lashing Systems, Ltd.*

Wire turnbuckles

REF. I.L.S.	DIAMETER B	ROD LENGTH L	BOW DIAMETER A	BREAKING LOAD
	mm	mm	mm	tons
M24	24	400 500	16 16	15
M30	30	400 500	18 18	19
M39	39	400 500	25 25	28

Also, there are types of special-purpose turnbuckles with special fittings and modifications (such as in the container trade, for instance) with much greater strengths than those given above. Again, the manufacturers' literature should be consulted if such equipment is to be brought into use.

Container lashing bottle-screws

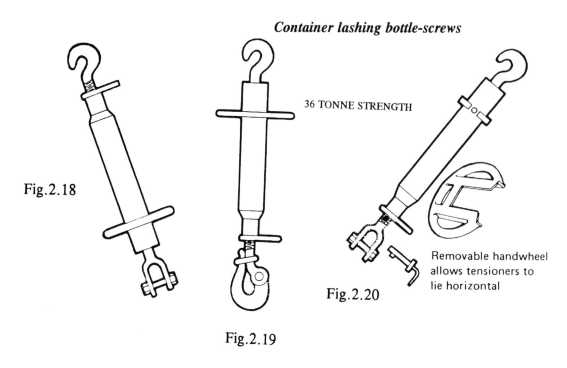

Fig.2.18

36 TONNE STRENGTH

Fig.2.20

Removable handwheel allows tensioners to lie horizontal

Fig.2.19

Sources: Various

Fig.2.21

Solid body bottle-screw

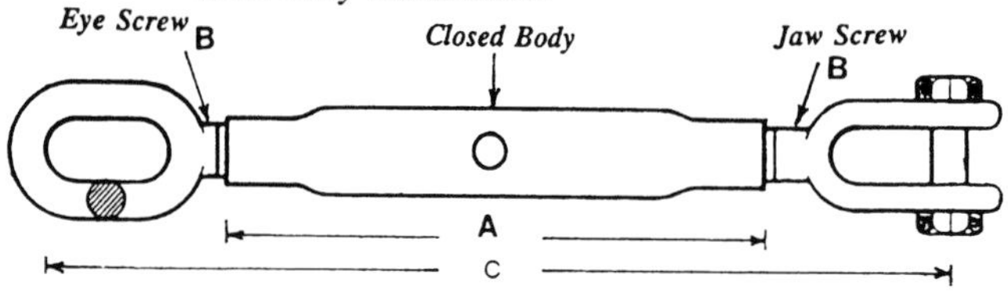

Eye Screw B   Closed Body   Jaw Screw B

A

C

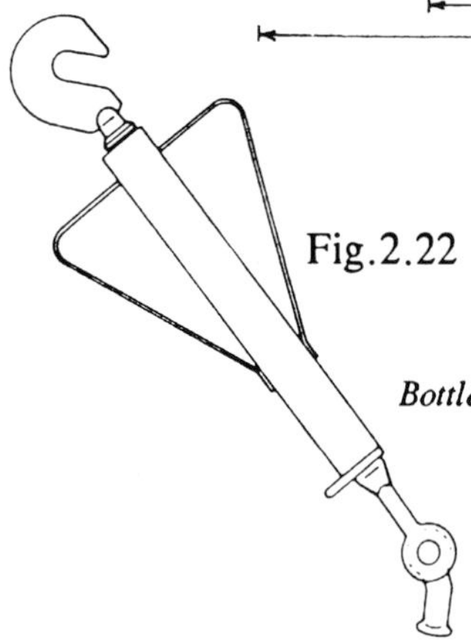

Fig.2.22

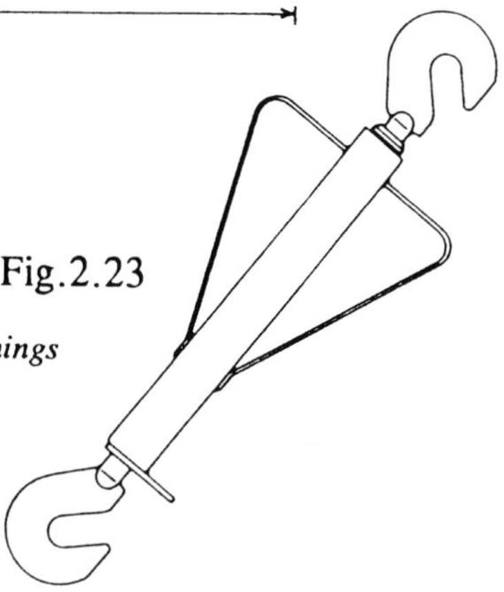

Fig.2.23

Bottle-screws for chain lashings

Fig.2.24

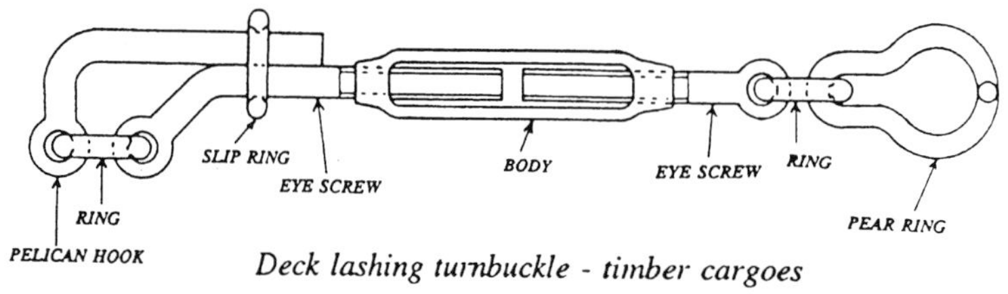

SLIP RING   EYE SCREW   BODY   EYE SCREW   RING

RING   PEAR RING

PELICAN HOOK

Deck lashing turnbuckle - timber cargoes

Pre-Tension

The question of pre-tension arises in deck cargo lashing considerations. Tests with rigging-screws effected by the author prior to the printing of the first edition, and again under his supervision in 1992, returned the results hereunder. All tests were made using 16mm diameter 6 x 12 galvanised wire made up in ½ double grommets using six bulldog-grips. Tension was attained by using a steel turning bar of length similar to a fair-sized marlin-spike of the type carried by riggers for continuous use, and tension was measured on an inset digital electronic load meter. The overall results may be generalised as:-

a.   The larger the screw diameter and the larger the thread, the higher the tension achieved.

b.   With screw diameter of between 22mm and 30mm maximum tension achieved was 2½ tonnes; settled back to 2 tonnes after several minutes.

c.   With screw diameter of between 17mm and 19mm maximum tension was 1.71 tonnes; settled back to 1.53 tonnes after several minutes.

d.   **Where many lashings are being set up, hand and arm fatigue set in quickly; it would therefore be unsafe to assume that pre-tensions in excess of 2 tonnes can be obtained when using equipment normal to the trade.**

e.   It is doubtful if hand-operated mechanical and/or hydraulic tightening equipment, such as "speed-clinchers", can achieve such pre-tension without risk of injury to the user.

f.   It is accepted that, with very large bottle-screws and long turning levers such as are used to set up the mast-stays on heavy-lift derricks, it is possible to attain pre-tension well in excess of 3 tonnes, but such arrangements would not apply to lashing items of deck cargo.

The prime rules for using turnbuckles may be stated by saying:

*   Always use them with the pulling forces acting in one straight line.

*   Never allow them to become the fulcrum of angled forces no matter how slight.

*   Make sure the screws are at adequate extension when the securing of the cargo is finalised, thereby providing scope for further tightening if this should prove necessary during the voyage as the cargo and lashing arrangements settle down.

*   Below-decks, and where high torque upon a main lashing is involved, the eyes of the turnbuckle should be seized/stopped against its own body to prevent the screws working back under load during the course of the voyage, because it may not prove possible to check and/or re-tension below-deck lashings once cargo loading has completed and hatches are secured.

*   With deck-cargo wire lashings, however, where inspection and re-tightening of the securing arrangements is a daily requirement, the locking and/or stopping-back of the turnbuckles, bottle-screws, and similar, may prove to be a burdensome and immensely time-consuming hindrance in instances where a hundred or more lashings demand attention in heavy weather conditions.

See Figs.2.18 to 2.24 on page 42 and colour Plate D at the end of this Chapter.

Sea Fastenings and Cribbaging

As remarked in Chapter 1, if items of deck cargo could be bolted or welded to the deck in the manner adopted for permanent deck fittings and machinery there would be little requirement for lashings of wire and chain; and in instances of awkward, large, and heavy cargo items where lashing facilities are limited or inappropriate, some alternative and semi-permanent arrangements may be necessary. Collectively, such arrangements are known as sea fastenings, and they may be constructed from any one or more steel section types and shapes. The object is to fasten down securely against rolling and pitching stresses.

Take, for instance, a large lattice-type crane jib - Fig.2.25 - which can only be accommodated on the forecastle of extended type which carries the weather-deck hatchways for the nos.1 and 2 upper 'tween decks - Fig.2.26.

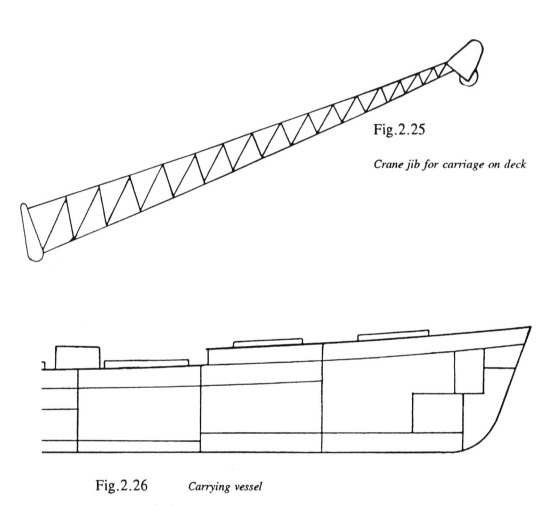

Fig.2.25

Crane jib for carriage on deck

Fig.2.26   *Carrying vessel*

Limited wire lashing points are insufficient, so sea fastenings will be used, together with cribbing (or cribbaging) to support the jib along its non-parallel length. The material for the sea fastenings and cribbaging may comprise of steel channels, steel girders of `H' section, steel angle bar, flat steel plate, steel girders of `T' section and box section, all of whatever sizes are convenient and available. Timber used is normally second-hand rail sleepers or heavy baulks of 12" x 12" pine (305 x 305mm), together with smaller sized timber to take up the narrower spaces. Apart from welded attachments, firm connections are made using rag-bolts through timber-to-timber, and rag-bolts through angle-bar to timber. Timber-to-timber connections may also be achieved using shipwrights' large metal staples.

Building Cribbaging Arrangements

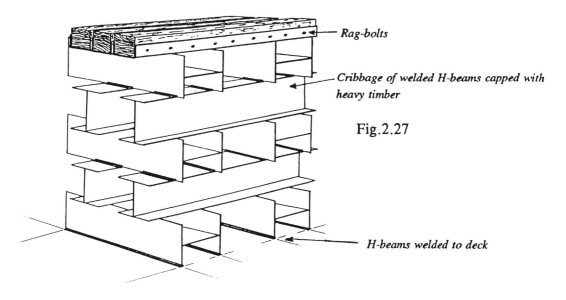

Rag-bolts

Cribbage of welded H-beams capped with heavy timber

Fig.2.27

H-beams welded to deck

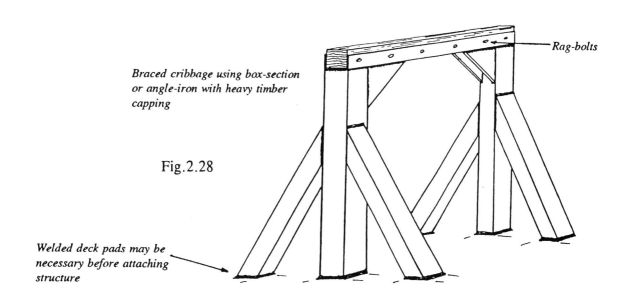

Braced cribbage using box-section or angle-iron with heavy timber capping

Fig.2.28

Rag-bolts

Welded deck pads may be necessary before attaching structure

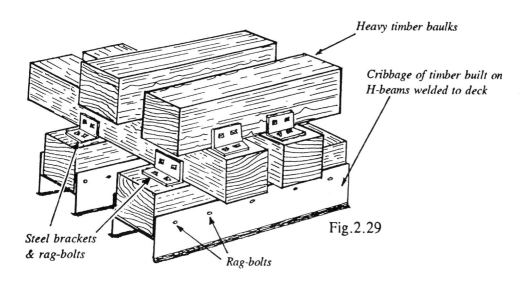

Heavy timber baulks

Cribbage of timber built on H-beams welded to deck

Steel brackets & rag-bolts

Rag-bolts

Fig.2.29

Cribbaging arrangements to accept the leading end of the crane jib might look something like Figs.2.27, 2.28 and 2.29. Note that the crib structure itself must be secured to the deck by welded connections. Several such structures of various heights and widths will be required along the jib's length: similar to Fig.2.27 away from the hatchway, but generally reducing to good timber dunnage used densely where the jib crosses the hatch covers' fore-and-aft length.

When all cribbaging and hatch cover dunnaging are complete and levelled along a tight sight-line the jib can be loaded and landed carefully into its sea-going position. Any minor deficiencies in the cribbing/dunnage levels can be taken up with broad planking of suitable thickness - all of which must be substantially nailed in place.

The steel sea fastenings can then be fitted and welded in place as illustrated in Figs.2.30 and 2.31, although the steel sections illustrated should not be considered the only type acceptable. Fig.2.32, for instance, illustrates an extensive mix of sea fastenings used to secure 195-tonne cat-cracking units (See, also, Chapter 3 for comments on weld connections.)

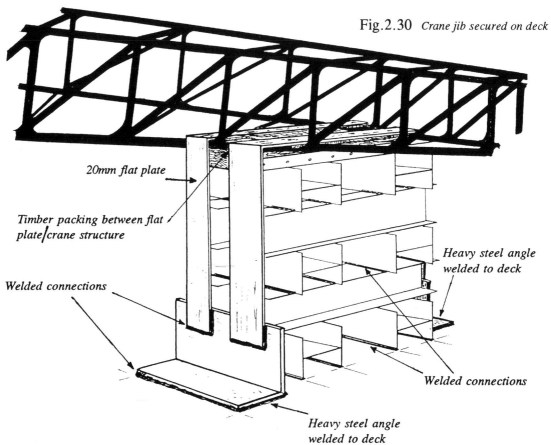

Fig.2.30 *Crane jib secured on deck*

20mm flat plate

Timber packing between flat plate/crane structure

Welded connections

Heavy steel angle welded to deck

Welded connections

Heavy steel angle welded to deck

Fire and Explosion Hazards

Before any welding is effected on board the vessel it is of the utmost importance to obtain a "hot work" certificate from the port/harbour authority. Make sure that the port/harbour authorities are in possession of ALL RELEVANT INFORMATION RELATING TO YOUR SHIP AND ITS CARGO. **DO NOT NEGLECT THIS RULE!**

Make sure that the welding contractors and/or the ship's officers and crew are competent to carry out and/or adequately supervise the welding work. In the space below the weather-deck, place not less than two reliable men, each supplied with two (2) suitable portable fire-extinguishers. In the space below the weather-deck, spread purpose-made thick asbestos sheeting immediately beneath each point where welding is being effected. Do not allow two areas of welding if only one area can be protected by the asbestos sheet below. Rig fire hoses on deck, with adjustable spray/jet nozzles, and with full water pressure on the deck fire-line.

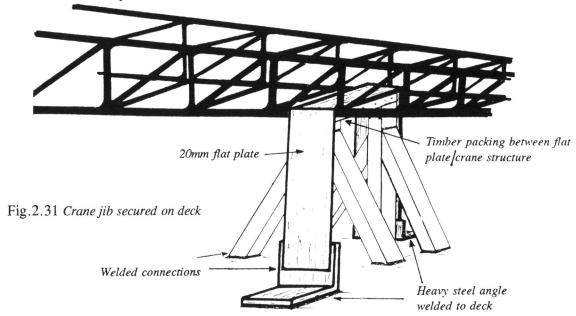

20mm flat plate

Timber packing between flat plate/crane structure

Fig.2.31 *Crane jib secured on deck*

Welded connections

Heavy steel angle welded to deck

On completion of all "hot work", maintain a watchman in the space below for at least four hours thereafter. A ship's officer should be directed to effect a thorough examination in the spaces below before those spaces are closed and/or battened-down. IF IN DOUBT - DON'T WELD. If any reader considers the foregoing rules to be unrealistic, the author will be pleased to provide details of instances where by-passing such common-sense requirements has resulted in catastrophic ship-board fires on the one hand, and catastrophic explosions and loss of life on the other!

Fig. 2.32 - *Cat-cracking units - 195 tonnes, plus - secured with a mix of sea-fastenings.* (*Photo: Gordon Line*)

DECIMAL AND METRIC CONVERSION TABLE
(Courtesy The CROSBY Group Inc.)

Fractional Equivalent (in.)	Decimal Equivalent (in.)	Metric Equivalent (mm)	Fractional Equivalent (in.)	Decimal Equivalent (in.)	Metric Equivalent (mm)
1/64	.0156	.397	33/64	.5156	13.097
1/32	.0312	.794	17/32	.5312	13.494
3/64	.0469	1.191	35/64	.5469	13.891
1/16	.0625	1.588	9/16	.5625	14.288
5/64	.0781	1.984	37/64	.5781	14.684
3/32	.0938	2.381	19/32	.5938	15.081
7/64	.1094	2.778	39/64	.6094	15.478
1/8	.1250	3.175	5/8	.6250	15.875
9/64	.1406	3.572	41/64	.6406	16.272
5/32	.1562	3.969	21/32	.6562	16.669
11/64	.1719	4.366	43/64	.6719	17.065
3/16	.1875	4.762	11/16	.6875	17.462
13/64	.2031	5.159	45/64	.7031	17.859
7/32	.2188	5.556	23/32	.7188	18.256
15/64	.2344	5.953	47/64	.7344	18.653
1/4	.2500	6.350	3/4	.7500	19.050
17/64	.2656	6.747	49/64	.7656	19.447
9/32	.2812	7.144	25/32	.7812	19.844
19/64	.2969	7.541	51/64	.7969	20.241
5/16	.3125	7.938	13/16	.8125	20.638
21/64	.3281	8.334	53/64	.8281	21.034
11/32	.3438	8.731	27/32	.8438	21.431
23/64	.3594	9.128	55/64	.8594	21.828
3/8	.3750	9.525	7/8	.8750	22.225
25/64	.3906	9.922	57/64	.8906	22.622
13/32	.4062	10.319	29/32	.9062	23.019
27/64	.4219	10.716	59/64	.9219	23.416
7/16	.4375	11.112	15/16	.9375	23.812
29/64	.4531	11.509	61/64	.9531	24.209
15/32	.4688	11.906	31/32	.9688	24.606
31/64	.4844	12.303	63/64	.9844	25.003
1/2	.5000	12.700	1	1.0000	25.400

Mass Conversions
To convert from U.S. tons to metric tons multiply by .907185
To convert from metric tons to U.S. tons multiply by 1.10231
To convert from metric tons to pounds multiply by 2204.62
To convert from metric tons to kilograms multiply by 1000
To convert from pounds to kilograms multiply by .453592
To convert from kilograms to pounds multiply by 2.20462

Temperature Conversion
To convert from degree fahrenheit to degree celsius use
$Tc = 5/9 \ (Tf-32)$
To convert from degree celsius to degree fahrenheit use
$Tf = 9/5(Tc)+32$

See Addendum No.1 at the end of this book for full Conversion Tables.

CHAPTER 3

Strength of Lashing Arrangements

Eyes - Splices and Grips

In some instances lashing wires are supplied pre-cut to length and with eyes and/or attachment devices already formed in one or both ends. (See Fig.3.01, for instance.) Such purpose-made items are usually sold with certificates stating the test-load and nominal break-load applicable. For general lashing purposes, however, the wire is usually supplied in coils and must be cut to length aboard the ship with the eyes and attachment devices formed and fitted on site as required. It is to this latter practice that the following considerations apply.

The eye may be formed by splicing the strands of the wire back into the lay of the standing part, as shown in Fig.3.02, around a thimble - Fig.3.03. There are several methods of achieving this result. All are time-consuming and, even if effected with the exercise of great skill and care, they all reduce the strength of the wire in the tucked area to about 80% of its nominal breaking-load. In instances where the eyes are formed with less skill and care the strands may pull or slip at loads of no more than 50% of the breaking-load of the wire.

For this reason bulldog-grips - Figs.3.04 and 3.05 - and their close cousin Crosby-clips - Fig.3.03 - Figs.3.06 and 3.07 - were invented, the use of which allows eyes to be formed quickly and securely in wire ropes by relatively unskilled persons providing a few simple rules are followed. Figs.3.08 and 3.09, respectively, show the correct method and the incorrect method of making eyes in wire ropes using bulldog-grips. It is the author's experience that the simple most predominant factor associated with the failure of cargo lashings is the incorrect application of bulldog-grips. Seamanship and rigging books, manufacturers' information material, and many years of instructive propaganda have all promulgated the correct methods to adopt; but with little apparent beneficial results; the learning curve remains stubbornly flat, and the task of getting the work done properly is as difficult today as it must have been when bulldog-grips first came on the market.

The strength of eyes formed by bulldog-grips has for years been a matter of speculation in some quarters. On the other hand, several publications attempt to give guidance on the subject. Empirical tests made several years ago by the author - over a range of wire-and-grip configurations - indicated that the perfect eye around a thimble, made and tested under perfect conditions, will hold at 90% to 100% of the nominal breaking-load (NBL) of the wire before slipping and/or fracturing. On the other hand, departures from the ideal will result in slippage at much reduced loads.

In the original Monograph plates i to ix were used to illustrate nine wrong ways to make-up a bulldog-gripped eye. Those plates - with different numbering and extended captions - were reproduced in this book's First and Second Editions, and again in this Third Edition. - and comprise less than half of a batch of 20 eyes in which none were made-up correctly. A rigging foreman was provided with detailed drawings of how a cargo was to be stowed, secured, and lashed, together with sketches illustrating clearly the correct way to use bulldog-grips. Two hours later he and his men had prepared the first batch of wires involving 20 bulldog-gripped eyes, none of which conformed to the sketches. Asked to explain, the foreman said he was going by the seamanship books and always did it that way. Which way? Each of 20 eyes were wrongly made-up, and each was wrongly made-up in a different manner; none were in line with any seamanship book! (See Figs.3.10 to 3.18 on the following pages.)

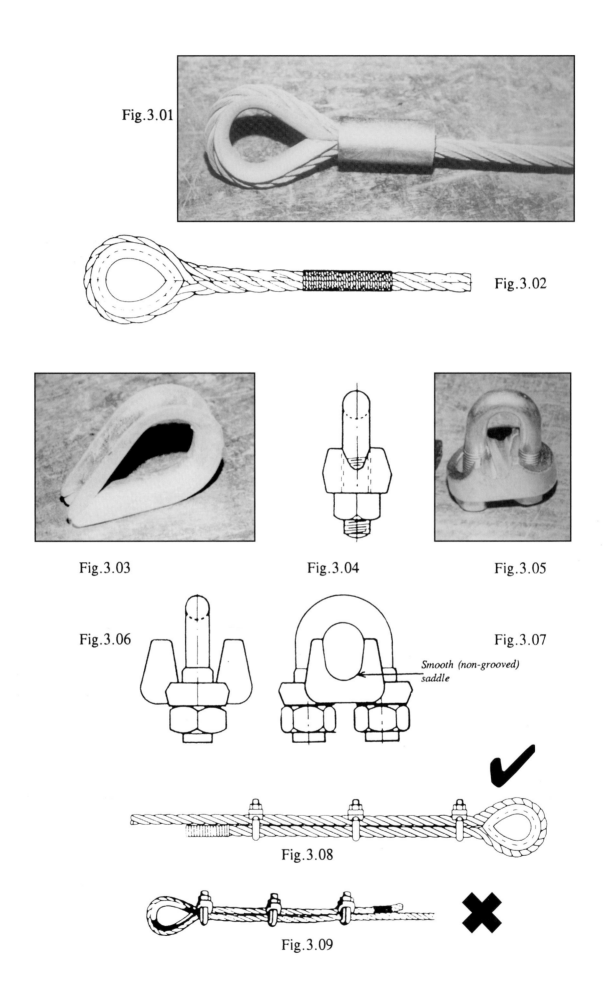

Fig.3.01

Fig.3.02

Fig.3.03

Fig.3.04

Fig.3.05

Fig.3.06

Fig.3.07

Smooth (non-grooved) saddle

Fig.3.08

Fig.3.09

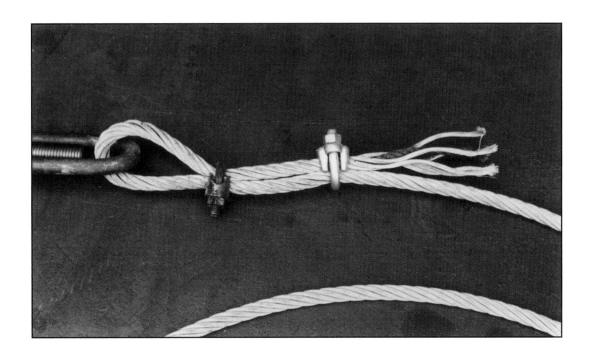

Fig.3.10   *The worst of all worlds: two non-matching grips applied in opposite directions and the cut end opening up. This eye will slip at loads of 0.3NBL tonne or less.*

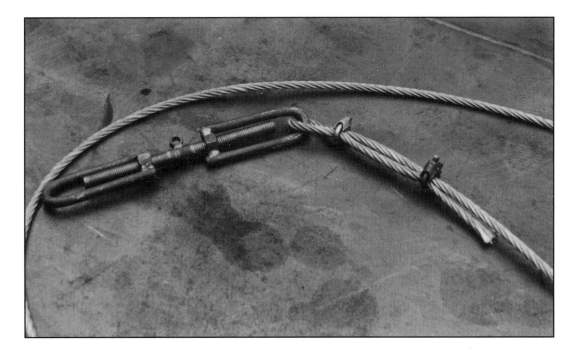

Fig.3.11   *Two grips, only, applied in the correct direction but too far apart and the cut end not whipped. The eye will hold to about 0.6NBL to start with, but may slip suddenly at about 0.3NBL as the cut end unlays. Here is a good example of a well-made hamburger turnbuckle: break-load in excess of 12 tonnes.*

Fig.3.12   *Three grips in the wrong direction, the second and last applied to wire which has opened up through lack of whipping. This eye will slip at loads of 0.4NBL and less.*

Fig.3.13   *Three grips - two of one type, one of another - applied in the correct direction, too close together, and over dead wire which has opened up and is not whipped. This eye will slip suddenly at loads of 0.4NBL and less.*

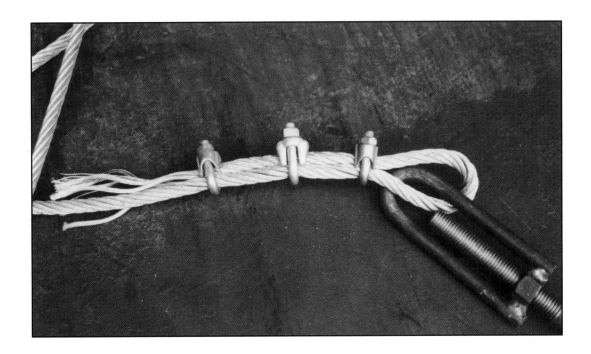

Fig.3.14   *Three grips used in the wrong direction - two of one type, one of another - the end grip pressing on wire which has opened up, and the cut end not whipped or taped. The eye shown here will start to slip at loads below 0.5NBL.*

Fig.3.15   *Three grips - each of a different type - all applied in the wrong direction, the end grip too near the cut end and the cut end not whipped or taped. This eye will hold to about 0.6NBL to start with, but may start to slip at lower loads as the cut end unlays.*

Fig.3.16 *Another example of a well-made hamburger turnbuckle, but all three grips applied in the wrong direction and the cut end not whipped or taped. This eye should not be trusted at loads greater than 0.5NBL.*

Fig.3.17 *The first two grips are the right distance apart, but applied the wrong way round; the third grip is the correct way round but too far from the second grip and is attempting to clamp wire which is opening up at the non-whipped cut end. Slippage is likely to occur at loads not in excess of 0.4NBL.*

Fig.3.18   *Three bulldog-grips - two of one type, one of another - applied in the correct direction, but slightly too close together (they should be 96mm apart for this 16mm dia. wire), and the cut end has not been whipped or taped. Will hold well to start with - 0.7NBL - but will start to slip at about 0.5NBL if cut end unlays.*

The eyes were all eventually made-up as illustrated in Plate A at the front of this book and as shown in Fig.3.19. This experience will find its echoes around the world, and illustrates the sheer perversity of responsible workmen who should know better.

Fig.3.19   *Soft eye - three correct-sized grips all used in the one correct direction.*

The experience is not uncommon, and is related here principally for the benefit of ships' masters and chief officers. When you see something being done badly or wrongly, stop the work and have it re-done correctly. When rigging foremen, stevedore superintendents and charterers' supercargoes insist on doing things wrongly and say they have always done it that way successfully, tell them they've just been lucky! Then make them do it correctly.

More recently the author organised and supervised an additional comprehensive range of bulldog-grip tests in 16mm and 18mm wire rope lashing configurations at the licensed test-beds of Abel Foxall Lifting Gear Limited, of Liverpool. The specification for the more than 100 tests was carefully drawn up, strictly adhered to, and fully monitored. The configurations were made-up by six different people under the direction of the author, his colleague Charles Bliault, and an experienced foreman. Ring-spanners were used to tighten the nuts on bulldog-grips. The configurations used were as illustrated in Figs. Figs.3.19, 3.20 and 3.21.

Sincere thanks are offered to Thomas Miller Defence who financed the tests and with whose agreement the results are included in condensed form in this Chapter.

It is here stressed that the tests made, the results obtained, and the recommendations which here arise apply only to marine cargo lashings; they should never be applied to lifting gear or statutory wire rope arrangements.

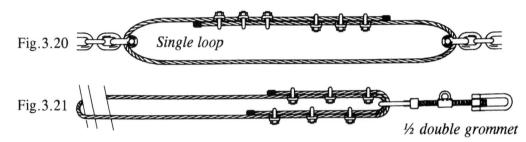

Fig.3.20   *Single loop*

Fig.3.21   *½ double grommet*

Also, it is recognised that, for eyes, thimbles should be used, and that four (or more) grips will provide a higher slip-load than will three grips; but the realities of actually getting a cargo lashed almost preclude thimbles and the use of four grips per eye. It is difficult enough to get lashing gangs and ships' crews to use three grips per eye without thimbles. For that reason, all physical tests undertaken were in "soft" eyes (no thimbles) and used no more than three grips per eye - scaled upward for single loops and half-double grommets as shown above - so as to provide reliable data on what was most likely to be the practical realities.

One of the practical realities is Table 1 of the CSS Code/CSM Regulations wherein the "breaking strength" and "MSL" to be assigned to lashing arrangements formed by the use of bulldog-grips is completely ignored even though this form of lashing termination is by far the most common where deck cargoes are involved. Also, as mentioned earlier herein, the term "breaking strength" is not currently defined in that Code or in those Regulations, even though the term is used repeatedly therein, so I would suggest that the following definition would cover all types of materials and terminations and would also provide some rationale to the MSL Table 1 applications:-

*"In the CSS Code and in the Cargo Securing Manual Regulations the term **"breaking strength"** shall mean the point at which the component, material or element can no longer support or sustain the load. Such breaking strength shall be the value as provided by the manufacturers/suppliers to the component, material or element **when new**. In the instance of bulldog-grip connections the 'slip load' shall equate with the breaking strength for each type of gripped termination deployed."*

It would be of assistance to ships' officers and others, if the Code/CSM Regulations then set out a 'Table' covering the different make-ups/slip loads using bulldog-grips as illustrated in Figs.3.22 to 3.40, hereof. Alternatively, for the IMO to instigate its own monitored tests under laboratory/test bed conditions, and use those results in a suitable 'Table'. In the absence of such a definition and an applicable slip-load 'Table', I suggest that the breaking strength definition, the bulldog-grip configurations and the slip-loads assigned to them in this book will be found fully safe and adequate when applied in a balanced, common-sense, manner in conjunction with the three-times-rule.

Using new, galvanised steel, marine wire rope with bulldog-grip terminations and loops, the aspects and recommendations arising from my own tests may be put concisely as follows:-

Bulldog-grip Terminations
1.   For all sizes of wire from **8mm** to **19mm** diameter, use not less than **three** grips at each eye; for wires of **20mm** to **32mm** diameter, use not less than four grips per eye; for wires of **33mm** to **38mm** diameter, use not less than five grips at each eye and upwards. **Using**

less numbers of grips than here recommended can seriously impair the holding effectiveness of the eye. The Table hereunder provides a quick reference.

TABLE 9 - Recommended Minimum Number of Wire Rope Grips for Each Eye

Diameter of Wire Rope mm	Wire Rope Grips
Up to and including 19	3
Over 19, up to and including 32	4
Over 32, up to and including 38	5
Over 38, up to and including 44	6
Over 44, up to and including 56	7

Again, it must be stressed that these recommendations are for cargo lashing purposes, only. Lifting gear and other statutory applications may require a minimum of 6 grips and upwards, respectively, and may not even allow such terminations.

2. Bulldog-grips have a grooved surface in the bridge piece which is suitable for a standard wire rope of right-hand lay having six strands. Crosby-grips have a smooth surface in the bridge piece. The grips should not be used with ropes of left-hand lay or different construction.

3. Before cutting the wire to length, whip or securely tape both sides of the cutting point. The two cut ends will then not tend to unlay, and a good, firm eye can be made without wasting material or time. (See colour Plate E between Chapters 2 and 3.)

4. The first grip must be close up to the thimble - or at the neck of the eye if a thimble is not used - and the other grips must be spaced approximately six rope diameters apart, i.e. 96mm (3¾") apart on a 16mm diameter wire; 108mm (4¼") apart on an 18mm diameter wire, for instance.

5. The grips must all face in the same direction and must be fitted with the saddle (or bridge) applied to the working/hauling part of the rope; the U-bolt (or bow) must be applied on the tail/dead-end of the rope, as illustrated in Figs.3.19, 3.20 and 3.21. **Applying the grips in reduced numbers and in other directions can seriously impair the holding effectiveness of the eye.**

6. Ideally, all nuts should be tightened using a torque-wrench so as to give tightening values in accordance with the manufacturers' instructions. This is feasible in covered workshop conditions but, on an exposed deck in the dark and rain of a winter's night, it is sufficient to take all nuts hard-up with a ring spanner. Thereafter, all eye terminations should be checked after one or two loadings and the nuts hardened-up again if necessary. This latter practice should never be neglected. The very nature of the grips and the wire means that one is compressing the other; the flattening effect of that compression may continue to some very slight degree after the nuts have been first applied firmly.

7. Under test, when the gripped connection starts to slip, it first goes quickly; the rate of slip then reduces, but slip does not stop until the load is removed.

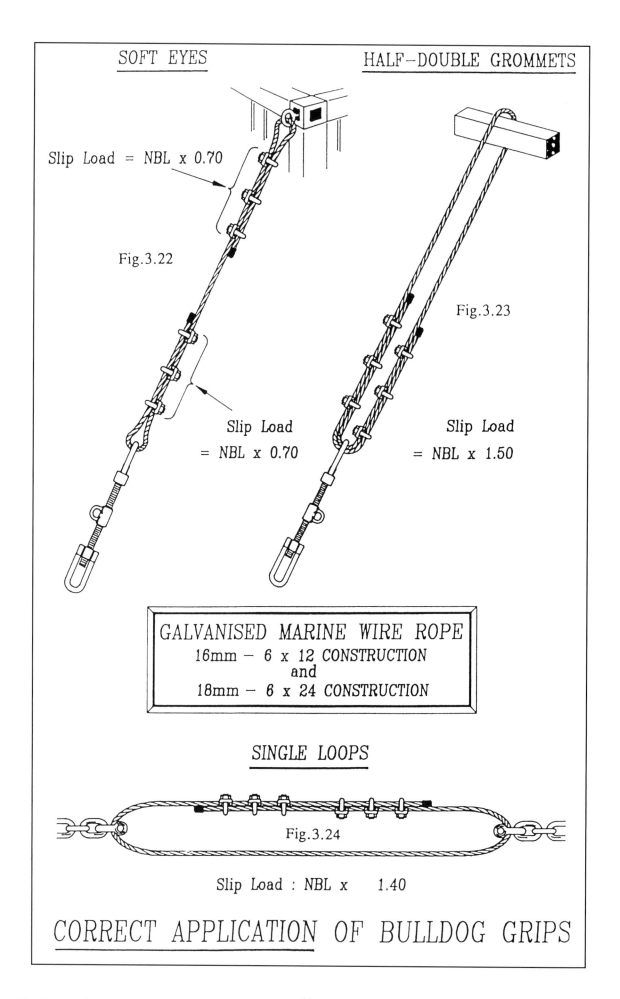

SOFT EYES   HALF—DOUBLE GROMMETS

Slip Load = NBL x 0.70

Fig.3.22

Fig.3.23

Slip Load
= NBL x 0.70

Slip Load
= NBL x 1.50

GALVANISED MARINE WIRE ROPE
16mm — 6 x 12 CONSTRUCTION
and
18mm — 6 x 24 CONSTRUCTION

SINGLE LOOPS

Fig.3.24

Slip Load : NBL x   1.40

CORRECT APPLICATION OF BULLDOG GRIPS

8.   With three grips used in the correct manner and with the eye formed around the correct sized thimble (a hard eye) the eye **will not fail or slip at loads less than** 7 tonnef for 16mm, 9 tonnef for 18mm, and 10 tonnef for 19mm diameter wires of 6 x 12 construction; quite simply at about 90% of the nominal break-load..

9.   With three grips used in the correct manner but without a thimble (a soft eye), this being by far the most common configuration likely to arise in practical, on-site, lashing arrangements, the eye can be **expected to slip** at loads **at, or slightly in excess of:** 5½ tonnef for 16mm, 7 tonnef for 18mm, and 7.7 tonnef for 19mm diameter wires of 6 x 12 construction: quite simply at about 70% of the nominal break-load. (See Fig.3.22.) **It would not be unreasonable to call this the "slip-load" or the "holding power" of the eye, and it is so called throughout this book.**

10.   The practice of using half-double grommets is widespread, but rigging gangs and ships' crews frequently assume such arrangement will provide a holding power of twice the break-load of the wire. Tests proved such assumption to be wrong. In a half-double grommet, with six grips used correctly as illustrated in Fig.3.23, the **slip-load** will be about 11½ tonnef for 16mm, 14½ tonnef for 18mm, and 16¼ tonnef for 19mm diameter wires of 6 x 12 construction: quite simply about 1½ times the nominal break-load. The holding power decreases as the number of grips is reduced. (See Figs.3.31 to 3.35, and 3.40, on later pages. **See, also, Addendum No.5 at the end of this book for MSL's, etc.)**

11.   The practice of using bulldog-grips to join two ends of wire rope together to form a single loop is to be avoided, and is not approved by the manufacturers of either wire rope or bulldog-grips. Rigging gangs and ships' crews frequently assume such arrangement will provide a holding power of twice the break-load of the wire. Tests proved such assumption to be wrong. Bearing in mind the content of (5) above, it follows that, where an attempt is made to join two ends of wire in a loop with the grips, there is no tail/dead-end involved: both parts are working/hauling parts and so there is a failure of the mechanical principles on which the grips are designed. It is, however, appreciated that circumstances may demand some such arrangement, and so tests were carried out on a range of made-up loops. The results were more favourable than expected when six grips were used. In a single loop, with six grips used correctly as illustrated in Fig.3.24, the **slip-load** will be about 10.8 tonnef for 16mm, 13.7 tonnef for 18mm, and 15¼ tonnef for 19mm diameter wires of 6 x 12 construction: quite simply about 1.4 of the nominal break-load. The holding power decreases as the number of grips is reduced. (See Figs.3.36 to 3.39, on later pages.)

12.   In a soft eye with two grips, and with one or both used in the reverse manner - Figs.3.25, 3.26 and 3.27 - the eye can be **expected to slip at loads of about** 3.8 tonnef for 16mm, 4.9 tonnef for 18mm, and 5.4 tonnef for 19mm diameter wires of 6 x 12 construction. These may be considered the least desirable configurations. However, if used, do not allow their holding power to be greater than half the nominal break-load of the wire.

13.   In soft eyes using only one grip the slip-load was 0.25NBL with the grip positioned correctly - Fig.3.29; 0.18NBL with the grip used in reverse - Fig.3.30. In effect, in the first instance, 16mm wire of 6 x 12 construction will slip at just under 2 tonnef; in the second instance it will slip at just under 1.4 tonnef. As referred to earlier in Chapter 2, a turnbuckle with a thread diameter of 24mm or more can set a pre-tension of about 2 tonnes.

If such a turnbuckle was attached to an eye made-up as shown in Figs.3.29/3.30, tension in the wire could not be attained - the eye would just keep slipping at the grip!

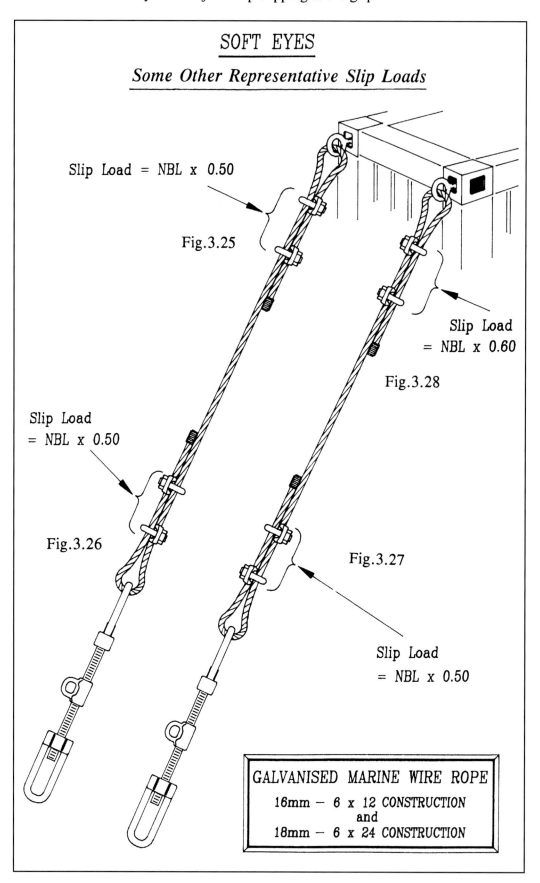

SOFT EYES

Some Other Representative Slip Loads

Slip Load = NBL x 0.50

Fig.3.25

Slip Load = NBL x 0.60

Fig.3.28

Slip Load = NBL x 0.50

Fig.3.26

Fig.3.27

Slip Load = NBL x 0.50

GALVANISED MARINE WIRE ROPE
16mm — 6 x 12 CONSTRUCTION
and
18mm — 6 x 24 CONSTRUCTION

SOFT EYES

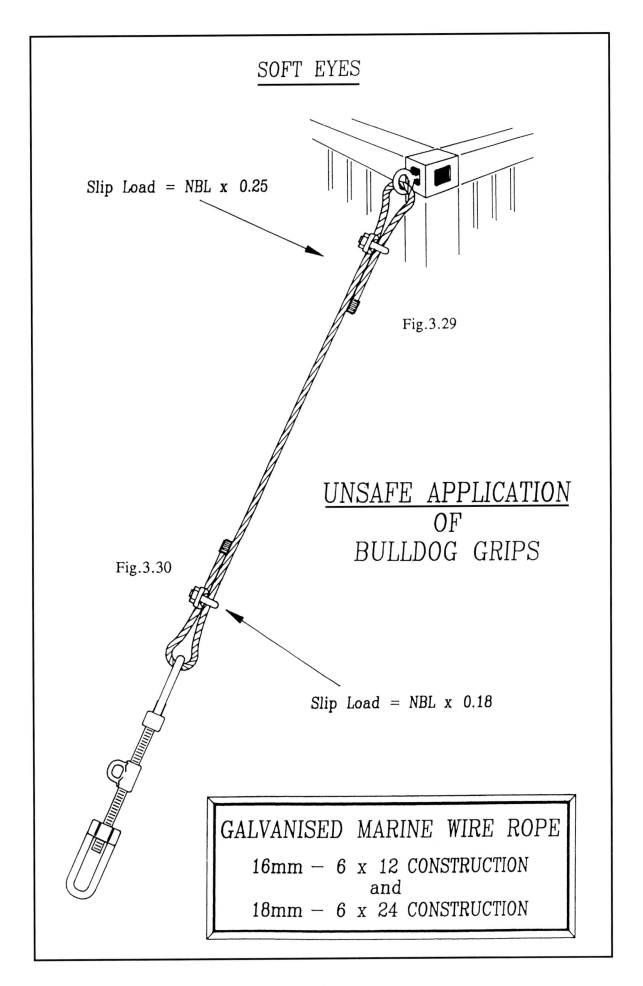

Slip Load = NBL x 0.25

Fig.3.29

UNSAFE APPLICATION
OF
BULLDOG GRIPS

Fig.3.30

Slip Load = NBL x 0.18

GALVANISED MARINE WIRE ROPE

16mm — 6 x 12 CONSTRUCTION
and
18mm — 6 x 24 CONSTRUCTION

HALF-DOUBLE GROMMETS

Some Other Representative Slip Loads

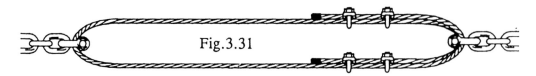

Fig.3.31

Slip Load : NBL x 1.00

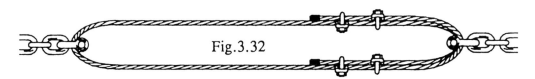

Fig.3.32

Slip Load : NBL x 1.00

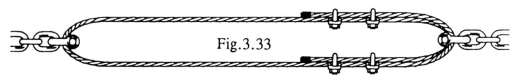

Fig.3.33

Slip Load : NBL x 1.00

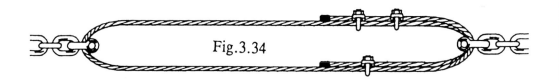

Fig.3.34

Slip Load : NBL x 0.70

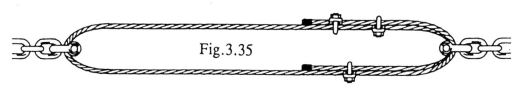

Fig.3.35

Slip Load : NBL x 0.70

SINGLE LOOPS

Some Other Representative Slip Loads

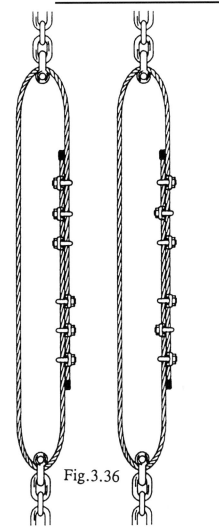

Fig.3.36

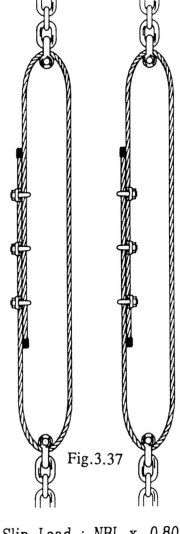

Fig.3.37

Slip Load : NBL x 1.40

Slip Load : NBL x 0.80

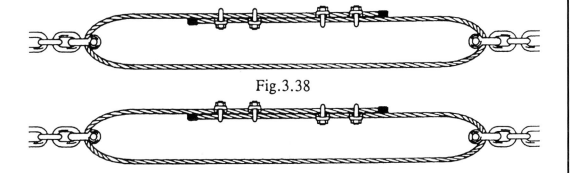

Fig.3.38

Slip Load : NBL x 1.00

SINGLE LOOPS   HALF-DOUBLE GROMMETS

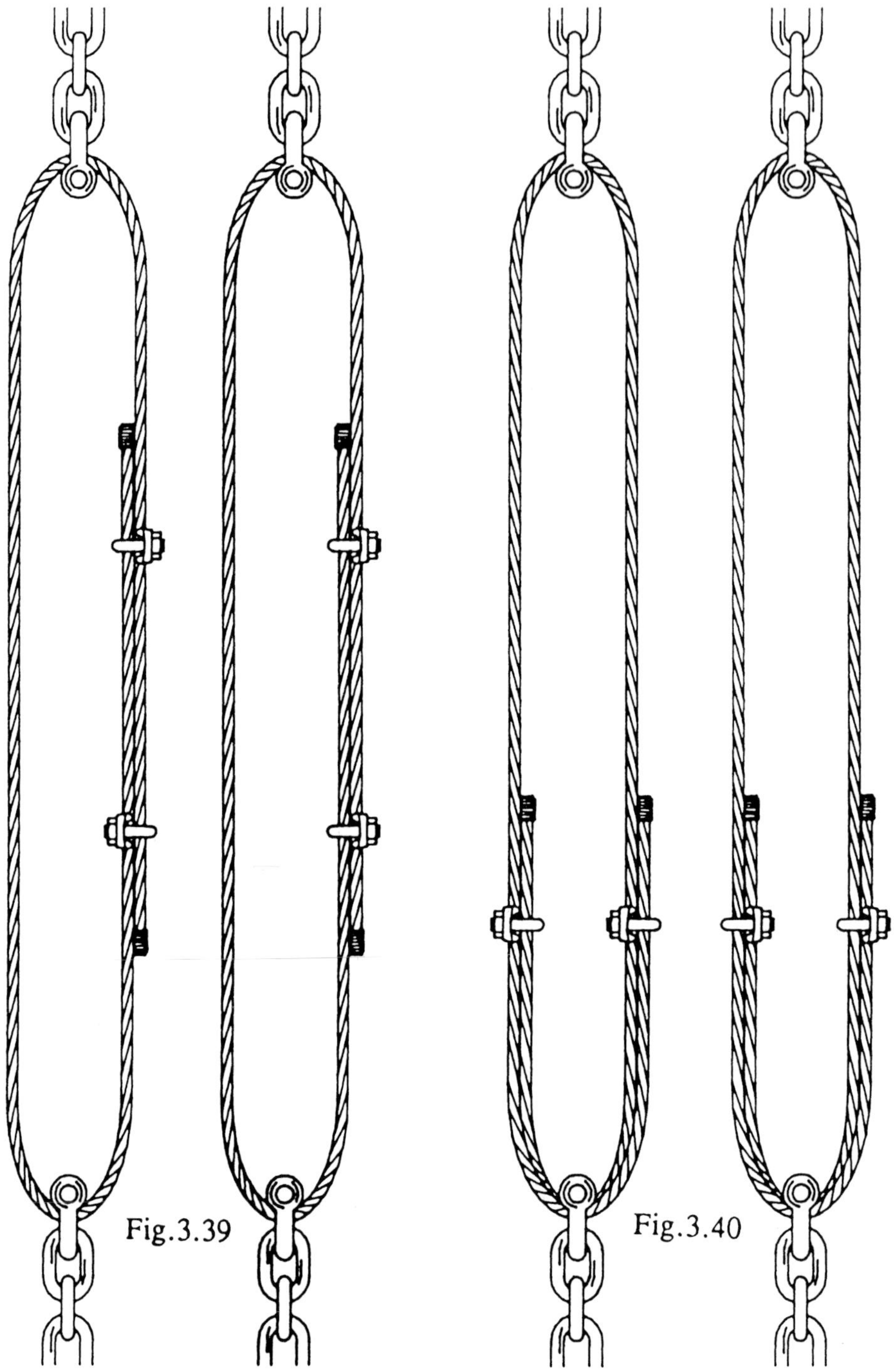

Fig.3.39   Fig.3.40

Slip Load : NBL x 0.40

NOT RECOMMENDED

Example 1 - Using the *3-times rule* and assuming that the components have **not** been tagged or otherwise identified as to MSL:-

The calculation for a 20-tonne load of cuboid shape and even distribution using single 16mm diameter wires of 6 x 12 construction with properly-formed soft eyes, shackles and hamburger turnbuckles, might lay out as follows:-

i. Lay out good timber dunnage to spread the load evenly across the deck and/or hatch cover, using a calculated grating arrangement if necessary. Make sure that such loading is not greater than that shown as permissible on the vessel's Capacity and/or General Arrangement Plans. (See pages 5,6 & 7.)

ii. 20 x 3 = 60 tonnef = holding power of lashings: ie, total NBL or BS or slip-load.

iii. Effective holding power/slip-load of soft eyes in 16mm wire of 6 x 12 construction equates with 0.7 NBL 7.75 = 5½ tonnef. (See Fig. 3.22, page 60.)

iv. 5.5 x 1/1.22 = 4.5 tonnef downward in transverse lashings. (See Fig.1.13, page 17.)

v. 5.5 x 1/1.04 = 5.3 tonnef downward in fore-and-aft lashings.(See Fig.1.13, page 17.)

vi. The average of 4.5 and 5.3 = 4.9 tonnef. (Say, 5 tonnef).

vii. 60/5 =12 lashings in all: 6 transverse downward (3 on each side) and 6 fore-and-aft downward (3 at each end), with base angles of about 55° and 73°, respectively.

viii. Check that the fixed securing terminals are at least of the same BS, and then select turnbuckles and shackles of at least equal matching holding power.

ix. From Tables 7A, 7B, 7C or 7D (Chapter 2, pages 38, 39 & 40) select a D shackle if only one lashing to attach, and a Bow shackle where two lashings will attach - and here we are looking for BS's of 5½ tonnes or better.

a) From Table 7A select a shackle with a SWL of at least 5½/4 tonnes (1.375 tonnes). A small D shackle with a 19mm dia. pin (dimension `D' - **not 'd'**) will give a SWL of 1.77 tonnes, equivalent (times 4) to an approximate BS of 7.08 tonnes:- use that size of small D shackle for single lashings. (The 16mm pin will provide only 4.04 tonnef BS.)

b) From Table 7D select a shackle with a SWL of at least **11/4 tonnes (2.75 tonnes) because it's going to take two lashings**. A large Bow shackle with a 22mm dia. pin is the nearest, providing a SWL of 2.79 tonnes, equivalent (times 4) to an approximate BS of 11.16 tonnes:- use that size of large Bow shackle for the twin lashings. (The 22mm pin will provide only 8.12 tonnef BS.)

x. From Table 8B, page 41, select the correct size hamburger turnbuckles, assuming that each lashing will be provided with its own turnbuckle, ie, one with a 24mm dia. screw. However, as mentioned earlier in Chapter 2, rigorous tests on well-crafted, non-certificated hamburgers returned failure values of not less than 12 tonnes, so it would seem reasonable to use those if they were well-made and free of defects for single and twin lashings for the cargo unit weight of 20 tonnes used in this example.(In the event you were going to use a "closed-body" bottle or rigging screw, you could use the 29mm shown in Table 8A (2.8x4=11.2 tonnes) for twin lashings, or the smaller 22mm dia. (1.66x4=6.64) for the single lashings. Additionally, other details relating to rigging-screws can be found in Addendum 5 at the end of this book.)

Example 2 - Here make reference to Chapter 2, Table 2, and Chapter 3, Figs. 3.22, 3.23 and 3.24 on page 58.

Using 16mm 6 x 12 wire, calculate the slip-load when using: a) soft eye, b) a single loop and, c) a half-double grommet - each in the best and correct manner.

From Table 2:- 16mm wire 6 x 12 - NBL = 7.75 tonnef.

> a.   soft eye = NBL x 0.7 = 7.75 x 0.7, so slip-load =5.425 tonnef (say 5.5 tonnef). This equates with BS.
> b.   single loop = NBL x 1.4 = 7.75 x 1.4, so slip-load =10.85 tonnef (say 10.9 tonnef). This equates with BS.
> c.   half-double grommet = NBL x 1.5 = 7.75 x 1.5, so slip-load =11.625 tonnef (say 11.6 tonnef). This equates with BS.

Example 3 - See Figs. 3.22 to 3.40, inclusive, and Table 2 in Chapter 2.

If you had only 12 bulldog-grips to fit 18mm wire of 6 x 12 construction, how could you use those grips to provide the greatest number of lashings with the highest aggregate slip-load?

From Table 2:- 18mm wire 6 x 12 - NBL = 9.80 tonnef.

Using soft eyes with 3 grips at each end (Fig.3.22) would provide **two** lashings each of slip-load NBL x 0.7 = 9.80 x 0.7 = 6.86 tonnef. (Not twice 6.86, because each eye will slip at the same load, but two such lashings would provide a total BS of 13.72 tonnef,)

Using half-double grommets each with 6 grips (Fig.3.23) would provide **two** lashings each of slip-load NBL x 1.5 = 9.8 x 1.5 = 14.7 tonnef. (Again, not twice 14.7, for the same reason, but two such lashings would provide a total BS of 29.4 tonnef.)

Using single loops each with 6 grips (Fig.3.24) would provide **two** lashings each of slip-load NBL x 1.4 = 9.8 x 1.4 = 13.72 tonnef. (Two such lashings would provide a total BS of 27.44 tonnef.)

So grip-for-grip the half-double grommet looks the best at 29.4 tonnef. but using 6 grips per grommet still only gives **two** lashings, and that's hardly likely to be sufficient. So can we use a make-up with a lower single slip-load but a better balance of lashing numbers?

If 4 grips per grommet were used (Fig.3.33) the result would be **three** lashings each of 9.8 x 1, a total BS of 29.4 tonnef.

If 3 grips per grommet were used as shown in Figs.3.35, the result would be **four** lashings each of slip-load NBL x 0.7 = 9.8 x 0.7 = 6.86 tonnef, a total BS of 27.44 tonnef.

And if two grips per grommet were used as shown in Fig.3.40, the result would be **six** lashings each of 9.8 x 0.4 = 3.92 tonnef, a total BS of 3.92 x 6 = 23.52 tonnef.

So although the Fig.3.23 and Fig.33 configurations provide the best single lashing strengths, it would most likely prove more efficient to use **six** lashings each of 3.92 tonnef slip-load - Fig.3.40 - (a total BS of 23.52 tonnef) rather than less lashing numbers with a slightly higher total BS.

Note: This example emphasises the importance of calculating the total breaking strengths of the components you are using. Personally, I would avoid, like the plague, the use of anything approaching the likes of Figs.3.39 or 3.40, but if you are short of the necessary gear, calculate the best option, and allow the results accordingly; and it is so important to allow no more than the appropriate slip-load.

Example 4 - Use Table 1, Chapter 1, page 20.

With a lashing slip-load of 5.5 tonnef, find the base angles in lashings to provide: a) a vertical and transverse restraint of 3.89 tonnef, b) a vertical and fore-and-aft restraint of 2.32 tonnef, c) a horizontal restraint for fore-and-aft and transverse lashings each to provide a vertical restraint of 3.15 tonnef.

a = 45°; b = 65°; c = 35° in the transverse direction (horizontal restraint 4.50 tonnef);

55° in the fore-and-aft direction (horizontal restraint 3.15 tonnef).

(See, also, Tables 9, 10 and 11 later in this Chapter 3.)

Example 5 - Use Tables 2, 7A,7B, 7C & 7D, 8A and 8B, and refer to page 62.

Using wire of 20mm dia. 6 x 24 construction, what size of solid bottle-screw and hamburger turnbuckle and suitable connecting shackles would you use with a single half-double grommet lashing made up as shown in Fig.3.33?

From Table 2, page 26 - 20mm 6 x 24 wire has a NBL of 16.2 tonnef.

From Fig.3.33, a half-double grommet made up correctly (note the position of the bulldog-grips) will provide a slip-load (holding power or BS) of NBL x 1 = 16.2 tonnef.

From Table 8A you could use a solid bottle screw of 32mm screw dia. (3.82x4 = 15.28 tonnef) and downgrade the BS to that value - which is probably what I would do) or go for the 38mm dia. screw and a BS of 5.21x4 = 20.84 tonnef. Using Table 8B, you could use a hamburger turnbuckle of screw diameter 39mm, providing a BS of 28 tonnef. However, if I was downgrading the BS to nearer 15 tonnef, I would use either the 24mm at 15 tonnef BS or the 30mm at 19 tonnef BS. (You can now see why using wire of greater than 16mm diameter requires much larger connecting components, and why a little latitude and common sense need to prevail if costs are to be kept reasonable without compromising safety standards.)

From Table 7A select a shackle whose SWLx4 is nearest to, but not less than, 16.2 tonnef, ie, the 25mm pin at SWL 4.57 tonnef = 18.28 tonnef BS, which is the lightest shackle to match the lashing's slip-load of 16.2 tonnef. (However, if you were prepared to downgrade each lashing to 14.12 tonnef BS, you could use the smaller 25mm dia. pin shackles. Again, an example of balancing lashing strengths to the components available. Be flexible without being careless.)

Example 6

The 40-tonne, 10m long, cylindrical pressure unit shown in Fig.3.41 below, is to be carried on the port side weather-deck of a Panamax bulker of 66000 tonnes deadweight and beam 32m. The vessel's departure GM is pre-calculated as a rather large 2.35m. The permissible loading on the weather-deck is shown on the Capacity Plan as 3.1 tonnes/m². The pressure unit may only be supported beneath externally at the three places marked on its external surface, each place coincident with strong transverse internal wash-plates. There are only eight lashing-lugs - four each side - each capable of safely sustaining a straight pull of 7 tonnes.

Instructions are to support the unit
beneath at the three marked places, only.

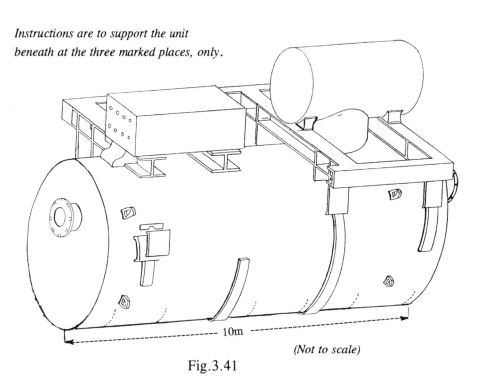

(Not to scale)

Fig.3.41

Procedure A (ignoring the MSL Table 1 application)

a.   Calculate the roll period.
b.   Decide what rule for lashing strength to apply.
c.   How many lashings will be used, and of what construction.
d.   Calculate the load spread area and type of dunnage to be used.
e.   Decide how the unit will be cradled.

Start:

a.   Roll period $T = \dfrac{C \times B}{\sqrt{GM}}$ (Chapter 1 - pp.9 to 11)

$$T = \frac{0.7 \times 32}{\sqrt{2.35}}$$

T = <u>14.6 seconds roll period</u>

b.   A roll period of 14.6 seconds is less adverse than 13 seconds, so it is reasonable to apply the 3-times rule. (Chapter 1 - pp. 9 to 17.)

c.   Unit mass for lashing purposes = 40 x 3 = 120 tonnef = minimum total BS required.

The lashings which attach to the lugs should not have a direct pull slip-load much in excess of 7 tonnef; but those lugs provide the only safe means of attaching lashings with forward and aft motion-restraint components. Here we encounter the first of the "connection" problems.

We know from Chapter 2, p.43, that pre-tension in excess of 2 tonnes is not easily attainable with the ordinary sizes of turnbuckle likely to be used in day-to-day cargo lashing operations; so it is reasonable to attach two lashings to each lug, angled equally in a forward and aft direction, and ensuring that the individual slip-load of each lashing does not exceed 7 tonnes.

Refer to Chapter 1, pp.15 to 19, from which it would appear reasonable to utilise Fig.1.15 - the 45°/45° triangle - in which each lashing will provide 71% of its holding power in a longitudinal direction and 71% in a transverse direction, as indicated in Fig.3.42, below.

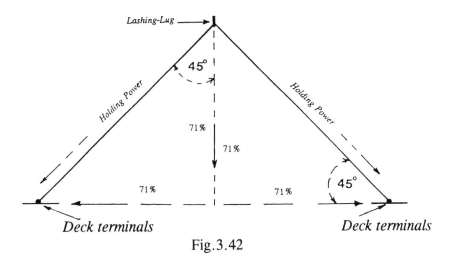

Fig.3.42

Consult Table 2, Chapter 2, p.26:- the 18mm 6 x 12 wire has a NBL of 9.8 tonnef, and when used with the Fig.3.22 (page 58) connection (soft eyes at each end) will provide a slip-load (BS) of 9.8x 0.7 = 6.86 tonnef. Eight lashings each of 6.86 tonnef = 54.88 tonnef, say 55 tonnef. Use bottle-screws or hamburger turnbuckles of not less than 22mm screw diameter. (See Tables 8A and 8B with some approximate interpolation.)

Each pair of lug lashings will be attached by a single large Bow-shackle - with pin through the lug - having a BS of not less than 7 tonnes. Table 7D, p.40, indicates a shackle with a pin diameter of 22mm, ie, SWL 2.03x4 = 8.12 tonnef. Use that type and size of shackle.

Now it could be said - with 16 lug lashings rather than 8 - that we should allow their aggregate holding power to be 16 x 6.86 = 109.76 (say 110) tonnef, but the lugs are safe to a load of 7 tonnes each, so we must use that as a governing factor. Hence, 7 x 8 = 56 tonnef is all that can be allowed by way of safe holding power of the lug lashings.

Taking 56 from 120 leaves 64 tonnes of additional lashing strength to apply without using the lashing-lugs on the unit. It is unsafe to take lashings around the unit's structural projections without prior knowledge of their strength or susceptibility to damage; so only circumferential lashings can be used, and only in areas of known strength - say one each side of the three internal wash-plates - six in all; so 64/6 = 10.66 tonnes slip-load per each circumferential lashing. If each of the circumferential body lashings is made-up with soft eyes with three grips at each termination, as shown in Fig.3.22, the slip-load will be NBL x 0.7 per lashing, not NBL x 0.7 x 2. There is, however, some advantage gained with dunnage and chocking which will vary in each instance, and some mechanical advantage is gained by the "wrap-around" application of the lashings; but the value of that advantage would need to be calculated for any specific diameter of cylinder; so, for this type of securing problem, any allowance for frictional and mechanical advantages can be ignored - the 3-times rule, properly employed, will suffice.

Consult Table 2, Chapter 2, p.26, again: The 18mm 6 x 19 wire has a NBL of 14.4 tonnef. With a Fig.3.22 soft eye such wire will give a slip-load of 14.4 x 0.7 = 10.08 tonnef (say 10.1) of which 6 such terminations will provide 10.1 x 6 = 60.6 (say 61) tonnef. This is 3 tonnef short of the 64 tonnef required by the arithmetic, but this is not an exact science, and frictional and mechanical advantages **do** play a part, so I would use those lashings rather than increase unnecessarily the size (and cost) of the individual components. Use hamburger turnbuckles of 22mm screw diameter or upward, or bottle-screws of 29mm screw diameter.

d.   The weight spread area must allow for 40 + 5% = 42 tonnes. (Chapter 1, pp.5 to 7.) The weather-deck's permissible loading is 3.1 tonne/m²; so 42/3.1 = 13.55m² minimum for the dunnage area. The unit is 10m long, so if the dunnage length is restricted to 10m, the width must be a minimum of 13.55/10 = 1.36m, say 1.4m when constructed, thus providing a loading of 42/(10x1.4) = 3 tonnes/m². Also, it must be remembered that the unit has only three acceptable support points.

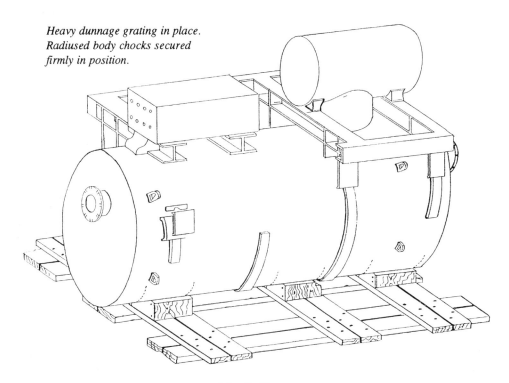

Heavy dunnage grating in place.
Radiused body chocks secured
firmly in position.

Fig.3.43

As illustrated in Fig. 3.43 on the previous page, use 9" x 3" (230 x 75mm white pine deals - or similar - in pairs:- 6 in pairs longitudinally each about 310mm (12") apart; 6 in pairs transversely - nailed to the longitudinals to form a grating. Use 6 large radiused chocks, one at each side of the three cross-bearers, to cradle the unit, each chock to be firmly secured in place when loading is complete and before lashing begins. The final lashing and securing of the 40-tonne cargo unit should look as shown in Fig.3.44, below.

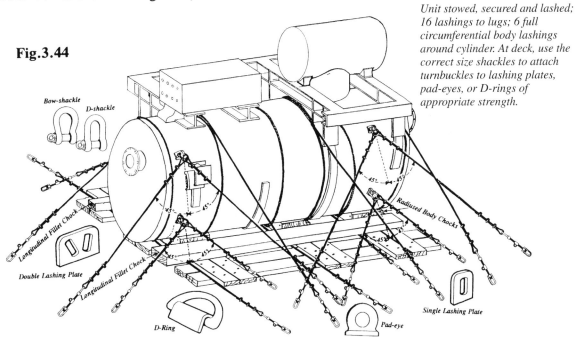

Fig.3.44

Unit stowed, secured and lashed; 16 lashings to lugs; 6 full circumferential body lashings around cylinder. At deck, use the correct size shackles to attach turnbuckles to lashing plates, pad-eyes, or D-rings of appropriate strength.

It is worth considering why the circumferential body lashings have been applied in Fig.3.44 as they have, bearing in mind that such method is different from the "preferred method" advocated in the IMO Code of Safe Practice for Cargo Stowage and Securing, and as carried forward into the CSM Regulations. (Here, please refer back to pages xix, xx and xxi of the **INTRODUCTION** preceding Chapter 1.) The IMO "preferred method" - when applied to a cylinder - would look like Fig. X2, where both ends of each lashing are made fast on the same side: Nos. 1 & 3 on the port side; Nos. 2 & 4 on the starboard side.

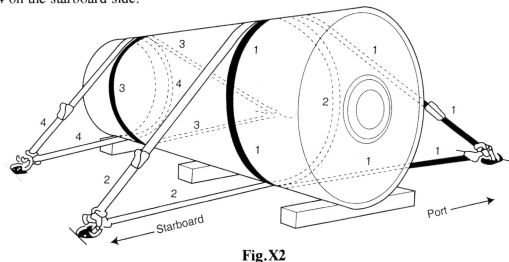

Fig.X2

If any one of the four lashings or their end connections should fail in the IMO application, the cylinder would become free from one transverse restraint, initiating an unbalanced arrangement as shown in Fig.X3 on the next page where I indicate that lashing No.3 has broken.

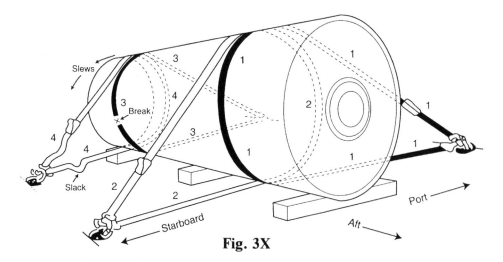

Fig. 3X

With lashing No.3 broken and adrift, lashing No4 then goes slack leaving nothing to check the forward end of the cylinder (in my sketch) from swinging and slewing to starboard (in my sketch); and that slewing effect will be added to by the pull exerted by the port side/aft end lashing No.1.

In effect, once a single lashing component fails in the IMO "preferred method" the securing system becomes unbalanced and the cargo item becomes susceptible to loss overboard.

An alternative, a more efficient and, in my opinion, a better method is illustrated in Fig.4.X, below.

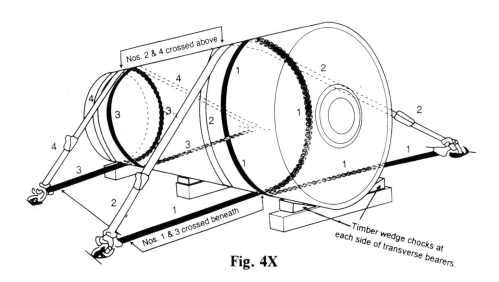

Fig. 4X

The lashings pass circumferentially around the cylinder, crossing over the upper surface/under the lower surface in pairs. From this it follows that if one component fails the system remains securely in balance. There is no tendency for the cargo unit to slew or for the other lashings to go slack.

Shaped timber wedge chocks should be considered an essential feature in the securing of such cargo items. And, depending upon the length and weight of the cylinder, I would probably use a pair of additional lashings at mid-length, much as illustrated in Fig.3.44, earlier herein.

I expect the IMO will take some time to issue any correcting amendment in this connection; so, in the meantime, I shall be advocating Fig.4X as the safest and most seamanlike method of securing this type of cylinder.

Important Caution

A word of caution before deciding to use half-double grommets (at NBL x 1.5) and single loops (at NBL x 1.4) as opposed to single eyes (at NBL x 0.7). At one terminal **end** in the instance of a half-double grommet, and at each terminal **end** in the instance of a single loop, there is no more material than at the terminal end of a soft eye.

If a properly made-up single loop breaks adrift, you have immediately lost twice the holding power allowable for a soft eye; if a properly made-up half-double grommet breaks adrift, you have lost more than twice the holding power allowable for a soft eye; so it is most important to ensure that the terminal ends are connected by shackles or some other form of smooth, non-sharp-edged, component.

For instance, say that for convenience and time saving you choose to use 12 half-double grommets of 16mm 6 x 12 wire to secure a 46-tonne item, rather than 25 single eyes. If one of the half-double grommets fractures at a poor terminal connection you lose 8.3% of the total holding power; if a soft eye had failed you would have lost only 4% of the total holding power. As remarked earlier, lashing and securing of deck cargoes is not an exact science. It is frequently a case of a balanced trade-off, but the trade-off should be based on information and a few quick calculations the basis for which this book hopefully provides.

D-Rings, Lashing-Lugs, Pad-Eyes, Etc.

Many a well-stowed, well-secured deck cargo started to break adrift because the lashing terminal points were either too weak to start with or overloaded with too many lashings. To spend the time and trouble to complete a well-balanced stowage and lashing arrangement as illustrated in Example 6 and Figs.3.42 to 3.44, and then to lose the cargo because deck terminal lashing points failed. would be unfortunate in the extreme.

The most unfortunate combination of events occurs where the lashing lug itself and its attaching welding are of ample strength, but the sub-structure to which the lug is welded is of much reduced strength. This situation arises where heavy lugs are attached to lightweight deck plating or bulwark plating on a ship, or to relatively thin plating forming the casing of a high-value piece of machinery.

One of the most useful (and now more common) deck lashing terminal points is the D-ring made of drop-forged steel, in either single or double construction. The dimensions of such rings govern their intrinsic strength together with the length, type and depth of weld attachment. The constructions shown in Figs.3.45, 3.46 and 3.47, for instance, illustrate that

    a.   A single D-ring with a 15-tonne break-load will have weld-runs of 100mm length each side of the connecting saddle.

    b.   A single D-ring with a 20-tonne break-load will have weld-runs of 130mm length on each side of the connecting saddle.

    c.   A single and a double D-ring with a 36-tonne break-load will have weld-runs of 140mm length on each side of the connecting saddle.

All for drop-forged material of yield strength well in excess of ordinary mild steel. But it is not only deck terminal points which fail; the lugs on the cargo itself may fail from similar causes, so due consideration must be given to their strength, also.

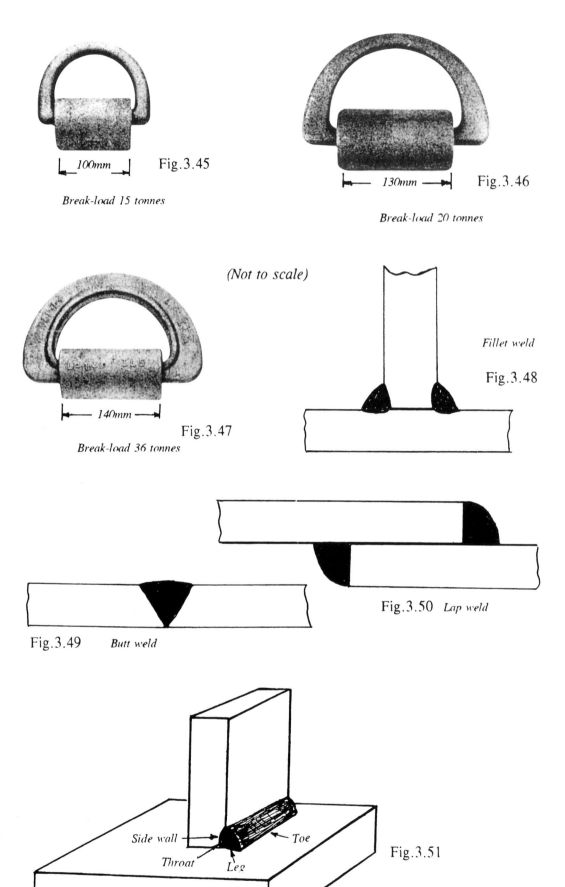

Fig.3.45

Break-load 15 tonnes

Fig.3.46

Break-load 20 tonnes

(Not to scale)

Fillet weld

Fig.3.48

Fig.3.47

Break-load 36 tonnes

Fig.3.50 *Lap weld*

Fig.3.49 *Butt weld*

Side wall

Throat

Leg

Toe

Fig.3.51

Shore-based engineers consistently under-estimate the forces likely to be generated in the lashing lugs on their machines arising from the pitching, pounding, scending, and rolling motions of a ship in severe adverse weather conditions. Vertical accelerations of as much as 2g may be experienced momentarily in the forward part of the ship; that is why the "3-times rule" is no more than adequate when securing deck cargoes. Over the years the author and his colleagues have been called upon many times to investigate the failures of lashing point arrangements, and a single typical instance may serve to make the point.

The external lifting lugs on heavy, high-value, transformer units were of rounded triangular shape - 45mm thick, short straight leg 180mm, welded long-leg 690mm - as illustrated in colour Plate F between Chapters 4 and 5. Of themselves, when properly welded, they had a direct (in plane) break-load in excess of 100 tonnes. There were no instructions to prohibit their use for lashing/securing purposes, and they were so used on the ship. Within 24 hours of the ship putting to sea the transformer units were adrift. The lashings had been applied at near right-angles to the planes of the lugs and the lugs had simply torn adrift at the sub-structure, as shown in colour Plate F. It was then seen that the sub-structure provided by the transformer tank walls to which the lugs attached was of no more than 10mm thickness.

Analyses confirmed the lugs and tank walls to be of general constructional mild steel free of defects and that the welds had been fully and correctly completed. Calculations confirmed, however, that if forces at the eye were applied at right-angles to the plane of the lug, then the sub-structure would fail at loads of about 3 tonnef! Saving a few dollars by not applying adequate reinforcement to the sub-structure resulted in a damage claim of several millions of dollars.

The important thing to remember when assessing the weld connections for D-rings, or any other form of welded terminal, is that constructional and Classification considerations require that the yield strength of the weld connections shall be at least equal to the intrinsic yield strength of the material welded. Ordinary shipbuilding mild steel, for instance, has a yield strength of about $235N/mm^2$; so it follows that an ordinary mild steel lashing plate of, say, 20mm thickness should not be welded to ordinary mild steel plating of less thickness. In other words, unless the yield strength and thickness of the sub-structure are known to be the same or better than the proposed lashing plate, play for safety. If necessary, decrease the size and increase the number of the lashing plates, and reinforce the sub-structure when terminal points are required to be welded to any part of a ship's structure.

Lloyd's Register, for instance, recommend that eye plates (lashing plates) are not to be welded to the upper side of the sheerstrake nor, in general, are they to penetrate the strength deck plating. Deck, bulwark or other plating is to be of sufficient thickness to withstand any shear forces that may be incurred in way of eye plates (lashing plates) due to asymmetrical loading of the eye plate (lashing plate), and such plating is to be stiffened as necessary to prevent deformation under direct eye plate (lashing plate) loadings.

It is not the intention of this book to provide the mathematics of the strengths of welds and structural steelwork. However, one or two rough guides do not come amiss, and may assist when "make do" has to be done quickly and without expert technical staff. Figs.3.48 to 3.51 illustrate the terms and types of welds likely to be encountered in lashing work.

For instance, in simple terms it is safe to assume that ordinary mild steel of shipbuilding quality will have a yield strength of about $24kgf/mm^2$.

Consider an ordinary mild steel plate of 20mm thickness as shown in Fig.3.52, properly welded to a sub-structure of similar steel 25mm thick. An eye has been cut smoothly to create a lashing terminal.

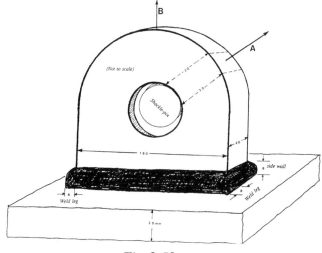

Fig.3.52

Assume that the shear yield strength of the weld is no better and no worse than the shear yield strength of the steel, i.e. 24kgf/mm², and assume the dimensions given in Fig.3.52 to be correct. Assume pull stress is in the direction of the arrow - A. (Or in any direction in which that shackle-pin bears evenly on the inside wall of the eye as shown.)

Then for lashing plate eye: area of section under load = 2 (20 x 20) = 800mm².

800mm² @ 24kgf/mm² = 19200kgf shear yield strength, ie, 19.20 tonnef.

(Note: This would equate with a MSL of 9.6 tonnef under the CSS Code Table 1).

Consider now the shear yield stress of the weld when subjected to a direct pull in the direction of the arrow - B. The side wall will be under shear loading over an area as shown in Fig.3.53.

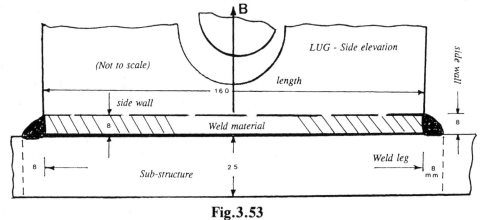

Fig.3.53

Then the weld side wall area = 2 (160 x 8) + 2 (20 x 8) = 2560 + 320 = 2880mm².

2880mm² @ 24kgf/mm² = 69120kgf shear yield strength, i.e, 69.12 tonnef.

(Note: This would equate with a MSL of 34.56 tonnef under the CSS Code Table 1).

So the weld is roughly 3½ times as strong as the material in the lashing terminal when subjected to direct shear stress loading. Such a large differential will diminish when the loading on the weld is not direct, ie, when other than in the direction of arrow B; but not to the extent of taking it as low as the shear yield strength of the eye.

But what of the sub-structure to which the lashing terminal is to be welded, whether it be intrinsic to the cargo unit or part of the ship's structure?

As illustrated in Figs.3.53 and 3.54 for direct load:

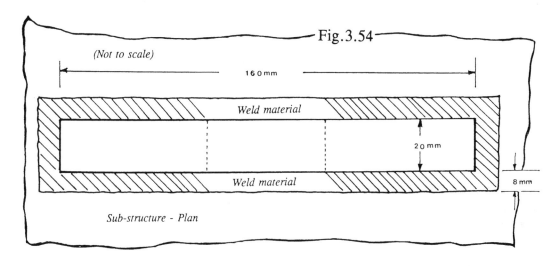

Fig.3.54

Area of section of sub-structure under shear stress = 2 (160 x 25) + 2 (20 x 25)
$$= 9000 mm^2.$$

9000mm^2 @ 24kgf/mm^2 = 216000kgf yield strength, ie, 216.0 tonnef.

(Note: This will equate with a MSL of 108 tonnef under the CSS Code Table 1, but it is the lashing plate eye at Fig.3.52 which would be the governing strength component.)

So the sub-structure, under direct shear stress, will have a shear yield strength roughly three times greater than the lashing terminal weld and roughly eleven times greater than the terminal eye. Hence, the Fig,3.52 lashing eye, efficiently welded to this sub-structure, will provide a breaking strength of 19.2 tonnef and a MSL of 9.6 tonnef with no risk of failure to the sub-structure - **provided the pull stress is in the direct plane of the lug: if the pull stress deviates to one side of the plane of the lug bending moments are generated with the often catastrophic results illustrated in Plate F**.

There is, of course, a wide range of ready-made lashing plates, together with ready-made pad-eyes with both circular and rectangular base plates, marketed as to standard sizes and strengths, all obtainable from specialist manufacturers such as Coubro & Scrutton Ltd., International Lashing Systems, MacGregor-Conver GmbH,, Peck & Hale Ltd., Line Fast Corporation, the Crosby Group Inc., and others too numerous to mention. A few samples of lashing plates are illustrated in Figs.3.55 to 3.61, on page 78, while Fig.3.62 and its following Table 10 provides details of rectangular-base standard eye-plates.

Lashing Terminals

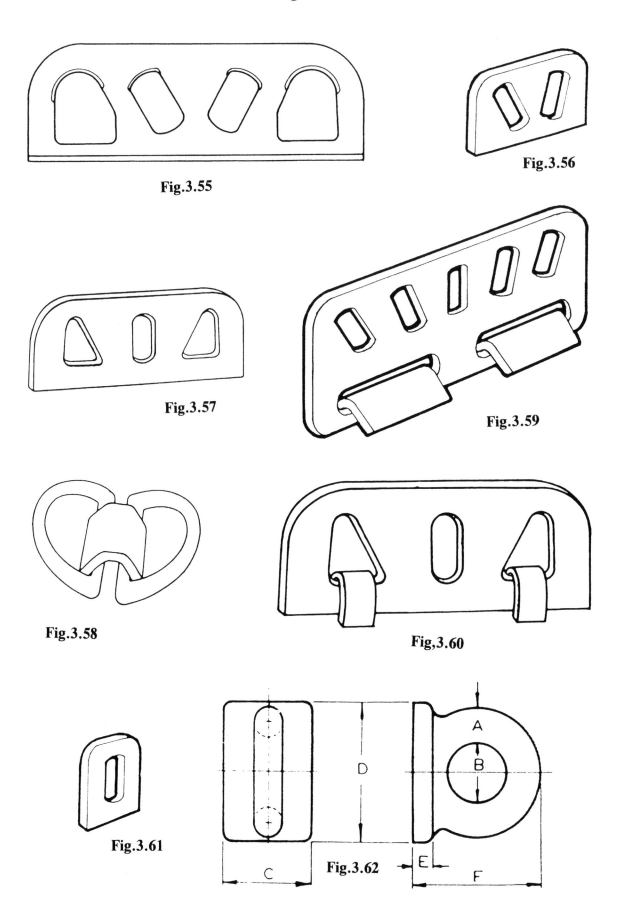

Fig.3.55

Fig.3.56

Fig.3.57

Fig.3.59

Fig.3.58

Fig,3.60

Fig.3.61

Fig.3.62

TABLE 10 - **Proof-Loads For Pad-Eyes**

Pattern Number	NATO Number	Dia. of Material in Eye		Dia. of Eye		BASE PLATES						Total Height		Proof Test	
		A		B		C		D		E		F		Tons	Kgs.
		in.	mm	in.	mm	in.	mm	in.	mm	in.	mm	in.	mm		
4014	5140	3/8	10	3/4	19	1	25	1 3/4	45	1/4	6	1 1/2	38	1 3/4	1,750
4015	5141	1/2	13	1	25	1 3/8	35	2 1/4	57	5/16	8	2	50	3 1/8	3,125
4016	5142	5/8	16	1 1/4	32	1 3/4	45	2 7/8	73	3/8	10	2 1/2	64	4 7/8	4,875
4017	5143	3/4	19	1 1/2	38	2	50	3 3/8	86	7/16	11	3	77	7	9,562
4018		7/8	22	1 3/4	45	2 3/8	60	4	102	1/2	13	3 1/2	89	9 9/16	7,000
4019	5144	1	25	2	50	2 3/4	70	4 1/2	115	5/8	16	4	102	12 1/2	12,500
4020		1 1/8	28	2 1/4	57	3	77	5 1/8	130	11/16	17	4 1/2	115	15 3/4	15,750
4021	5145	1 1/4	32	2 1/2	64	3 3/8	86	5 5/8	142	3/4	19	5	127	19 1/2	19,500
4022		1 3/8	35	2 3/4	70	3 3/4	96	6 1/4	158	13/16	20	5 1/2	140	23 3/8	23,375
4023	5146	1 1/2	38	3	77	4	102	6 3/4	171	7/8	22	6	153	28 1/8	28,125
4025	5147	1 3/4	45	3 1/2	89	4 3/4	120	7 7/8	200	1 1/16	27	7	178	38 1/4	38,225
4027	5148	2	50	4	102	5 3/8	136	9	229	1 3/16	30	8	204	50	50,000

(SOURCE: Taylor Pallister & Co. Ltd.)

(For the purposes of Table 1 of the CSS Code, the values under the two **Proof Test** columns can be taken as equivalent to at least the appropriate MSL. The pad-eye Table 10, however, includes two errors: Firstly, the column headed **Tons** should read **Tonnes**. Secondly, in the column headed **Kgs** the values in the fourth and fifth lines down have become transposed - they should match the values (in tonnes) in the next column adjacent.)

Fire and Explosion Hazards

The need for care, thought and planning before any welding of lashing terminals takes place cannot be too greatly emphasised, bearing in mind that the attachment of such terminals may occur when stowage of below-decks cargo is well advanced or maybe completed. With such aspects in mind, the last part of Chapter 2 is here repeated in full.

Before any welding is effected on board the vessel it is of the utmost importance to obtain a "hot work" certificate from the port/harbour authority. Make sure that the port/harbour authorities are in possession of ALL RELEVANT INFORMATION RELATING TO YOUR SHIP AND ITS CARGO. **DO NOT NEGLECT THIS RULE!**

Make sure that the welding contractors and/or the ship's officers and crew are competent to carry out and/or adequately supervise the welding work.

In the space below the weather-deck, place not less than two reliable men, each supplied with two (2) suitable portable fire-extinguishers. In the space below the weather-deck, spread purpose-made thick asbestos sheeting immediately beneath each point where welding is being effected. Do not allow two areas of welding if only one area can be protected by the asbestos sheet below. Rig fire hoses on deck, with adjustable spray/jet nozzles, and with full water pressure on the deck fire-line On completion of all "hot work", maintain a watchman in the space below for at least four hours thereafter. A ship's officer should be directed to effect a thorough examination in the spaces below before those spaces are closed and/or battened-down. IF IN DOUBT - DON'T WELD! If any reader considers the foregoing rules to be unrealistic, the author will be pleased to provide details of instances where by-passing such common-sense requirements has resulted in catastrophic shipboard fires on the one hand, and catastrophic explosions and loss of life on the other!

Additional Lashing Angle Tables

Reverting back to Chapter 1, it will be recalled that Table 1 provided a quick means of assessing vertical and transverse restraints for lashings with a holding power of 5.5 tonnef. Hereunder, three additional Tables are provided for half-double grommets and soft eyes of holding power (slip-load) greater than 5.5 tonnef.

TABLE 11 - Correctly Made Half-Double Grommet In 16mm 6 x 12 Wire. Lashing Holding Power (Slip-load) 11.625 Tonnef. Vertical, Transverse & Fore-and-Aft Restraints.

Base Angle Degrees	Peak Angle Degrees	Lashing Holding Power (Slip-load) Tonnef	Vertical Restraint Tonnef	Transverse and Fore-and-Aft Restraint Tonnef
0	90	11.625	0.00	11.625
5	85	11.625	1.013	11.581
10	80	11.625	2.019	11.448
15	75	11.625	3.009	11.229
20	70	11.625	3.976	10.924
25	65	11.625	4.913	10.536
30	60	11.625	5.813	10.068
35	55	11.625	6.668	9.523
40	50	11.625	7.472	8.905
45	45	11.625	8.220	8.220
50	40	11.625	8.905	7.472
55	35	11.625	9.523	6.668
60	30	11.625	10.068	5.813
65	25	11.625	10.536	4.913
70	20	11.625	10.924	3.976
75	15	11.625	11.229	3.009

For single loops with 6 grips: in 16mm 6 x 12 wire use Table 11 values multiplied by 0.934.

TABLE 12 - Correctly Made Soft Eye In 18mm 6 x 24 Wire.
Lashing Holding Power (Slip-load) 9.24 Tonnef.
Vertical, Transverse & Fore-and-Aft Restraints.

Base Angle Degrees	Peak Angle Degrees	Lashing Holding Power (Slip-load) Tonnef	Vertical Restraint Tonnef	Transverse and Fore-and-Aft Restraint Tonnef
0	90	9.24	0.00	9.24
5	85	9.24	0.81	9.20
10	80	9.24	1.60	9.06
15	75	9.24	2.39	8.93
20	70	9.24	3.16	8.68
25	65	9.24	3.90	8.37
30	60	9.24	4.62	8.00
35	55	9.24	5.30	7.57
40	50	9.24	5.94	7.08
45	45	9.24	6.53	6.53
50	40	9.24	7.08	5.94
55	35	9.24	7.57	5.30
60	30	9.24	8.00	4.62
65	25	9.24	8.37	3.90
70	20	9.24	8.68	3.16
75	15	9.24	8.93	2.39

It will be appreciated that Table 1, on p.17 earlier in the book, is for the smaller diameter 16mm 6 x 12 wire made up correctly with a soft eye. As indicated in the associated drawing above, *correctly* means using not less than three bulldog-grips of the right size all applied with the bridge on the 'working' part and the bow on the 'static' part of the eye. For those persons with a mind to do it, Tables can be created for eyes using only two bulldog-grips by following the lay-out and principles indicated here - useful if you have no alternative due to shortage of grips or some other unwanted circumstance.

TABLE 13 -Correctly Made Half-Double Grommet In 18mm 6 x 24 Wire.
Lashing Holding Power (Slip-load) 19.8 Tonnef.
Vertical, Transverse & Fore-and-Aft Restraints.

Base Angle Degrees	Peak Angle Degrees	Lashing Holding Power (Slip-load) Tonnef	Vertical Restraint Tonnef	Transverse and Fore-and-Aft Restraint Tonnef
0	90	19.80	0.00	19.80
5	85	19.80	1.73	19.72
10	80	19.80	3.44	19.50
15	75	19.80	5.12	19.13
20	70	19.80	6.77	18.61
25	65	19.80	8.37	17.95
30	60	19.80	9.90	17.15
35	55	19.80	11.36	16.22
40	50	19.80	12.73	15.17
45	45	19.80	14.00	14.00
50	40	19.80	15.17	12.73
55	35	19.80	16.22	11.36
60	30	19.80	17.15	9.90
65	25	19.80	17.95	8.37
70	20	19.80	18.61	6.77
75	15	19.80	19.13	5.12

For single loops, made correctly with 6 grips as shown:

in 18mm 6 x 24 wire use Table 13 values multiplied by 0.934.

The numbers in these Tables do not plot as straight lines: the lines are slightly curved. Nevertheless, for the degree of accuracy required, it is acceptable to treat the tabular values as linear, thus allowing direct interpolation between any 5 degree step. A simple example of such interpolation is provided on the next page.

Example:

In Table 12, what would be the approximate a) vertical and b) transverse restraints in lashings with a 28° base angle?

a) At 25°, vertical restraint = 3.90 tonnef; and at 30°, vertical restraint = 4.62 tonnef.

$$\therefore \text{ at } 28° \text{ vertical restraint} = 3.9 + \frac{(4.62 - 3.90) \times (28 - 25)}{5}$$

$$= 3.9 + \frac{0.72 \times 3}{5} = 3.9 + 0.43 = \underline{4.33 \text{ tonnef.}}$$

b) At 25°, transverse restraint = 8.37 tonnef; and at 30° transverse restraint = 8.00 tonnef.

$$\therefore \text{ at } 28° \text{ transverse restraint} = 8.37 - \frac{(8.37 - 8.00) \times (28 - 25)}{5}$$

$$= 8.37 - \frac{0.37 \times 3}{5} = 8.37 - 0.22 = \underline{8.15 \text{ tonnef.}}$$

#########

Plastic-Covered Wire - The Dangers
Colour Plate G, between Chapters 4 and 5, illustrates plastic (PVC) coated galvanised standard marine wire rope of 18mm diameter of 6 x 24 construction. It is commonly used to form gripes and tricing pennants for ships' lifeboats, the tarpaulin holding-down arrangements across traditional timber-and-canvas hatch covers, and applications where the strength of the wire is required without its cutting/chaffing characteristics. Its application for securing cargo items is undoubtedly appealing, but it must be used with care and consideration.

In a series of tests effected by the author at the test-bed premises of R. Perry & Co. Ltd. of Birkenhead, financed by Thomas Miller Defence, it was clear from the outset that eyes, single loops, and half-double grommets made-up with this wire, using bulldog-grips, without fully stripping away the PVC coating first, would fail at relatively very low slip-loads. The PVC coating here involved was coloured blue, but red, yellow, green and clear coatings are not uncommon. A series of 96 individual tests had been planned, as had been followed with all the previous tests. In the event, three soft eye, five single loops, and five half-double grommets, only, were tested because the failure rate was so obvious.

Soft eyes were made-up, tape-marked, and measured using 3 grips, and similarly for 2-grip and 1-grip configurations. **In round terms, instantaneous slip occurred at loads of no more than half those for uncoated wire of the same size and construction**. The PVC coating simply puckered, split, and slid along the wire with the bulldog-grips, as shown in the uppermost view in colour Plate G.

Single loops were made-up, tape-marked, and measured using 6 grips, and similarly for 4-grip and 3-grip configurations. In those instances, the PVC did not pucker and split; rather the interior wire simply slipped along inside the coating, as illustrated in the centre view in colour Plate G. **In round terms, instantaneous slip occurred at loads of little better than two-fifths of those for uncoated wire of the same size and construction.**

Half-double grommets were made-up, tape-marked, and measured using 6 grips, and similarly for 4-grip and 3-grip configurations, as illustrated in the lowermost view in colour Plate G. **The results were widely scattered: at best no better than two-fifths, at worst no better than one-quarter of slip-loads in uncoated wire of the same size and construction.** The wire simply slipped along inside the coating as in the instances of single loops.

From the foregoing it follows that if plastic-covered wire is to be used in any context make sure that all the coating is fully stripped away clear of any contact with bulldog-grips and clear along the line of the opposing lengths of wire in contact.

****

CHAPTER 4

Timber Deck Cargoes

Codes Of Practice

There continues to be a steady incidence of the loss overboard of timber deck cargoes, sometimes with catastrophic results for ship and crew. It is therefore more important than ever to ensure that the stowage and securing of timber deck cargoes does not fall short of any currently accepted recommendations, Codes, or Regulations.

A Code of Safe Practice for Ships Carrying Timber Deck Cargoes was formulated by the IMO sub-committee on Containers and Cargoes and was approved by the Maritime Safety Committee in November 1973. IMO recommended that Governments should implement the Code and authorised the Maritime Safety Committee to update it when necessary. A Supplement to the Code contained various amendments, followed by the consolidated 1974 edition, and subsequently by a second edition in 1981.

Later, a further revision was adopted by Resolution A.715(17) and this was published by IMO as the Code of Safe Practice for Ships Carrying Timber Deck Cargoes, 1991. That Code is different in several respects from the earlier versions. As things stand at the beginning of the year 2002, a vessel loading a timber deck cargo should comply with the IMO "Code of Safe Practice for Ships Carrying Timber Deck Cargoes, 1991"(with the included interpretation of Regulation 44 of the International Convention on Load Lines) with any Amendments which may follow, together with all relevant requirements set out in her Cargo Securing Manual, mandatory since 1st January 1998.

Those involved with the stowage and carriage of timber deck cargoes should have a full knowledge and understanding of that 1991 Code, which is obtainable from the International Maritime Organisation, 4 Albert Embankment, London SE1 7SR.

The Practical Applications

The provisions contained in the IMO 1991 Code are recommended for all vessels of 24m or more in length engaged in the carriage of "Timber Deck Cargoes" - a phrase defined as meaning a timber cargo carried on an uncovered part of a freeboard or superstructure deck, and includes logs and sawn timber whether loose or packaged. The following basic factors need to be considered:-

1. The type and compactness of timber cargo, e.g. logs, cants, ragged-end packages, square (or flush) both ends, etc.

2. Type of vessel: timber load line or not.

3. Strength, pitch and tending of lashings.

4. Height of cargo above weather-deck level.

5. Height of cargo and stability considerations.

6. Measures to deliberately jettison cargo.

7. Keeping clear all sounding and air pipes, and valves, necessary for the working of the ship.

8. Ensuring means of safe access to all parts of the ship.

9.   Keeping cargo hold ventilators clear for operation.

10.   Fully closing all screw-down overboard drain valves fitted to topside ballast tanks,
        keeping them accessible for the working of the ship at all times.

11.   The issuing of "Under-Deck" and/or "On Deck" Bills of Lading.

12.   Hatch covers and other openings to spaces below decks should be securely
        closed and battened-down.

13.   Hatches and decks, and the cargo itself during loading, should be kept
        free of any accumulations of ice and snow.

14.   Have all deck lashings, uprights, etc., in position before loading commences.
        (This will be necessary anyway if a pre-loading examination of securing
        equipment is required by local officials at the loading port.)

15.   The cargo must not interfere in any way with the navigation and necessary
        working of the ship.

16.   Upon completion of loading, and before sailing, a thorough inspection of the
        ship should be carried out. Soundings within the ship should also be taken to
        verify that no structural damage has occurred causing an ingress of water.

Types of Timber Cargo

Packaged timber should not be stowed on deck if the bundles are ragged at both ends. Generally speaking, only bundles square at both ends should be used for weather-deck stowages. It is recognised, however, that the Far East trade demands the stowage of a proportion of packages which are square at one end and ragged at the other. Wherever possible, every care should be taken to ensure that ragged ends are kept to a minimum, stowed inboard of the perimeter, and that broken stowage is avoided. **The Code does not allow athwartship packages to extend to the extreme sides of the on-deck stowage. Packages stowed athwartships must be contained within side walls formed by square-ended packages stowed fore-and-aft**. Where failure to do this has resulted in loss of packaged timber, cargo interests have been successful in recovery litigation against the ship. (See Fig.4.01, on the following page, for example, and Section F, pages xxii and xxiii of the **INTRODUCTION** to the CSM preceding Chapter 1.)

Logs may come in a variety of lengths and be of widely varying diameter; and **Cants** are defined as logs which are "slab cut", that is, they are ripped lengthwise so that the resulting thick pieces have two opposing parallel flat sides and in some cases a third side which is sawn flat.

Any omissions from the lashing arrangements recommended in the Code could lead to loss of cargo. For the securing of logs and cants cargoes - uprights, hog wires, and wiggle-wires are required, all in addition to securing wires or chains pitched at the correct distance apart. The 1991 Code should be consulted in full before loading a timber cargo.

Timber Load Lines
Many vessels are marked with special timber load lines in addition to the normal load lines. (See Fig.4.02). The timber lines are calculated on the premise that a full timber deck cargo will be carried, and an entirely separate set of cross-curves of stability is produced for the full timber deck

Photo: Gordon Line.

Fig.4.01   *Transverse packages must be kept within sides of square-ended packages stowed fore-and-aft. This photograph illustrates the results of ignoring that recommendation. Here, and at an adjacent hatch cover, part of the transverse stowed packages and part of the fore-and-aft-stowed packages were lost overboard due to the excessive shift of those transverse packages which had been stowed right out to the ship's sides.*

cargo condition. The timber lines allow the vessel to load to a deeper draught (and hence a larger displacement) than would otherwise be the case.

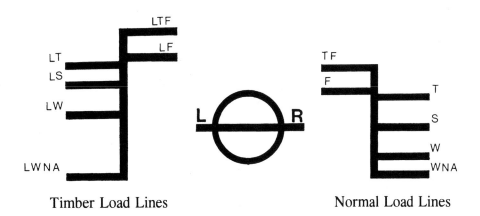

Fig.4.02   Timber Load Lines   Normal Load Lines

Disputes have arisen between shipmasters and charterers as to the strict application of the timber load lines. The following guidelines should be applied:-

a.   When a ship is assigned timber load lines then, in order to load to those marks, the vessel must be loaded with a timber deck cargo which is correctly stowed and fully secured in accordance with the International Load Line Rules and the IMO Code of Safe Practice for Ships Carrying Timber Deck Cargoes, 1991.

b.   Those Rules and that Code require that the timber be stowed as solidly as possible to at least the standard height of the superstructure. For instance, in ships of 125m or more in length this means to a uniform height of not less than 2.3m. In ships under 125m in length, the stow should reach a uniform height of not less than the height of the break of the forecastle head.

c.   **If the timber is stowed to a lesser height than above or is not correctly stowed in any other way - i.e. not the full length of the well or not from side to side - then the ship is not permitted to load to the timber line.**

d.   When timber is correctly stowed on deck as referred to at (a) and (b), above, the ship may load to the timber load line irrespective of the quantity or type of cargo stowed below decks. The reduction in freeboard enjoyed by a ship which is assigned timber load lines is permitted because of the buoyancy contribution of the timber deck cargo to the ship's stability characteristics.(Importantly in this connection, see the third and fourth paragraphs under the heading **Height of Cargo and Stability Considerations,** later in this Chapter.)

e.   When a full timber cargo is carried on deck and the ship is loaded to the timber load line, the statical stability curve may be derived from the cross-curves of stability. **When the timber deck cargo is not correctly stowed, due to deficient height or other reason, the statical stability curve must be derived from the cross-curves computed for the ship without timber deck cargo.**

Pitch, Strength and Tending of Lashings

The IMO Code confirms Regulation 44 of the International Convention on Load Lines 1966, and the spacing of the transverse lashings should be determined by the maximum height of the cargo above the weather-deck. The straightforward interpretation applies to a compact stow of square-ended bundles (flush at both ends) or near square-ended bundles, or compactly-stowed loose timber - **secured throughout its length by independent lashings** - in the following manner:-

1.   For a height of 4m (13 feet) and below, the spacing of lashings should be not more than 3m (9.8 feet). (Fig.4.03 shows an unacceptable attempt to comply with this standard).

2.   For heights above 4m (13 feet) the spacing should be not more than 1.5 metres (4.9 feet).

3.   The distance apart from an end bulkhead of a superstructure to the first eye-plate shall be not more than 2m (6.6ft). Eye-plates and lashings shall be provided 0.6m (23½in) and 1.5m (4.9ft) from the ends of timber deck cargoes where there is no bulkhead. Fig.4.04 illustrates the provision of permanent terminal points to accommodate this requirement.

4.   When timber is in lengths less than 3.6 metres (11.8 feet) the spacing of the lashings shall be reduced or other provisions made to suit the length of timber. In any event, the spacing of the lashings should be such that the two lashing at each end of each length of continuous deck stow are positioned as close as practicable to the extreme ends of the timber deck cargo

5.   Height - means the height above the weather-deck at the ship's side adjacent to the cargo, and must include the height of hatchway coamings and hatch covers.

Fig.4.03   *Using lashing wires through the drain holes in the side plates of side post foot restraints (or similar) does not provide acceptable terminal connections.*

Fig. 4.04   *Permanent lashing terminals at forward end (aft end similar) closed down to 0.6m spacing to comply with paragraph 6 of Regulation 44 of the Load Line Rules, 1966 - still in force as of January 2002.*

6. Under the terms of some of the earlier Codes (and possibly still today in some National regulations) when timber was stowed to a height of more than 4m but less than 6m, the required lashings' spacing could be interpolated linearly between 1.5 metres and 3 metres, as shown hereunder:-

Given that up to 4m height the maximum lashing pitch will be 3m; that at 6m height the maximum pitch will be 1.5m, then pitch of lashings between 4m and 6m will be -

$$\text{Pitch} = 3 - \left(\left[\frac{h-4}{2} \right] 1.5 \right) \quad \text{where } h = \text{height of cargo above the weather-deck at ship's side.}$$

For instance, if the height of the cargo was 4.95m, the lashing pitch would be -

$$3 - \left(\left[\frac{4.95-4}{2} \right] 1.5 \right) \quad = \quad 3 - \left(\frac{0.95}{2} \times 1.5 \right)$$

$$= 3 - (0.475 \times 1.5) = 3 - 0.7125 = \mathbf{2.2875, \; say \; 2.29m.}$$

Or, to put it more simply: For timber cargo heights above 4m and not greater than 6m, the pitch of lashings decreases by 3cm for every 4cm increase in cargo height.

This was **not** a very clever recommendation, to say the least, and it resulted in many unsafe lashing arrangements while attempting to meet the calculated spacing. **It should be borne in mind that the IMO 1991 Code does not permit this form of interpolation. The 1991 Code now requires 3m spacing up to 4 metres height, and 1.5 metres thereafter. Hence, it makes it more straightforward for all vessels likely to carry timber deck cargoes to be provided with permanent lashing points pitched at intervals not greater than 1.5m.**

The stowage of timber deck cargo should be tight and compact. Where packages are involved, they should be square-ended (flush) at both ends so far as this is possible. Broken stowage and unused spaces should be avoided.

The Code requires the rigging of uprights at the ship's sides in the presence of a deck cargo of **logs**; but there is no specific requirement for uprights to be used for packaged timber cargo, although some National administrations occasionally insist on their use. In fact, many large modern vessels engaged in the trade have no provision for the fitting and rigging of uprights. **The Code does not allow uprights to be used instead of, or partly in place of, lashings. Where uprights are used in the presence of logs and/or packaged timber, such use must be in addition to the full number of lashings properly pitched and of full strength.** (And see later in this Chapter).

Wires or chains used for lashings should have a break-load of not less than 13.6 tonnef (133kN), spaced apart as indicated on pages 88 and 90, hereof. With wire and grips the Code recommends **that four grips per eye are used** and, if that is done around a thimble, the holding power of the eye will be better than NBL x 0.9, so 6 x 24 wire rope of 19mm diameter will be acceptable.

Where soft eyes made-up correctly with three grips and no thimbles are used, the slip-load/holding power will be about 70% of the wire's nominal break-load; so the NBL of the wire should be at least 100 (13.6/70) =19.43 tonnef, of which 70% equals 13.6 tonnef. This means that a 6 x 19 wire of say 19mm diameter (¾") can be used, although it is not as flexible - diameter for diameter - as wire of 6 x 24 construction.

Every lashing should be provided with a device - pear-rings and chains attached to long turnbuckles, for instance - or some other component system, suitable to permit the length of the lashings to be adjusted. (See Figs.4.05, 4.06 and 4.07). These should be of breaking strength not less than that of the other components. The lowest MSL/SWL component in the system will be considered to be the MSL/SWL of the entire system.

Steel chain with an approved MSL/SWL of 6.8 tonnes and above, complies with the Code and the strengths of lashing components set out in the CSM. Shackles should be of equivalent strength.

The IMO Code recommends that rounded angle pieces of suitable material and design should be used along the upper outboard edge of the stow to bear the stress and permit free reeving of the lashings.

More complex additional securing arrangements are required for cants, and reference should be made to the drawings and illustrations given in Appendix A of the Code.

At sea, lashings and securing arrangements should be tended daily, adjusting to take up any slack which may occur as the cargo shakes-down and consolidates. It is essential to enter in the ship's deck log book the times and dates of checking, together with comments on what was found and what was done, including the application of additional lashings when that action is prudent. **Where intermediate ports of discharge are involved, great care must be taken to ensure that the remaining deck cargo is levelled out and re-secured in accordance with the spirit of the Code.** Where failure to do this has resulted in loss of packaged timber, cargo interests have been successful in recovery litigation against the ship.

Disasters Follow Transverse Stowages To Outer Wings
There have, for instance, been cases in which one, if not the only, cause of loss has been the popping out and sliding overboard of packages stowed athwartships to the outer wings of the stow, thereby generating a rapid collapse of the stow and loss overboard of the greater mass of the cargo. (Fig.4.01 and Fig.4.09, for instance.) In those cases, the respondents in litigation have argued that such stowage is in keeping with the Code. They have not always been successful.

The problem here lies in the correct answers to the questions: What is a packaged timber deck cargo and where are its "wings"?

Deck cargo is, simply, cargo carried on the weather-deck. This includes the weather-deck hatch covers which, in many modern vessels, extend so far to port and to starboard as effectively to exclude the area of the actual weather-deck for cargo-carrying purposes. This may be self-evident, yet it becomes of some importance when considering what constitutes the "wings" of a stow. When packages can be stowed "on the deck", then clearly the wings of the stow will be out to the ship's sides. Where the packages are placed on hatch covers, alone, then the outer edges of that stow become its " wings".

What the Code Says.
The Code requires that each package shall be **secured by at least two transverse lashings** which shall be pitched (spaced) 3m apart for heights not exceeding 4m, and 1.5m apart for cargo heights above

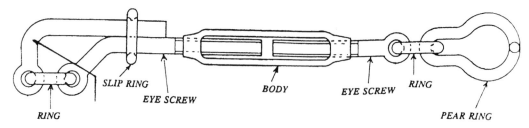

SLIP RING

EYE SCREW

BODY

EYE SCREW

RING

PEAR RING

RING

Fig. 4.05 *Timber rigging-screw with pelican hook slip at one end and pear-ring for chain length adjustments at other end. The hook slip can be knocked clear to jettison the cargo. (But see later in this Chapter.) Some such arrangement is still required under Regulation 44 of the International Convention on Load Lines 1966. See, also, Fig.4.06 and Fig. 4.07.*

Fig.4.06 *At rear: standard pelican slip-hook and pear link. At near view: turnbuckle screw-bar with circular jaw for taking up slack and shortening chain span.*

Fig. 4.07 *The correct use of timber rigging-screws, pear-links and chains pitched 1.2m apart. View shows pre-slung packaged timber.*

4m - all measured above the weather-deck edge at the ship's sides. **When the outboard stow is in lengths of less than 3.6m, the spacing of the lashings should be reduced as necessary.** That's clear enough; but how is paragraph **2.8** of Appendix A of the Code - here quoted in full - to be applied? (To save repetition, refer to Section F, pages xxii and xxiii of the **INTRODUCTION** to the CSM preceding Chapter 1)

"**2.8** *Due to the system of athwartship lashing, the stowage of packages should generally be in the fore-and-aft direction; the wings of the upper two tiers should always be in a fore-and-aft direction. It is advisable to have one or more non-adjacent tiers stowed athwartships when above the level of the hatches in order to produce a binding effect within the cargo. Also, athwartship packages should be carried above the hatches to interlock the load. If packages with great differences in length are to be loaded, the longest packages should be stowed fore-and-aft outboard. Short packages should be confined to the inner portions of the stowage. Only packages flush at both ends can be stowed athwartships (see figures 11, 12 and 13). "*

To most ship masters, and to myself, it is self-evident that the word "*tier*" means "a single package height"; so if a tier is one package high and **ALL** "*outboard* " packages are to be stowed in a fore-and-aft direction there is no problem with *figure 13*. But what of *figure 12?*

It seems to confirm that a "tier" equals a one package height and, bearing in mind the direction of the packages actually on the deck, that *figure 12* is a cross-section looking forward and aft. But does it show the correct way or the wrong way to stow packages athwartships?

Whichever way you look at *figure 12*, with its athwartship packages extending right out to the ship's side, it is contrary to paragraph **2.8** (quoted above) and in conflict with *figure 13* wherein the outboard packages are clearly stowed in a fore-and-aft direction. And no master or stevedore would contemplate attempting to stow four tiers of interlocked packages canted steeply inboard as shown in *figure 12*. The Code should be corrected to remove such confusing inconsistences.

The Unwanted End Result.
The cross-sectional end widths of packaged timber varies depending upon the country of origin. From the Far East and South America they can be as much as 1.5m wide. From Canada and the U.S.A., they are more likely to be almost standard at about 1.2m, stowing at about 1.25m. From this it follows that, in a four-pack high stowage, not exceeding 4m height, lashings pitched 3m apart would catch no more than random package ends if stowed athwartships to the "wings".

Where, say, the stowage was six packages high and 4m **or more** in height, the lashings would be pitched 1.5m apart. On a long hatch cover overstowed with Canadian and/or West Coast U.S.A., packages, **12 package ends would not be restrained by any lashing at all (30%), another 12 ends would be caught by no more than one lashing adversely skewed much closer to one side than the other (30%), and the balance of packages (40%) would be restrained by only one lashing at roughly mid-width,** as illustrated in Fig.4.08 on the following page. This is contrary to paragraph **4.3.4** of the Code, which says:

"**4.3.4** *When the outboard stow of the timber deck cargo is in lengths of less than 3.6m, the spacing of the lashings should be reduced as necessary or other suitable provisions made to suit the length of timber.*

The tendency for the transverse packages to slide overboard is pronounced when rolling heavily in a seaway. This, in turn, creates general slackness in the stowage and in the lashings. In a recent case which came to trial, where packages had been stowed athwartships to the outer wings and the lashings were 1.5m apart, the learned judge held that:

" The evidence however shows that not a single lashing component fractured or broke. Only one pear link was found to have elongated. This very localized damage is not consistent with dynamic forces uniformly exerted on every lashing, as they would be in a unitized stow. It indicates that a localized force was exerted on one lashing, which could only have occurred as the stow began to break up. In this respect I accept........that the generally intact and unbroken state of the lashing suit suggests that there was a gradual deterioration of the stow. This deterioration probably began with the slippage of one or two packages out of the stow due to the very heavy rolling and pitching motion...... followed by a rapid domino-like disintegration of the stow as the rapid roll of the ship propelled the packages into the sea. "

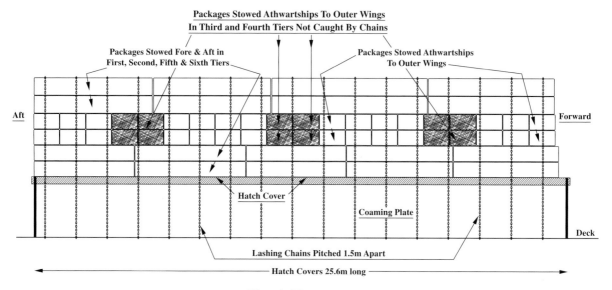

Fig. 4.08

Fig. 4.09

Arrow points to space where the major part of a package stowed athwartships has "popped out" from the stow.

Photo: Gordon Line

Personally, I am of the view that all packages at the sides (wings) of the stow should be placed in a fore-and-aft direction, in keeping with the intent of the Code. In the event, however, that the practice continues of stowing packages athwartships out to the extreme sides of a timber deck stow - and in order to avoid a contradiction in terms - the pitch of lashings should be closed down to about 50cm. With lashings so pitched the ends of packages would always be restrained by one, and mostly by two, lashings. To continue with anything less is contrary to the principles of prudent and sensible cargo care

Height of Cargo Above Weather-Deck Level

If the timber deck cargo is to be carried through Tropical or Summer Zones only, the following points should be observed:-

i.   that the height of the cargo does not restrict or impair visibility from the bridge. (In this connection reference should be made to Notice No.M.1264 of January 1987 - Navigation Bridge Visibility, reproduced as Addendum No.3, hereof.)

ii.   that, for any given height of cargo, its weight shall not exceed the designed maximum permissible loading on weather-decks and hatch covers and,

iii.   that any forward facing profile of the timber deck stowage does not present overhanging shoulders to a head sea.

If a timber deck cargo is to be carried through a Winter Zone, or a Seasonal Winter Zone in winter, the height of the cargo above the weather-deck should not exceed one-third of the extreme breadth of the ship. For instance, if the extreme breadth of the vessel was 15m, the height of the timber deck cargo should not exceed 5m. Similarly, a vessel of extreme breadth 21m could stow the cargo to 7m above the weather-deck, providing this did not contravene any of the other requirements of the Code. (See, also, under "**Timber Load Lines**", earlier.)

Height and Weight of Deck Cargo and Stability Considerations

As mentioned earlier in Chapter 1, and as dealt with more fully in Chapter 6, the weight of the deck cargo should not exceed the maximum permissible loading of weather-decks and hatch covers, and everyone involved with the loading and safe carriage of timber deck cargoes should be fully conversant with the stability requirements as set out in the IMO Code, the ship's "Standard Conditions" Stability Book, and the Cargo Securing Manual.

It is important that the correct weight of the cargo is known and allowed for in the stability calculations. Instances have occurred where, because the ship's Stability Book has indicated a given height of timber deck cargo as representing a given weight, the master and charterers have assumed that any timber cargo of the same height will have the same weight. This assumption has proved to be wrongly based and, in some instances, has resulted in serious adverse consequences.

For instance, from the remains of a packaged timber export cargo which had suffered extensive loss overboard, samples were cut from 14 timbers clearly different from each other, but shipped collectively as Sawn Brazilian Hardwood. Scientific analysis showed that 78% of the deck cargo - **by weight** - had specific gravities of between 1.0 and 1.4. Of those samples, 73% sank like stones in salt water of s.g.1.025. The inherent average s.g. for the deck cargo timber was 1.080 - e.g.

in its dry state denser than ocean salt water at s.g. 1.033. This timber was three times heavier per unit volume than the vessel's stability data allowed for, but no-one had informed the master or owners even though the shippers were fully aware of the cargo's excessive density!

If the cargo lashings had not failed due to contributory causes when the cargo shifted, the vessel would have continued to roll from the listed angle - in circumstances were the timber had become a "**sinking**" factor rather than the intended buoyancy factor - and it is highly probable that the ship would have capsized. (See colour Plate L.) In this instance a considerable proportion of the cargo was lost and the main-deck plating was torn open in several places. To re-establish her seaworthiness the vessel had to put in to a port of refuge for extensive repairs and re-stowage/re-securing of the packaged timber remaining, all at great cost.

To summarise: A packaged timber deck cargo of s.g. as high as 0.8 may not be so unusual as to require any special alert, bearing in mind that it can still provide some measure of positive buoyancy to a heavily listed ship. A packaged timber deck cargo of s.g. in excess of 1.033 - as occurs with Sawn Brazilian Hardwoods - provides no measure of positive buoyancy; rather, where a significant shift of cargo occurs creating a significant list and lashings do not part, such timber may well be causative of the ship capsizing.

The shipping industry should be alerted to these possible hazards.

Draught Surveys
Draught surveys should be conducted by the ship's officers at regular intervals to check the weights of cargo coming on board. This is necessary particularly when all the under-deck cargo has been loaded and before "on-deck" cargo loading commences. Such draught surveys, although subject to all their associated vagaries, if effected carefully will provide acceptable information for "on-deck weight" and stability purposes, and may well indicate that transverse lashings should be increased in number and/or strength to compensate for excessive weight. Addendum 6 at the end of this book provides a "short form" for calculation of deadweight/displacement, and may be found of assistance where the ship is not provided with a relevant computer programme.

The calculation of the metacentric height (GM) of a ship provides some measure of transverse stability, but additional calculations need to be made to produce the curve of statical stability (the GZ graph). The ship's stability characteristics can then be established for various angles of heel, and can be compared with the minimum characteristics required by the Load Line Rules, the vessel's Stability Book, and the Cargo Securing Manual.

The author is aware of, and has drawn the attention of others to, written instructions issued by some charterers or shippers requiring that the "*metacentric height (GM) should be maintained at one-and-a-half per cent of the vessel's beam and should never exceed 2ft (61cm)*". The author considers such instructions to be poorly-worded, incomplete, and positively dangerous in the instance of vessels of less than 10m beam where 1½% would produce a GM of less than 0.15m where 0.15m may be the statutory minimum. Ship masters should follow the IMO Code, and call for expert advice if they face instructions to the contrary. Paragraph 2.5 of Chapter 2 of the Code says:-
"*2.5 However, excessive initial stability should be avoided as it will result in rapid and violent motion in heavy seas which will impose large sliding and racking forces on the cargo causing*

high stresses on the lashings. Operational experience indicates that metacentric height should preferably not exceed 3% of the breadth in order to prevent excessive accelerations in rolling provided that the relevant stability criteria are satisfied. This recommendation may not apply to all ships and the master should take into consideration the stability information obtained from the ship's stability manual. " (In my opinion, this recommendation provides sound and prudent advice.)

Also, when making departure draught and load-port/arrival port stability calculations in winter time, some allowance must be made for absorption of water shipped on board and, when sub-zero temperatures are to be expected, for the increased weight due to accumulation of ice. The ship's stability booklet/loading instructions usually provides some guidance but, in the event it does not, then an increase in weight equal to 10% of the timber deck cargo weight should be allowed as acting at a height above the weather-deck equal to half the height of the deck cargo.

Disasters Follow Excessive Cargo Heights

The possible dangers relating to transverse stowage of packages to outer wings and the problems arising from dense timber cargoes have been earlier considered. We look now at the dangers which arise from lack of firm, clear, guidance as to the closing down of lashings' pitch where cargo heights become excessive.

As earlier parts of this Chapter have explained, the1991 Code requires that lashings shall be pitched 3m apart for cargo heights up to 4m, and 1.5m apart for cargo heights above 4m, measured above the weather deck at sides. In the previous (1978) edition of the Code, paragraph 5.4 stated: *"Where the height of timber deck cargo exceeds 6 metres the strength of the lashings should be to the satisfaction of the Administration. "* This was not very helpful, and has been omitted from the 1991 Code, but it did put everyone concerned on notice that something additional in the lashings' holding power might be a good idea. As it now stands, for heights above 6m, the lashings can remain at a 1.5m spacing with little hint that closer spacing and/or increased lashing strength should be considered.

I consider this to be a most unsatisfactory situation, and it is salutary to consider the additional weight effects as timber cargo heights increase on a large, modern, timber carrier in which the horizontal hatch covers are, say, 2.8m above the weather-deck at sides.

In such an instance, and assuming all the timber to be of more-or-less normal specific gravity:- when the upper surface of the cargo is 4m above the deck, only 1.2m of that height is cargo, and the lashings need be no closer spaced than 3m. Going to 6m height gives 3.2m vertical measurement of cargo with the lashings closed down by a factor of 2, to 1.5m spacing, yet cargo weight has increased by a factor of 2.66.

Going to, say, 8.9m overall height, gives 6.1m vertical measurement of cargo, with the lashings' spacing remaining at 1.5m; **yet cargo weight has increased by a factor of 5.08.** When cargo height goes to 10m - a not unknown occurrence - **the weight of cargo has increased by a factor of 6 with no requirement to increase strength of, or to reduce the pitch of, the securing lashings.**

There appears to be little justification for relying on under-strength lashings. Additional to other contributory causes, Figs.4.01 and Fig. 4.09 illustrate the catastrophic failure of a packaged timber deck cargo where the cargo height above the weather deck was 8.9m and the standard transverse lashings were pitched at 1.5m. All in keeping with the Code of Safe Practice, but highly unsafe and dangerous!

There is nothing in the Code to prevent increasing the lashings' strength and/or decreasing the pitch. Some traders do weld additional interspaced pad-eyes or D-rings before loading commences, thereby reducing the lashings' pitch to 0.75 and doubling the holding power of the 1.5m spacing; but the majority do not.

Also, at 10m height, and with 7.2m of that height made up of cargo, the down-acting force on the hatch covers may well exceed the vessel's designed permissible hatch cover load. This, in turn, will create a deflection in the hatch cover panels greater than that for which they were designed; excessive flexing may occur, causing the cargo to vibrate towards slackness, and may thus be a contributory factor in the overall loss of the cargo.

So far as I am aware, there is no record of any National Administration enforcing a reduced lashing' pitch even in instances where packaged timber cargo height has achieved 10m. Combined with other adverse factors, during the years 1982 to 1994 this lack in numbers/strength of lashings contributed to not less than 21 vessel incidents of loss of, or severe shift of, packaged timber deck cargoes shipped from West Coast Canadian and/or United States ports - certainly more if all were known and had been reported. This can hardly be considered a satisfactory state of affairs so far as cargo interests and their insurers are concerned.

Tiers and Modules.
In the IMO 1991 Code there is no mention of anything sounding like a "module" yet, in some instances involving packaged timber, shippers and charterers have attempted to make the words "module" and "tier" mean the same thing. This has resulted in some very questionable stowage practices followed by at least two major losses of packaged timber deck cargo.

What Does The Code Say?
With respect to packaged timber, the first reference to "tiers" occurs in Appendix A, paragraph **2.8**: "*....the wings of the upper two tiers should always be in the fore-and-aft direction. It is advisable to have one or more non - adjacent tiers stowed athwartships when above the level of the hatches.* The first reference to "tier" is at paragraph **2.9**: "*....a level and firm working surface should be prepared on each working tier.* And at paragraph **2.12**: "*When placed in upper tiers, heavy pieces of timber tend to work loose at sea.... "* And at paragraph **2.13**: "*When the final tier is loaded on a large number of tiers, it may be stepped in from the outer edge of the stow.... "*
The context is clear: a *"tier"* means a single package height. No mention of "modules" at all.

Where the Code says *"non-adjacent tiers stowed athwartships"* the loading port practice was to load **adjacent** tiers athwartships and out to the far sides of the stow, arguing that a "module" - without dunnage or stickers between the adjacent packages - equalled one "tier". The first two-package-high modules were all stowed fore-and-aft, then the next two-package-high modules were all stowed athwartships out to the limits of the port and starboard sides of the stow, then the next set of modules went fore-and-aft, then the next athwartships, and the final modules went fore-and-aft. By any reasonable reckoning, that was 10 tiers of packaged timber with adjacent tiers stowed athwartships, contrary to the intent of the IMO Code. Fig. 4.10 illustrates a typical 8-tiers/4-module stowage of the type here referred to.

Wrong & Dangerous
Athwartship Packages Should Not Extend To The Far Wings Of The Stow.
Tiers Stowed Athwartship Should Be Non-Adjacent.

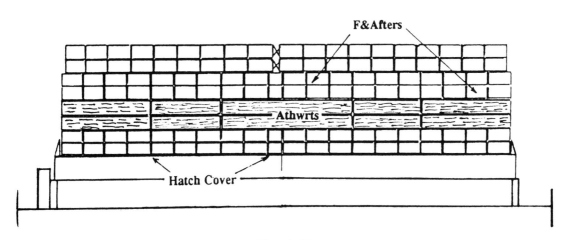

Fig. 4.10

Chambers Twentieth Century Dictionary defines "tier" as rank, or layer, especially **one** of several placed **one** above the other, a commonsense definition with which most people would agree. To describe a two-package height as a " tier" is straining the language beyond its reasonable limits.

The attempt to make "module" equal "tier" rested solely on commercial considerations where heavy-lift gantry cranes can handle large blocks of packages. In furtherance of this concept, it was proposed as within reason to say that a four-package-high, or a six-package-high module could be defined as a "tier" if it was loaded and stowed as a "module". If that idea had gained credibility it is possible that four or six adjacent packages could have been stowed athwartships out to the wings of the stow!

Fortunately, the learned judge, in a recent case which considered this aspect, said in his judgement:
"This apparent inconsistency with the applicable operating standards was explained by the defendants as owing to a pure question of semantics. Indeed, it appears as though the term "tier", which commonly refers to " one of a series of rows placed one above another", has come to be understood on the West Coast as two layers placed one above another which together are said to form a single tier. In this parlance, the cargo in issue, while made up of ten layers of packages, consisted in five tiers, and as such the cargo would not have had " one or more non-adjacent tiers stowed athwartships." .... In short, while it is undoubtedly more efficient to load packages in modules, this practice curtails the use of established methods to secure the stow and otherwise contributes nothing to its integrity. In so stating, I stress the fact that the modules, once deposited on board the ship, cease to be modules as their composite packages are no longer bound in any way. There is therefore no such thing as a module o packages once it has been loaded on board the ship, and hence no rational basis for identifying the existence of a tier by reference to such modules in applying the Code."

The judgment here is so clear that it needs no expansion: The Codes do not comprehend a "module". And, as was also explained earlier herein, athwartship packages should never extend to the far sides of the stow and packaged timber which goes to 9 or 10m above the weather-deck requires lashing arrangements additional to those specified in the Codes if the cargo is to survive an ocean crossing intact. Fig.4.11, below, illustrates just one of a number of Code-supported, logical, 8-tier/4-module methods of stowing correctly the packages shown in Fig. 4.10.

An Acceptable Correct Stowage - In Accordance With The 1991 Code.
All Athwartship Packages Are Contained Within Side Walls of Fore-and-Afters.
All Athwartship Packages Are Stowed As Single Tiers.

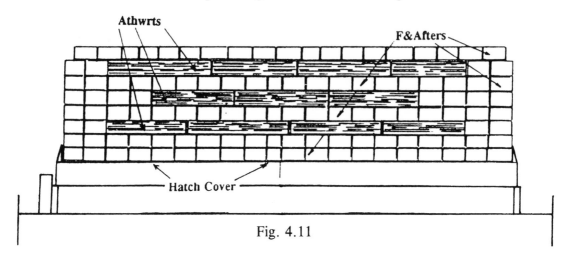

Fig. 4.11

In closing, it should be said that I have not yet seen any conclusive evidence to support the recommended practice of stowing ANY packages athwartships. On the contrary, it seems that all packages stowed fore-and-aft produces less incidents of cargo shift or loss.

Uprights At Ship's Side - Packaged Timber Cargo
This aspect was touched upon earlier herein. Here we consider the question of whether or not to use vertical uprights at the ship's sides when carrying packaged timber cargo.

Section **4.2** of Chapter 4 of the 1991 Code says:

4.2   Uprights

4.2.1   Uprights should be fitted when required by the nature, height or character of the timber deck cargo.

4.2.2   When uprights are fitted, they should:

> *.1   be made of steel or other suitable material of adequate strength, taking into account the breadth of the deck cargo;*
> *.2   be spaced at intervals not exceeding 3 m;*
> *.3   be fixed to the deck by angles, metal sockets or equally efficient means; and*
> *.4   if deemed necessary, be further secured by a metal bracket to a strengthened point, i.e. bulwark, hatch coaming.*

Those phrases "......*fitted WHEN required ......*" and "......*WHEN uprights are fitted......*" leave a lot to be desired by way of a clear instruction. Where **LOG** cargoes are carried on the weather-deck, their nature makes the use of uprights almost mandatory (see later, herein), but there is no absolute requirement for vessels carrying packaged timber deck cargoes to utilise uprights. The Code on this point can safely be interpreted as allowing an almost complete discretion on the part of the carrier. In fact, it is now customary in the world-wide timber trade not to use uprights when carrying packaged timber, even in circumstances where the heights and weights of the cargo may reasonably be considered to be "excessive".

In this, I am not saying I agree with such option in the presence of excessive heights and weights of cargo. As looked at earlier herein, it is my view that excessive timber deck cargo heights/weights require something more positive in their securing arrangements - closing down the lashings' pitch to 0.75m AND deploying uprights, maybe, but not uprights without closing down the lashings' pitch!

It should be noted that the optional/discretionary use of uprights at the ship's sides, in the presence of packaged timber, does not in any way allow a decrease in the number and strength of cross-lashings required by the Code. If the height of cargo requires full strength lashings to be pitched at 3m or at 1.5m, then deploying uprights can only be considered as an "extra". **Uprights in the presence of weather-deck stowed timber packages cannot ever be deployed instead of, or in the place of, the pitch and strength of lashings as currently required by the Code.**

There are a number of recorded instances where uprights have been used in the presence of lashings pitched at 3m when the cargo heights required a lashing pitch of 1.5m, in the belief that the uprights compensated for the lack of lashings. This has resulted in catastrophic loss of cargo, extensive damage to the ships concerned, and major "port of refuge" costs. Don't do it!

As also mentioned earlier (and will be again with respect to Log cargoes later herein) when uprights are used they must be assisted by the rigging of hog wires. Do not use uprights, alone.

Carefully To Carry
In a small narrow-beamed vessel, a full timber deck cargo might comprise no more than 200 tonnes weight. The standard securing arrangements can handle that weight in relation to the narrow beam by keeping the cargo safely on board in one block if required. But, while the nature of timber cargoes has changed, the relative strength of the securing requirements has changed little, despite the fact that vessels with beams in excess of 31m (100ft) carry full cargoes of deck-stowed packaged timber. Take a vessel of 30m beam and, say, 39000 tonnes deadweight, for instance, with 4000 tonnes of packaged timber block-stowed on the weather-deck to a height of 4m. The length of the stow will be about 120m. The Code requires cross-lashings at 3 metre intervals: 41 in all. The weakest component of each lashing is required to bear an ultimate load of 13.6 tonnef. You don't need to be a mathematician to appreciate that 41 x 13.6 = 557.6 tonnes, ie, a holding power equal to only 14% of the static weight of the cargo.

It is difficult to rationalise that result with the general principles set out in the CSS Code and/or the CSM where the required breaking strength of the lashings for deck cargo items may be as much **four times** (400%) the static weight of the cargo. (See Chapter 1, and onward, earlier in this book.) Under the CSS Code, if 4000 tonnes of something other than timber were being carried on the weather-deck secured by chains, the required holding power of the lashings would be 16000 tonnes - more than 28 times greater than that required for the same weight in timber. The holding power required would be 12000 tonnes if the "3-times-rule" was applied.

It's not that the "3-times-rule" for deck cargoes is too much (experience proves it to be about right); rather, it is a case where the 1991 Code for securing timber deck cargoes is sometimes inadequate with respect to lashings' holding power when applied to modern, relatively fast, broad-beamed cargo vessels if the object is to keep the cargo on board in severe adverse weather conditions. (See colour Plate H.)

In some instances it may be that lashings pitched 3m apart on a 4m-high timber deck cargo on a vessel of 30m beam are being asked to bear a load three times greater than the same lashings for a 4m-high timber deck cargo on a vessel of 10m beam. Possibly, a sliding - or, better, a stepped scale, is needed in which **weight** and **height** of cargo and **beam of vessel** are set against a closer lashings' pitch and/or increase in strength of lashings and their attachments.

In a modern timber carrier, the hatch covers may be as much as 2.8m above deck level, so that, in a block of deck cargo of 6.1m height above the deck, only 3.3m of that height is cargo and the lashings need not be closer spaced than 1.5m. Going to 9.4m height gives 6.6m of cargo - the **volume and weight have doubled**, yet the lashings' spacing can remain at 1.5m without any increase in strength. This all seems devoid of reasonable cargo safety logic, and can hardly be considered a satisfactory state of affairs so far as cargo interests and their insurers are concerned.

If a starting point no more radical than a "½ times rule" could be agreed, the increase in overall lashing holding power would be dramatic - and that is only one-sixth of the "3-times-rule" recommended in this book for deck cargoes in general. Chapter 6, paragraph 6.2.2, of the Code does little to assist. As might be expected, the onus of preventing all adverse occurrences resides with the master:-

"6.2.2 In cases where severe weather and sea conditions are unavoidable, masters should be conscious of the need to reduce speed and/or alter course at an early stage in order to minimize the forces imposed on the cargo, structure and lashings. The lashings are not designed to provide a means of securing against imprudent ship handling in heavy weather. There can be no substitute for good seamanship."

Like many marine technical problems, one's view of them depends upon whether you are in the camp of the cargo interests, the corridors of the regulatory authority, the office of the shipowner, or the captain's cabin. Do we really want to secure timber deck cargoes, in line with other deck cargoes, so that they will neither move nor tend to go overboard?

The Code requirements for the jettison of cargo involve the use of senhouse slips (penguin hooks) which require personnel standing on top of the stow to release the individual lashings. This can only be achieved at considerable personal risk and may cause serious damage to the structure of the ship as, indeed, frequently occurs when the cargo goes overboard unassisted. This serves to emphasise the importance of ensuring at the outset of the voyage that the cargo will not shift. If, despite that care, the timber does shift, great caution must be exercised in any attempt made to jettison all or part of the cargo.

It is no news that slip-hooks jam, and sending somebody across the surface of the cargo to knock them free means that you lose a seaman for every block of cargo that goes overboard. A surveyor attending on board a listed timber vessel could see nothing to prevent someone knocking free the senhouse slips with a sledge-hammer, until he was handed the hammer and requested to demonstrate how it should be done. By the time he was in a position to use the hammer he realised that its successful application to the slips would result in him going overside with the cargo. He wisely decided that retreat was better than demonstration.

The slip-hooks on that cargo were in good condition, complied in all senses with the Code, and were in no way deformed; yet the sheer weight of the displaced cargo lying against the wire/chain lashings made it impossible for the slips to be released by men wielding heavy sledge-hammers from a large fenced cradle suspended from an overhead crane. In the event, the lashing wires had to be burned through with flame-cutting equipment used from the suspended cradle. A large volume of packaged timber cascaded on to the quayside!

In this connection, paragraph 6.3.3 of Chapter 6 of the Code says:-

"6.3.3 As any cargo shift will in most cases occur in adverse weather conditions, sending crew to release or tighten the lashings on a moving or shifted cargo may well represent a greater hazard than retaining an overhanging load. A moving or shifted timber deck cargo should only be jettisoned after careful consideration; jettisoning is unlikely to improve the situation as the whole cargo stack would probably not fall at once. Severe damage may also be sustained by the propeller if it is still turning when timber is jettisoned." All very true!

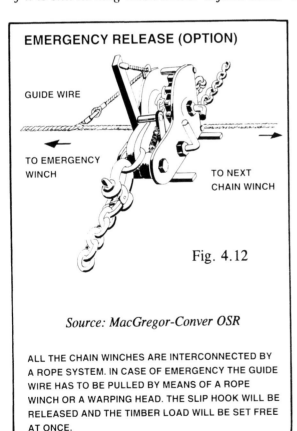

EMERGENCY RELEASE (OPTION)

GUIDE WIRE

TO EMERGENCY WINCH

TO NEXT CHAIN WINCH

Fig. 4.12

Source: MacGregor-Conver OSR

ALL THE CHAIN WINCHES ARE INTERCONNECTED BY A ROPE SYSTEM. IN CASE OF EMERGENCY THE GUIDE WIRE HAS TO BE PULLED BY MEANS OF A ROPE WINCH OR A WARPING HEAD. THE SLIP HOOK WILL BE RELEASED AND THE TIMBER LOAD WILL BE SET FREE AT ONCE.

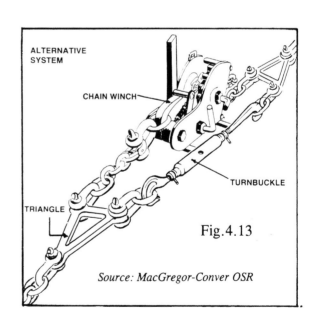

ALTERNATIVE SYSTEM

CHAIN WINCH

TURNBUCKLE

TRIANGLE

Fig.4.13

Source: MacGregor-Conver OSR

TURNBUCKLE FITTING TO TRIANGLE PLATE ALLOWS ON-GOING TIGHTENING OF LASHING. EMERGENCY REMOTE RELEASE CANNOT OPERATE WITH TURNBUCKLE FITTED AS SHOWN,

However, more than ten years ago I was asking if somebody could design and implement a remotely-operated safe method of deliberately jettisoning timber deck cargoes if and when such measures became necessary and desirable? Well, it has been drawn to my attention that the 1996 components catalogue of MacGregor-Conver OSR illustrates and markets such equipment, as illustrated in Fig.4.12 on the previous page, and that an alternative arrangement allows the addition of a turnbuckle, as illustrated in Fig.4.13, although if the turnbuckle is left in place the remote quick release system cannot operate. It is for the trade now to decide whether or not to take advantage of this system without waiting for mandatory requirements to do so.

Sounding Pipes, Air Pipes, and Ventilation
The safe working of a vessel in port or at sea depends largely upon the ability to obtain quick and safe access to all sounding pipe caps and air pipes. With this in mind, it is imperative that deck cargo should not be stowed over such pipes nor interfere with safe access to them, and that safe and efficient means of access be provided for all working parts of the ship, as required by the Code. Numerous instances continue to arise where ships are placed in danger because it is not possible to walk safely across the cargo to sound tanks or bilges, or effectively to close-off the upper apertures of air pipes as required by the Load Line Rules.

Care must be taken to ensure that all ventilators serving the cargo holds are kept clear and free for operation in the normal manner.

Hatchways fitted with steel covers are provided, more often than not, with drain holes from the coaming channels which, in turn, are fitted with drainage pipes. The lower open ends of these pipes are sometimes provided with loose canvas socks which close-off with the pressure of seas shipped on board, thereby acting as simple - but very efficient - non-return valves. (Never paint those socks. If you do, they will become stiff and will not close sides under pressure of water shipped across decks. Old, soft and supple canvas hose makes the best non-return valve.) Similarly, drain pipes are just as frequently fitted with patent non-return valves of one form or another which are designed to exclude water on deck from working back into the hatchway coaming channels. Before loading timber deck cargoes, masters should, therefore, ensure that all such non-return facilities are in efficient working order so that they do not require maintenance or supervision during the course of the voyage. **A well-found vessel was nearly lost because, when listed steeply due to a shift of cargo, water on deck flooded back into the Holds via patent non-return valves which failed to operate to exclude the water at angles of list greater than 15°.**

Bills of Lading
The continuing trade from tropical countries includes packages of "Kiln Dried" timber requiring under-deck stowage. Serious claims have arisen recently where kiln-dried timber has been stowed on the weather-deck for a voyage to Europe. Masters should ensure that all such timber is afforded below-deck stowage. Where charterers insist on carrying such timber on the weather-deck, masters should issue a clear letter of protest, ensure that all Mate's Receipts are claused accordingly, and instruct agents to similarly clause the Bills of Lading.

Logs
Logs as a deck cargo require a lashing system different from that employed for loose timber and/or packages, the full details of which may be found in the 1991 Code, Appendix A, Section 3, of which part is reproduced on the next page:-

"3.1 If logs are loaded on deck together with packaged timber, the two types of timber should not be intermixed.

3.2 Logs should generally be stowed in a fore-and-aft direction to give a slightly crowned top surface such that each log is adequately restrained from movement when the system of securing is in place and set up taut.

3.3 In order to achieve a compact stow, the butt of each log or sling of logs should not be in the same athwartship plane as those adjacent to it.

3.4 In order to achieve a more secure stowage of logs when stowed on deck, a continuous wire (hog wire) should be utilized at each hatch meeting the specifications of chapter 4 of this Code. Such hog wire should be installed in the following manner:

    .1 At approximately three quarters of the height of the uprights, the hog wire should be rove through a padeye attached to the uprights at this level so as to run transversely, connecting the respective port and starboard uprights. The hog lashing wire should not be too tight when laid so that it becomes taut when overstowed with other logs.

    .2 A second hog wire may be applied in a similar manner if the height of the hatch cover is less than 2 m. Such second hog wire should be installed approximately 1 m above the hatch covers.

    .3 The aim of having the hog wires applied in this manner is to assist in obtaining as even a tension as possible throughout, thus producing an inboard pull on the respective uprights."

A guidance note - also referred to in M.1469 - has been issued as a supplement to the Code, as follows:-

"Action to be taken by the Ship's Master"

1. The Master should be aware that, during the loading of logs, some vessels have listed up to 20°, causing concern that they might capsize. The major factor in this dangerous listing is failure to close screw-down overboard drain valves fitted to topside ballast tanks. The Master is advised to ensure that discharges, which must necessarily be closed at sea, such as gravity drains from topside ballast tanks, remain closed during the loading of timber.

2. Whilst the means of operation of valves are appropriately covered by relevant regulations in the International Convention on Load Lines 1966 and unified interpretations thereto, the Master is also advised to ensure the accessibility of the remote control screw-down valves in overboard drains of topside ballast tanks, both at port and during the voyage.

3. In keeping with the philosophy contained in resolution A.647(16), IMO Guidelines on Management for the Safe Operation of Ships and for Pollution Prevention, the owner and operator should take appropriate steps to implement safety measures by informing the shipmaster of the importance of maintaining safe operational procedures even when at dockside."

Sub-paragraph 3.4.3., makes clear that the restraining effect of the uprights depends heavily upon the strength and rigidity imparted to them by the weight of the logs "sitting" across the hog wires. Positive attention is here drawn to this aspect. If uprights are to be used, then hog wires **must** be rigged: **uprights must not be utilised without hog wires also being deployed correctly**. This requirement applies equally to a cargo of logs and to a cargo of packaged timber - uprights must include hog wires! (See Figs.4.14 and 4.15 on page 106, and Fig.4.16 on page 107.)

Fig. 4.14   *Rigging hog-wires for deck-stowed log cargo,*
               as required by the IMO 1991 Code of Safe Practice.

Photos: Captain Alan B. Baines, N.Z.

Fig. 4.15   *The correct use of wiggle-wires through snatch blocks - used to bind and*
               consolidate the log stow - independent of the number and pitch of cross-
               lashings required. Photo shows chain cross-lashings pitched 3m apart for stow
               not exceeding 4m in height above the weather-deck edge at the ship's side.

The correct use of hog-wires between deck side uprights with a deck cargo of logs.

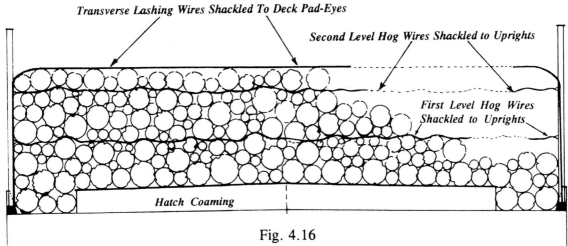

Transverse Lashing Wires Shackled To Deck Pad-Eyes

Second Level Hog Wires Shackled to Uprights

First Level Hog Wires Shackled to Uprights

Hatch Coaming

Fig. 4.16
Always Rig Hog Wires When Using The Deck Side Uprights For Logs, Packages & Loose Timber.

There are a number of different hand-operated load-binders available for timber deck cargoes, of which the ratchet type illustrated in Fig. 4.17 is just one, with lashing strength capacities up to 10 tonnes.

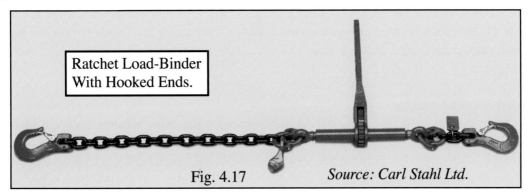

Ratchet Load-Binder With Hooked Ends.

Fig. 4.17   *Source: Carl Stahl Ltd.*

There are also power tensioners of one sort or another, hand-held but powered either mechanically or hydraulically. Fig. 4.18 shows just one such tool.

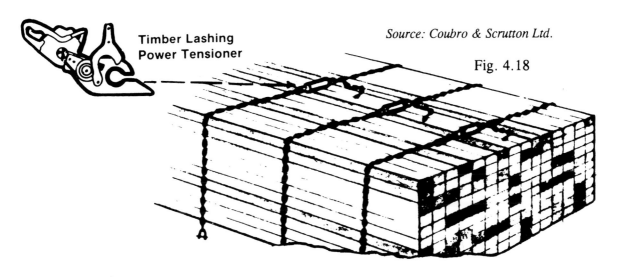

Timber Lashing Power Tensioner

Source: Coubro & Scrutton Ltd.

Fig. 4.18

These "speedy tensioners" allow turnbuckles to be rotated quickly until a limited degree of tension is attained. Bearing in mind the test results for rigging screws featured in Chapter 2, earlier herein, it is most unlikely that any of these "speedy tensioners" can safely achieve a tension in excess of 1.2 tonnes without the very probable risk of backlash injury to the user. Hence, when the "speedy tensioner" comes to a halt it will be necessary to take up the remaining "slack" by manual operation of the turnbuckle or rigging screw. Failure to do this will mean that the necessary pre-tension has not been attained in the lashings.

Manufacturers of all types of load-binders caution against the risk of whip-lash:- move the handle or clincher with care; keep yourself clear of the moving parts and of any loose chain that may be in the vicinity. While under tension the load-binder must not bear against an object, as this will cause side load; never use a handle extender, and never attempt to operate the binder with more than one person. At all times make sure your footing is secure.

Webbing For Timber Deck Cargoes
The IMO 1991 Code makes no provision for the use of webbing as a lashing material for timber deck cargoes, but I cannot see any objection to its use for that purpose. Breaking strengths of 13.6 tonnef are currently available, together with the appropriate accessories in compliance with the Code. (See colour Plate K, for instance.) Personally, I have experience of only one timber deck cargo secured with webbing lashings, and a high proportion of that cargo was lost overside during severe adverse weather conditions - **not** because of any failure with the webbing lashings - but because the terminals on the hatch side coaming plates with which the ship was fitted as part of her "as-built" structure pulled apart at their welded connections. That instance speaks well for the webbing, but poorly for the builder's shipyard.

A Word For The Master
Apart from the carriage of Containers in non-purpose built ships, timber deck cargoes tend to generate more friction as between the master, the charterer, the owner, and the charterer's supercargo, than any other commodity. This because of the opposing forces involved in using the minimum of charterer's material and keeping his costs low, aided and abetted by a supercargo who may or may not know much about such cargoes but intends to load whatever he can persuade the master to take within or outside the Code of Safe Practice - and the master aware of the necessity not to offend what may be a long-term charterer while attempting to ensure that the Code is followed and that the safety of his ship and its cargo are not compromised.

If you think that's too bald a statement, talk to the arbitrators of the London and New York Maritime Arbitrators' Associations, the Judges of the Admiralty and Commercial Courts, and with the lawyers who negotiate settlements before the cases even get to the stage of formal litigation, and you will find that the crux of the problem resides mainly in the paragraph above.

Masters who allow themselves to be persuaded to do less than is necessary in the line of securing arrangements - for whatever reason - become everybody's scapegoat when the cargo is lost overside, the ship's structural seaworthiness is breached, and the port of refuge, re-stowing and ship repair costs, plus delay due to deviation, all amount to incredible sums of money.

Stand your ground, I say, and have it done correctly.
****

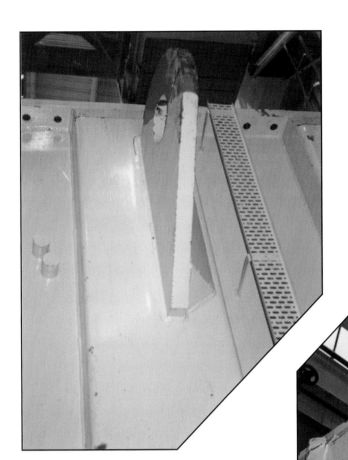

Heavy-duty mild steel lifting lug on transformer casing. Yield strength of lug is in excess of 100 tonnes if stress is applied correctly in the direct plane of the lug.

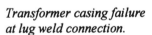

Transformer casing failure at lug weld connection.

(Photos: Arthur Todd)

Transformer casing torn at lug connection. Lashing tress applied at the eye was at 90° to the plane of the lug. This created a large bending moment at the lug-to-casing connection. Casing only 10mm thick, so casing metal tore in pattern here shown.

Plate F

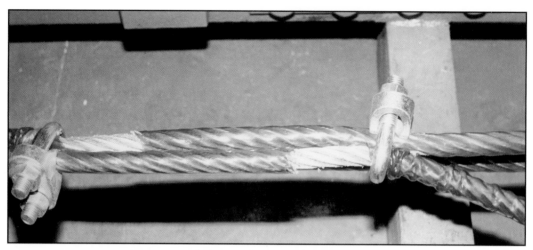

Coating splits and puckers; wire and grips slip quickly.

Wire slips inside coating at low loads.

For ½ double grommets, wire slipped inside coating at low loads.

<u>Plate G</u>

Full timber deck cargo breaking adrift and going overboard during North Atlantic winter conditions. (Photo: Ship's master)

Full timber deck cargo adrift after encounter with very severe storm and sea conditions off north-west Spain.

Plate H

On a general cargo vessel -ISO Containers stowed as deck cargo adrift after heavy weather.

Never *stow ISO Containers on their bottom rails or skirts.* ***Always*** *stow ISO Containers on their corner castings, only.*

When stowed like this, skirts and bottom rails collapse, and general slackness develops in the stow.

<u>***Plate I***</u>

CHAPTER 5

Vehicles on Ro-Ro Vessels

In 1991 a Code of Practice was published by HMSO, London, entitled: Roll-on/Roll-off Ships - Stowage and Securing of Vehicles. There have been a number of addenda and adjustments to the text since then, and the Fourth Impression, dated 1997, is the current version for reference purposes. It includes the standards developed by IMO, and provides guidance and information on safe procedures to be followed to reduce the risks to persons, ships and - by extension - to the vehicles and cargo contents themselves. The U.K. Health and Safety Executive were also consulted during the Code's preparation. The full text can be purchased at The Stationery Office Bookshops in London, Birmingham, Manchester, Belfast, Cardiff and Edinburgh; or by fax order to 0171 873 8200, price £9.50 net. Some of the recommendations contained therein are dealt with hereunder, and will be referred to as the 1997 Code. Also, reference is made herein to the Department of Transport Code of Practice Safety of Loads on Vehicles and the Swedish Transport Research Commission (TFK) report Securing Goods on Semi-Trailer, 1986. For the parts of those publications reproduced herein, due thanks and acknowledgements are extended.

Vehicle Definitions
A vehicle is defined as a vehicle with wheels or a track laying vehicle.

A flat-bed trailer is defined as a flat topped, open sided trailer or semi-trailer and includes a roll-trailer and a draw-bar trailer. (See Figs.5.01 to 5.05, below.)

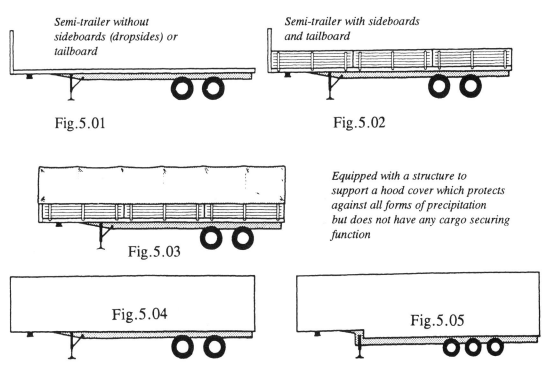

Semi-trailer without sideboards (dropsides) or tailboard

Fig.5.01

Semi-trailer with sideboards and tailboard

Fig.5.02

Fig.5.03

Equipped with a structure to support a hood cover which protects against all forms of precipitation but does not have any cargo securing function

Fig.5.04

Fig.5.05

Van body trailers: The load-carrying part comprises a platform and headboard or bulkhead. The platform is provided with fixed side walls and roof and has doors at the rear. If the van body is to be used as a complete cargo-blocking carrier, a pre-condition is that each side wall can withstand a load that is applied and distributed uniformly and perpendicular to the side of the body, and which is 40 per cent of the semi-trailer's maximum load weight. (Courtesy: TFK)

A freight vehicle is defined as a goods vehicle, flat-bed trailer, road train, articulated road train, combination of freight vehicles, or a tank vehicle. (See Figs.5.06, 5.07 and 5.08, below.)

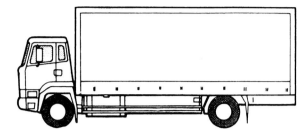

Fig.5.06

Fully-enclosed goods vehicle

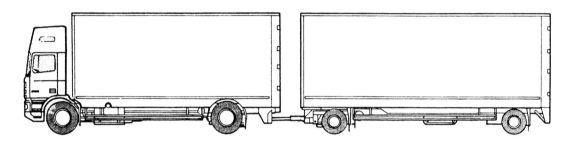

Fig.5.07 *Draw-bar combination*

Fig.5.08 *Draw-bar road train*

A semi-trailer is defined as a trailer which is designed to be coupled to a semi-trailer towing vehicle and to impose a substantial part of its total weight on the towing vehicle. (See Fig.5.09, below.)

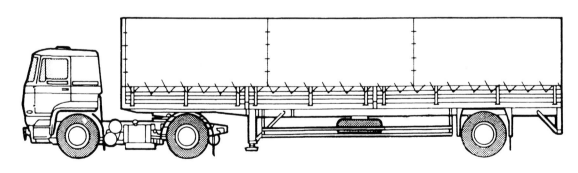

Fig.5.09

(Courtesy: Commercial Motor/Leyland DAF)

A tank vehicle is defined as a tank which is rigidly and permanently attached to the vehicle during all normal operations of loading, discharging, and transport, and is neither filled nor discharged on board and is driven on board by its own wheels. (Fig.5.10, for instance.)

Fig.5.10

Under the section relating to suitability for transport by sea, the Code of Practice advises that shippers, forwarding agents, road hauliers, and any other party presenting road vehicles for shipment, should appreciate that vehicles can be subjected to forces of great magnitude, particularly in the transverse direction and especially in adverse weather conditions. It is of importance for them to ensure that:

a.   Vehicles must be in sound structural condition, free of defects likely to affect their structural strength, and in good working order if they are to be driven on to or off the ship.

b.   Freight vehicles of more than 3.5 tonnes must be provided with an adequate number of accessible securing points of sufficient strength, located so as to ensure effective restraint of the freight vehicle by the lashings. (This refers to lashing points on the vehicle which will be used to secure the vehicle to the deck of the ship.)

c.   Semi-trailers are of adequate strength to withstand the loadings imposed by the use of trestles or similar devices. Semi-trailers should have, within the area of the king-pin, sufficient strength and space for a trestle to be located to allow safe storage prior to unhitching of the semi-trailer towing vehicle. The area of trestle location should be suitably marked on both sides.

d.   Supporting legs on semi-trailers which are specifically designed to support the semi-trailer during sea transport are clearly marked.

e.   Where jacks are used on a freight vehicle, the jacking-up positions on the chassis are strengthened and clearly marked.

f.   Refrigerated freight vehicles of more than 3.5 tonnes, with flush insulated undersides, should have jacking points especially fitted and marked to avoid damage to insulation.

g.   Freight vehicles designed to transport loads likely to have an adverse effect on their stability, such as hanging meat, have a means of neutralising the suspension system.

h.   Vehicles are provided with an effective braking system.

i.   Freight vehicles are provided with an adequate number of **securing points to enable the cargo to be adequately secured to them so as to withstand the forces which may arise during the sea transport.**

j.   **Loads carried on or within freight vehicles or containers are secured in a manner that will prevent them from moving when they are subjected to the worst conditions likely to be encountered at sea.** The publication, "Code of Practice, Safety of Loads on Vehicles", obtainable from any Stationery Office Bookshop, provides guidance as to how loads should be secured on vehicles. (See, also, IMO/ILO Guidelines for Packing Cargo in Freight Containers or Vehicles).

k.   Each freight vehicle is provided with documentation, to indicate its gross weight and any precautions which may have to be observed during sea transport.

l.   All dangerous goods, including those contained within groupage loads, are fully declared.

m.   The dangerous goods placards (large labels) required for the sea transport of dangerous goods on vehicles are clearly visible on the outside of the vehicle.

n.   The master receives adequate notice containing information about special vehicles, e.g. track laying vehicles, high-sided freight vehicles, earth moving plant, low loaders, **and freight vehicles carrying livestock**; and

o.   The recommendations in Merchant Shipping Notice No.M.1433 are followed regarding fuel in tanks.(See, also, MS Notice M 1437 of 1990 headed *"Portable tanks, Road tank Vehicles and Rail tank Wagons for the carriage by sea of Liquid Dangerous Goods and Liquified Gases"*).

The Code of Practice provides guidance on specific types of loads on freight vehicles. For instance, cargo carried on flat-bed trailers should be effectively secured, preferably with chains or suitable webbing fitted with tightening devices. Empty trailers carried on semi-trailers should be adequately secured to the carriage semi-trailer.

Steel plates, girders, and laminated boards will, if not properly secured, readily slide and may penetrate the sides of a freight vehicle or container. Such items require strong securing arrangements. They should be located in positions where they can do the least damage to the ship's internal structure and fittings if the securing arrangement fails.

Pipes, cylinders, and similarly shaped units of cargo require special attention. One of the most successful methods of securing is the use of a pipe-rack, nesting frame, or cradle in association with chain lashings and tightening devices.

Where there is doubt that a vehicle complies with the foregoing provisions, the master may, at his discretion, refuse to accept the vehicle for shipment, and the following aspects are worth noting.

Curtain-Sided Semi-Trailers on Ro-Ro Vessels

The carriage of high-sided, curtain-sided semi-trailers on ro-ro vessels is, within United Kingdom waters, a phenomenon almost exclusively experienced on the Irish sea crossings, apparently because the motorway bridges on United Kingdom and Ireland roads are generally higher than those experienced on European autobahns, thereby allowing in the U.K. a higher vehicle to be operated in a normal environment. It is accepted that the design concept of curtain-sided semi-trailers is applied to vehicles operating on European roads and elsewhere, but as the overall height of the vehicles in use in such countries is generally considerably lower than those found on United Kingdom road networks, similar difficulties are not currently encountered, although the situation may change in the future. Nevertheless, the following comments have international implications.

To fully understand the problem with curtain-sided semi-trailers it is necessary to look at their design concept. Traditionally, loads placed onto open platform semi-trailers needed to be secured in place/covered and protected against the weather. This was usually carried out by the driver roping and sheeting, in some instances with up to four sheets which, particularly in high wind situations, was both difficult and time-consuming. (See Fig.5.11.)

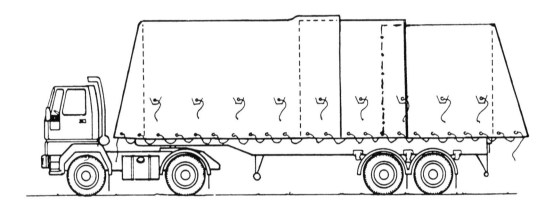

Fig.5.11   *Three sheets used to protect a vehicle load*
            (Adapted from "Safety of Loads on Vehicles" HMSO.)

In order to reduce the time and effort necessary to secure and cover cargo on vehicles, a curtain-sided semi-trailer was introduced, consisting of a platformed trailer fitted with a solid forward bulkhead (generally fibreglass-covered to reduce weight), a light perspex roof, and two rear doors similar in design to those fitted to ISO containers, although of much lighter construction. The sides of the box thus created are closed by tarpaulin curtains hanging on the equivalent of curtain rails and free to slide from end to end of the trailer. The bottom edges of the curtains are held in place by simple webbing-and-hook tensioning devices. A full side-curtain on a 40ft semi-trailer can generally be unhooked and slid to one side in a matter of minutes, thereby reducing considerably the turn-round time of a delivery/ pick-up vehicle. (See Fig.5.12.)

Fig.5.12

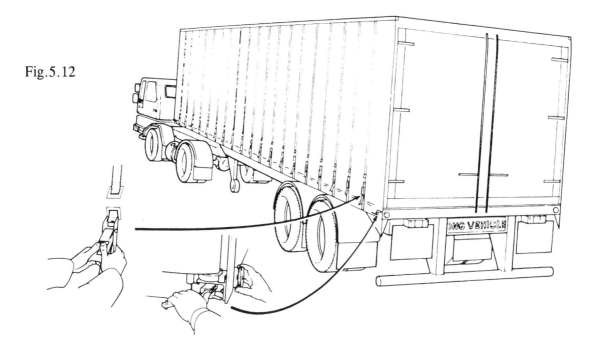

Curtain-sided semi-trailer
(Courtesy: "Safety of Loads on Vehicles" HMSO.)

In an effort to prevent sideways movement of cargo loaded onto the semi-trailer, webbing restraining straps are attached to a central ridge-bar running the full length of the unit just beneath the centreline of the roof. Generally of webbing, such restraints are fitted with a simple hook to allow them to be hooked over the edge of the semi-trailer platform if desired, together with tensioning devices of one form or another.

Despite the recommendations contained in the Code of Practice, there is a noticeable trend for cargo to be placed on curtain-sided semi-trailers secured by no more than the tensioned curtain sides. Indeed, there are publications which instruct heavy goods vehicle drivers to the effect that, unless the loads are abnormally heavy or awkward, securing of cargo within curtain-sided semi-trailers is not required. This is contrary to all common-sense and sound practice, contrary to the requirements of the Road Traffic Act 1991, Section 40A, and has created a number of otherwise avoidable casualties.

Indeed, the Code of Safe Practice for Safety of Loads On Road Vehicles clearly states that, with the exception of very light loads, all cargo should be securely fastened to the vehicle for normal road transit.

During recent years various difficulties have been experienced with cargo incorrectly or inadequately secured within curtain-sided semi-trailers resulting in, at best, movement and, at worst, capsize rotation of trailers, damage to other cargo, and delays to the carrying vessel while the problems are sorted out. Initially, such trailers were presented with no securing to the cargo but, as recommendations that the cargo should be secured to the trailer were acted upon, a secondary problem developed.

The restraining straps referred to on the previous page, attached as they are to the centre-line ridge pole directly beneath the roof, transfer a substantial portion of the cargo weight to a point higher above the trailer bed than the cargo's natural centre of gravity in conditions of heavy rolling; a situation which has caught ships' officers unaware, and which has resulted in trailers tipping over.

In the Code of Practice it is suggested that vehicles with high centres of gravity or unstable loads should be stowed in positions of minimal roll. Unfortunately, the predominance of curtain-sided semi-trailers being handled on certain sea routes means that such suggestions cannot readily be accommodated. One way round the difficulty would be for a return to the original design concept of curtain-sided semi-trailers, **where the cargo is secured downwards to the platform of the vehicle** as it would have been for an open vehicle; the curtain sides being used for their original intention of providing no more than a weather-proof cover. It is unlikely, however, that the curtain-sided semi-trailer will be readily abandoned, and so ships' officers should be cautious.

In line with the problem of securing normal cargoes, ie, palletised units, etc, there is an increasing difficulty encountered with regard to the usage of curtain-sided semi-trailers for the carriage of bulk cargoes such as bark, sawdust, etc. In such circumstances, the load is blown-loaded or gravity-fed into the trailers with lateral support comprising no more than the ordinary curtain sides. As a result of normal settlement and movement during road transit, alone (and excluding any rolling forces imposed at sea), curtain-sided semi-trailers can be seen on roads like pregnant cows, with bulging sidewards expansion of up to 1300mm. (See Fig.5.13.)

British Standard BS3951, Part 2, Section 2.4:1992 (ISO 1496-4:1991) dealing with the specifications for containers carrying bulk cargo, specifies that sidewards deflection of walls should be no more than 40mm. Whilst it is accepted that curtain-sided semi-trailers presented for shipment do not fall within the direct classification of ISO containers, similar common-sense considerations clearly should apply, for the safety of the vehicle, cargo and ship. It is, for instance, a requirement for vehicle lanes to be left between vehicles secured on ro-ro vessels clear enough and safe enough to enable crew members to make regular lashing checks. The bulging outwards of curtain sides on semi-trailers greatly prohibits such safe working.

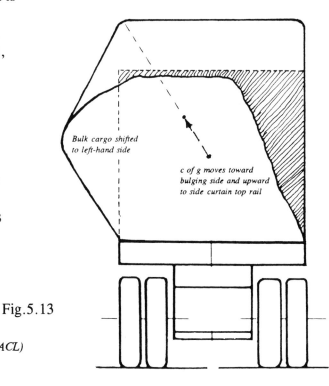

Bulk cargo shifted to left-hand side

c of g moves toward bulging side and upward to side curtain top rail

Fig.5.13

(Adapted from ACL)

Shippers should be advised that all cargoes carried on curtain-sided semi-trailers, whether conventional or bulk, should be so secured as to remain within the parallel lines of the vehicle platform without any reliance upon side curtain restraint.

Curtain-sided equipment developed principally for marine use, ie, curtain-sided containers and road ferry "tilt" semi-trailers, all have load restraints built into their structures, comprising steel gates and supports plus timber battens, beneath the outer curtains or tilt covers. (See Fig.5.14.)

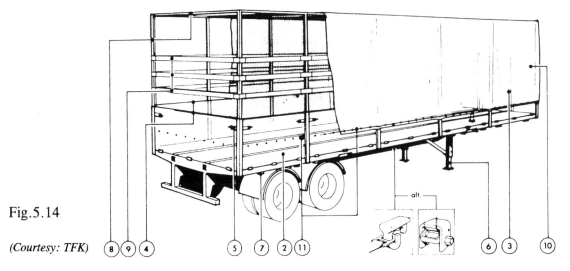

Fig.5.14

(Courtesy: TFK)

Shippers and road-hauliers should ensure that:-

a. The semi-trailer has been cleaned and, wherever applicable, is free from odour;
b. The load platform is in good condition;
c. The headboard is intact;
d. The sideboards (dropsides) and tailboards are intact;
e. The locking devices function correctly;
f. The landing legs are intact and in working order;
g. The load securing equipment is intact, clean, and in working order;
h. The cover stanchions are intact;
i. The cover laths are in place and intact;
j. The hood cover is intact;
k. The equipment for securing the cover is intact.

Sections in the 1997 Code dealing with securing and lashing arrangements are reproduced in part hereunder:-

Securing Arrangements
3.3.1   The ship should be provided with:
> ***.1   an adequate number of securing points of sufficient strength;***
> ***.2   a sufficient quantity of cargo securing gear of sufficient strength and, where***
> ***appropriate, sufficient reserve cargo securing gear; and***
> ***.3   a Cargo Securing Manual.*** (Note this new reference to the CSM).

Deck Securing Points
3.4.1   Securing points should be provided on the ship's deck for each vehicle and for each element of a combination of vehicles.

3.4.2   *The longitudinal and transverse spacing of securing points should be suitable for the mix of vehicles to be carried so that, where practicable, the optimum angles specified in paragraph 5.3.8 can be achieved.*

3.4.3   *The minimum strength without permanent deformation of each securing point for freight vehicles of more than 3.5 tonnes should be 120kN* (12.24 tonnef). *The strength of securing points designed to accommodate more than one lashing should be not less than the summation of the strength required for each lashing calculated at 120kN per lashing.*

3.4.4   *On ships which do not carry freight vehicles of more than 3.5 tonnes or which only occasionally carry vehicles, the spacing and strength of securing points should be such that the vehicles can be adequately secured.*

3.4.5   *Ship's mobile cargo handling equipment not fixed to the ship should be provided with adequate securing points.*

Lashing Arrangements
5.2.3   *Persons supervising the securing of vehicles should be conversant with the contents of the Cargo Securing Manual.*

5.3.1   *Lashings should have strength and elongation characteristics appropriate for the mass of the vehicle being secured.*

5.3.2   *Steel chain is the preferred means of lashing freight vehicles of more than 3.5 tonnes gross vehicle mass (GVM). When any other system or material is used it should have strength and elongation characteristics equivalent to those of steel chain.*

5.3.3   *Chains and associated elements (e.g. hooks, shackles, elephants' feet and tensioning devices) should be able to withstand a load of not less than 120kN without permanent deformation.*

5.3.4   *Where, exceptionally, wire ropes or other materials are used their breaking load should be at least 200kN* (20.39 tonnef).

5.3.5   *Hooks and other devices which are used for attaching a lashing to a securing point should be designed and applied in a manner which prevents them from disengaging from the aperture of the securing point if the lashing slackens during a voyage.*

5.3.6   *Lashings should be so designed and attached that, provided that there is safe access, it is possible to tighten them if they become slack.*

5.3.7   *Securing points provided on vehicles should be used for lashing purposes. Only one lashing should be attached to any one aperture, loop or lashing ring at each securing point. (See Section 5.2.7).*

5.3.8   *The lashings are most effective on a vehicle when they make an angle with the deck of between 30 and 60 degrees. When these optimum angles cannot be achieved additional lashings may be required.*

5.3.9   *Where practicable, the arrangement of lashings on both sides of a vehicle should be the same, and angled to provide some fore-and-aft restraint with an equal number pulling forward as are pulling aft.*

5.3.10   *Crossed lashings should, where practicable, not be used for securing freight vehicles because this disposition provides no restraint against tipping over at moderate angles of roll of the ship. With these vehicles, lashings should pass from a securing point on the vehicle to a deck securing point adjacent to the same side of the vehicle. Where there is concern about the possibility of low co-efficients of friction on vehicles such as solid wheeled trailers, additional crossed lashings may be used to restrain sliding.*

5.3.11 Bearing in mind the characteristics of the ship and the conditions expected on the intended voyage, the master should decide on the number of securing points and lashings, if any, to be used on each class of vehicle having regard to any vehicles which by the nature or disposition of their load may require particular attention.

Additional factors which may be present and which should be taken into account are:-

.1 The intended stowage arrangement including the presence of bulk liquids and hazardous cargoes.

.2 The weight and centres of gravity of the vehicles. High centres of gravity can substantially increase the lashing loads. With loads which evidently have a very high centre of gravity it may be necessary to utilise additional lashings attached at or near the top of the load.

.3 Factors which may reduce the co-efficients of friction between various bearing surfaces.

5.3.12 It is not possible to specify with certainty the maximum forces which may be exerted in the most severe conditions. If in doubt, or if very heavy weather is forecast, additional lashings should be fitted or appropriate operational measures, such as delaying sailing or altering course, taken to minimise the forces.

5.4 The standard lashing equipment used to secure vehicles in excess of 3.5 tonnes should be able to withstand a load of not less than 120kN without permanent deformation (see section 5.3.3). Lighter equipment used for lashing vehicles of less than 3.5 tonnes should be clearly marked to identify its strength where this is less than 120kN. Wherever possible the standard 120kN lashing equipment should be substantially different in appearance from the lighter equipment in order to prevent confusion between the two.(Note, however, that the 1997 Ro-Ro Code defines "strength" - when referring to a lashing or fitting - as the maximum load which the lashing or fitting can withstand without permanent deformation; whereas the CSM currently provides no such definition)

General
7.2.1 The Cargo Securing Manual should include the following general information:
(Sub-paragraphs .1, .2 & .3 not here quoted.)
.4 Information on the safe working load of standardised securing gear or information on the safe working load of every specific item of cargo securing gear. The specification of safe working loads should take full account of the stresses to which the securing gear may be subjected. With regard to lashings for securing vehicles to ships' decks it is not required to apply the same factors of safety used in determining the safe working load (SWL) of lifting gear. A vehicle lashing should not be subjected in use to a load value greater than 50% of its breaking load. This value is the "effective" safe working load of a lashing.

In broad terms the 1997 Code "strength" will be at a point possibly slightly greater than the "proof-load" referred to earlier herein, where the "proof-load" is half of the minimum breaking force and the SWL is normally taken as half the proof-load. The sub-paragraph *.4* quoted above would have been more helpful to the reader if it had omitted the last sentence and, instead, drawn attention to the fact the CSM Table 1 - MSL (maximum securing load) - values set a 50% breaking strength usage for most of the materials likely to be used in the securing of vehicles on ro-ro vessels, and that MSL's (maximum securing loads) should **not** be confused with SWL's (safe working loads).

Everyone involved with this aspect should remain alert to the proposed implementation of the CEN/EU Rules, wherein the term "Lashing Capacity" (LC) will mean 50% of break load (don't blame me for all these term changes - "breaking strength/break load/breaking force/et al" - I'm only quoting) and will not be confused with any earlier abbreviations such as SWL, MSL (maximum service load), or WLL(working load limit). All the IMO would be required to do to rationalise the matter and remove any chance of confusion is to scrap MSL and SWL and use LC. Also, whereas in the CSS Code and CSM Regulations the aspect of "proof load" is generally fudged, the proposed CEN/EU document will make clear that "proof-load will equal LC x 1.25" ie, 62½% of break-load, which ties in with one of the ISO Standards referred to earlier in the **INTRODUCTION** preceding Chapter 1.

In the instance of a chain lashing having a proof-load of 120kN, its SWL would generally be 60kN, and its nominal break-load could be anything between 192kN and 240kN (MSL 96kN to 120kN) depending upon which Standard it relied. (Again, see the **INTRODUCTION**). For ro-ro vehicle cargo lashing purposes, therefore, it seems safe to me to assume that the 1997 Code " strength" will equate with about 62½% of break-load (say two-thirds, roughly) and that MSL and "lashing load value" will be 50% of break-load. These distinctions should be remembered when attempting to make sense of the - sometimes - mystifying wording in Codes, Recommendations, Rules, and Regulations.

As most of the important aspects of the Cargo Securing Manual have been dealt with earlier herein, I shall not reiterate Section 7 of the 1997 Code which deals almost exclusively with the requirements of the CSM and should be consulted.

1997 Code - ANNEX - Vehicle Lashing Arrangements. (The full text of this ANNEX should be consulted by anyone involved in the operation of ro-ro vessels. Only limited parts are referred to herein.)

3. Illustrative Lashing Charts for Ships on Short Voyages

3.1 Paragraph 7.3.5.2 of the Code of Practice suggests a simplified method, applicable to ships carrying a limited number of cargo unit types on short sea voyages, for determining the lashings required as an alternative to the comprehensive advice given in paragraph 7.3.5.1. The illustrative lashing charts (of which that for 30 tonnes Gross Vehicle Mass is reproduced as Fig.5.16, hereunder) *show the minimum number of lashings of a given strength for a range of roll periods and a range of vertical heights above the waterline to resist the forces encountered in a defined case (20° roll angle, 5° pitch angle). The charts are based on typical tandem or triaxle semi-trailers and are based on typical trailer weights. The limit load of 9.5 tonnes* (per lashing) *used in the graphs gives a factor of safety of 2 in relation to the breaking load of typical grade 80 13mm alloy chains capable of withstanding a force of not less than 120kN without permanent deformation. This gives an effective safe working load of 95kN.*

To remain in keeping with the general context of such propositions, it is suggested that the last two sentences might read: "The limit load of 9.5 tonnef used in the graphs gives a safety factor in excess of 2 (50%) in relation to the breaking load of typical grade 80 13mm alloy chain with a nominal breaking load of 20 tonnef and a proof-load of 12.50 tonnef." Under other circumstances the SWL would be 6.25 tonnef, ie, a safety factor of 3.2 in relation to the chain's nominal breaking load. In other words, the use of the phrase "safe working load" in paragraph 3.1 may be confusing, whereas the phrase "limit load" is correctly used, is near enough in keeping with the CSM Table 1 and with the four paragraphs, above, following **7.2.1.**

3.2 Use of the Charts

3.2.1 The accelerations to which vehicles are subjected and, hence, the lashing forces developed, become more severe as the natural period of roll decreases.

A good estimate for the roll period of a ship is given by the formula:

$$T = \frac{0.7B}{\sqrt{GM}} \quad where \quad \begin{array}{l} T = roll\ period\ in\ seconds \\ B = moulded\ breadth\ in\ metres \\ GM = metacentric\ height\ in\ metres \end{array}$$

The metacentric height should be known for any condition of loading and the value for T may therefore be easily obtained.

(**TYPING ERRORS:** In the MCA publication "Instructions To Surveyors - Volume 1, 1999 " the above formula for roll period is shown wrongly as

$\dfrac{0.7B\ T}{\sqrt{GM}}$ when it should read as shown at **3.2.1,** above, ie, $T = \dfrac{0.7B}{\sqrt{GM}}$

and the word "to" in the second line below should read "for".)

3.2.2 The lashing charts are based upon a defined case of a ship undergoing a cyclic roll angle of 20 degrees in combination with a pitch of 5 degrees. It is assumed that a semi-trailer is positioned at the forward end and outboard lane of a typical ro/ro ship able to load standard trailers in six lanes. The charts show the number of lashings which should be required in the defined circumstances to ensure that a load on the lashings of 9.5 tonnes is not exceeded. (The disposition of the lashings relating to the charts is as shown in Fig.5.15 on page 121 and a chart for a 30 tonne trailer is reproduced at Fig. 5.16 on page 122)

3.2.3 The charts are drawn up for typical ranges of GVM (gross vehicle mass) *of semi-trailers up to the maximum weight currently permitted. For a 40 tonne gross train weight including tractor unit, it has been assumed that the corresponding trailer GVM is 32T.*

In order to use the charts for a particular case:

.1 Work out the roll period T, using the formula in paragraph 3.2.1 above.
(If, however, your vessel is provided with its own specific roll period data there is no reason, in my view, why you should not use that instead,)

.2 Select the chart for the appropriate vehicle GVM.

.3 Pick off T, the roll period.

.4 Pick off the height of the deck in question above the waterline.

.5 Find the intersection of roll period and height above the waterline (Steps .3 and .4).

.6   The minimum number of lashings recommended for the defined case is indicated by the limit line to the left of the point of intersection.

NOTE: Due to the difficulty in predicting dynamic accelerations and the complexity of dynamic calculations the lashing forces apply to rigid and unsprung cargo. Additional lashings may be required to resist dynamic forces.

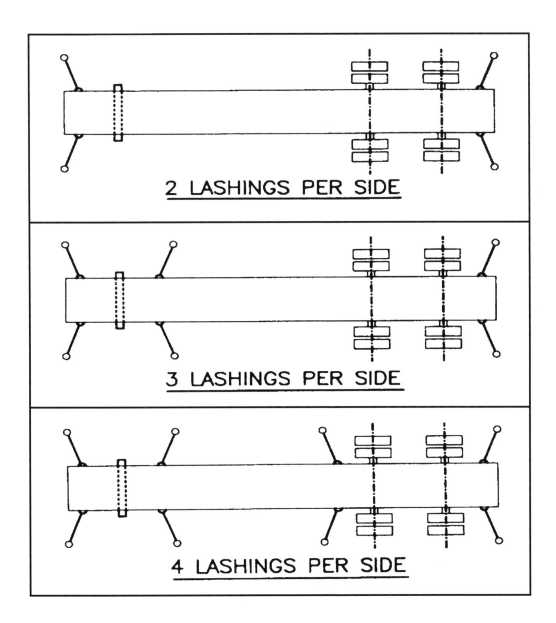

2 LASHINGS PER SIDE

3 LASHINGS PER SIDE

4 LASHINGS PER SIDE

ARRANGEMENT OF LASHINGS USED IN CALCULATIONS

Fig.5.15

Example:

A 30-tonne trailer is to be secured on an upper vehicle deck at a height 8 metres above the water-line. Roll period in the loaded/sailing condition is calculated as 9 seconds. How many lashings per side?

9.5 TONNE LOAD LIMIT LINES
FOR: 6 LANE RO/RO SHIP;
SEMI-TRAILER STOWED AT FORWARD
END OF OUTBOARD LANE;
ROLL ANGLE 20 DEGREES;
PITCH ANGLE 5 DEGREES

30 TONNE TRAILER

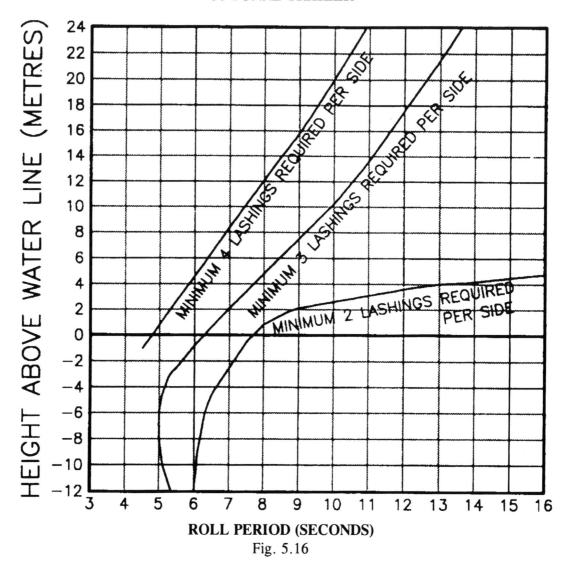

ROLL PERIOD (SECONDS)
Fig. 5.16

Take 8m horizontal line at left-hand side; locate its intersection with the vertical line extending upward from 9 seconds; move to the right (or left) until you pick up the nearest "lashings curve" - in this instance a minimum of 3 lashings (each of 9.5 tonne limit load) on each side of the vehicle. (If the intersection had been further to the left, then 4 each side would have been appropriate.)

It will be noted that 6 lashings each with a nominal break-load of, say, 19 tonnef, will provide a total nominal break-load of 114 tonnef, whereas the straightforward 3-times rule would require 30 x 3 equals 90 tonnef of lashings. This is because the Code's graph allows for a roll angle of 20° and this example uses a roll period as low as 9 seconds at 8m height above the water-line,whereas the 3-times rule allows for a roll angle of 30°, a roll period of not less than 13 seconds, and a height above the water-line of about 4m.(If a 13 second/20°roll angle at 4m is taken from the graph, the answer is 2 lashings on each side - a total of 76 tonnef.) **In summary, then, the Code's graphs can be relied upon to provide trustworthy guidelines, well on the side of safety, as well as a rapid and uncomplicated method of obtaining practical results.** Graphs for other Vehicle Mass Values will be found in the ANNEX to the 1997 Code.

A Useful Alternative
Prior to 1991 the most helpful recommendations for securing vehicles on ro-ro vessels could be found in Merchant Shipping Notice No.M.849. They were detailed, comprehensive, and too lengthy to be quoted here in full. That M. Notice has been withdrawn. The advice offered therein, however, was designed to minimise the risk of tipping and sliding, particularly of high-sided trailers full of cargo and with high centres of gravity. The Notice commenced with the words:-

> **"During recent years the Department has received a number of reports of damage caused by the shifting of vehicles and cargo units within the vehicle/cargo spaces of Ro-Ro ships. Fortunately none of the reported incidents has resulted in loss of life but only minor changes in the pattern of events may well have produced a situation in some of these instances from which a major casualty could have developed."**

Unfortunately, since those words were written the author knows of instances where injury to one officer and loss of life of another occurred because one of the lashing-lugs on the vehicle trailer was in poor condition and failed, with a subsequent domino effect of incidents finalising in catastrophic death. The risks accepted voluntarily as part of their job by ships' officers do not include - nor should they include - the knowledge or assessment of a weakened vehicle trailer lashing-lug. The efficient condition of such lugs is, and should remain, the outright responsibility of the shipper or - by extension - the relevant road transport operator. Some advice in this connection is contained earlier in this chapter. **It is important for everyone concerned to recognise that if a lashing chain is required to have a break-load in the range 19/20 tonnef it is equally important for each lashing-lug on the vehicle to have at least that break-load - possibly more. If ordinary mild steel round bar is used for the lug, the bar diameter would need to be at least 26mm, properly weld/attached to a strength member of the vehicle.**

The Annexe to the M. Notice - although now also withdrawn - provided a useful method by which to assess the tipping and sliding forces likely to be developed in vehicle lashings on ro-ro ships - and from that point decide whether to use the 3-times rule or something more, or something a little less, stringent. The method is demonstrated herein because the basic principles involved can be applied to all aspects of deck cargo in circumstances where the more general methods given earlier may not be wholly appropriate. It also has the happy characteristic of providing a solution by means of a scale drawing.

The method assumes, in the absence of any more precise information, that vehicles and/or units of cargo stowed on the decks of ro-ro ships will be subjected to the following forces:-

a.	Force parallel to and across the deck	=	1.0W
b.	Force normal to the deck	=	1.4W
c.	Force in the longitudinal direction	=	0.3W

Such forces are intended to represent the total to be applied in each direction; that is, they are the aggregate of the static and dynamic forces.

To examine the forces causing a vessel to tip sideways, for instance, moments are taken about the outer edge of the trailer wheel as illustrated in Fig.5.17. (For the non-mathematically inclined, don't be put-off by the word "moments": it just means the product of multiplying a weight by the length of the lever it's working on. When you push on the outside edge of a door which is 1.5m wide with a force of 3kg, the hinges become the fulcrum and the "moment" is 1.5 x 3 = 4.5m kg, said as: four point five metre-kilogrammes.)

The forces preventing tipping are the vertical downward force and the lashings (F_{LT}). If moments are taken about "A" - the outer edge of the wheel - the fulcrum position, the equation (from Fig.5.17) can be written as:-

$$F_{LT} \times L = (1.0W \times 2/3H) - (1.4W \times X)$$

transposes to

$$F_{LT} \times (X + Y) \sin \theta = W (0.67H - 1.4X)$$

transposes to

$$F_{LT} = \frac{W (0.67H - 1.4X)}{(X + Y) \sin \theta}$$

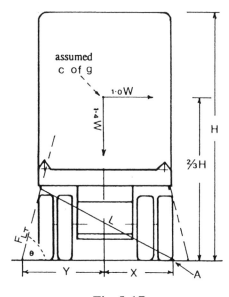

Fig.5.17

In Fig.5.17 there are: two factor "constants"; one elective factor "constant"; at least four physical distances which must be measured (either on site or from an accurate scale drawing); and one base angle (again, found by measurement on site, or from an accurate scale drawing or by trigonometry if some other values are known) as follows:-

a.   A `g' factor "constant" of 1.0W relating to the force acting parallel to and transversely across the deck;

b.   A `g' factor "constant" of 1.4W relating to the force acting vertically to the deck;

c.   A `g' factor "constant" of 0.3W relating to the force acting parallel to and longitudinally to the deck (not shown in Fig.5.17);

d.   An elective centre of gravity (c of g) "constant" of ⅔H. If the exact c of g of the unit as a whole is not known, and cannot accurately be calculated, the c of g is to be taken as being at a height above the deck of ⅔ the **overall** height of vehicle and body;

e.   Physical height `H': the overall height of vehicle and body;

f.   Physical length `X': the horizontal distance from the outer edge of the outer wheel to the centre line of the unit as a whole;

g.   Physical length `Y': the horizontal distance from the centre line of the unit to the deck level lashing terminal;

h.   Physical height of the trailer lashing terminal above the deck level.

Using squared graph paper and a reasonably large scale - 1:200 fits nicely on A4 paper, ie, 5cm = 1m - produce an outline drawing and measure (or calculate) the base angle θ.

Using the values given in Fig.5.18 and the enclosed formulae given in the box on the previous page, the tipping sideways force may be calculated:-

W = total weight of trailer and contents = 30 tonnes

H = 3.582m of which 0.67H = 2.40m

Y = 1.45m

X = 1.15m

X + Y = 2.60m

θ = 75° at trailer side lashings

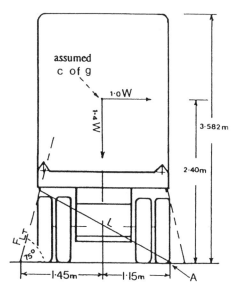

Fig.5.18

$$F_{LT} = \frac{W\ (0.67H - 1.4x)}{(X + Y)\ \mathrm{Sin}\ \theta} = \frac{30\ (2.4 - (1.4 \times 1.15))}{2.6\ \mathrm{Sin}\ 75°}$$

$$= \frac{30 \times 0.79}{2.5114}$$

Tipping forces = 9.437 tonnef - each way = 18.874 tonnef, in all

Where tipping forces are not properly allowed for and secured against, severe adverse weather conditions will exact the penalty shown in Fig.5.19.

Photo: Peter McClelland

Severe weather and inadequate side lashings

Fig.5.19

To examine the forces causing the vehicle to slide sideways, it is assumed that the trailer is supported by wheels at one end and by a trestle (or horse) at the other as shown in Fig.5.20.

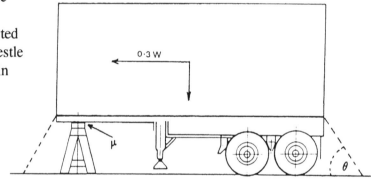

Fig.5.20 *(Adapted from ACL)*

In each instance sliding is resisted by the frictional resistance (denoted by the letter "μ") between trestle/trailer frame and tyre/deck and also the lashings shown as F_{LS} in Figs.5.21 and 5.22.

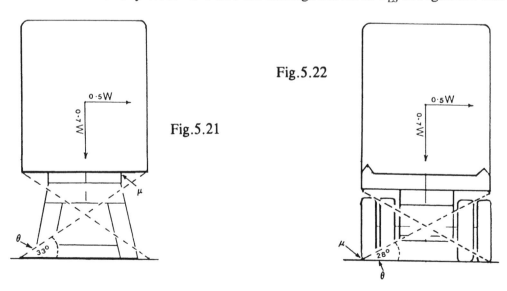

Fig.5.22

Fig.5.21

It is assumed that half the total forces act at each end of the trailer and that the co-efficient of friction between trestle and trailer frame (or trestle and deck) is 0.2, and between rubber wheels and the steel deck it is 0.4 - see, also, Chapter 1 on this topic - then, in the instance of Fig.5.21, the trestle end of the trailer, the effective sliding force

$$= \quad 0.5W - (0.7W \times \mu) \quad = \quad 0.5W - (0.7W \times 0.2) \quad = \quad 0.5W - 0.14W$$
$$= \quad 0.36W$$

Then the force in the lashing resisting sliding $= \quad F_{LS} \quad = \quad \dfrac{0.36W}{\cos \theta}$

Again, using squared graph paper, produce an outline drawing and measure (or calculate) the base angle θ. In this instance, use the values shown in Fig.5.21, so

$$F_{LS} = \dfrac{0.36 \times 30}{\cos 33} = \dfrac{10.8}{0.8387} = 12.877$$

So the force in the lashing resisting sliding at the trestle end = 12.877 tonnef.

In the instance of Fig.5.22 - the wheel end of the trailer - the effective sliding force

$$= \quad 0.5W - (0.7W \times \mu) \quad = \quad 0.5W - (0.7W \times 0.4) \quad = \quad 0.5W - 0.28W$$
$$= \quad 0.22W$$

Then the force in the lashing resisting sliding $= \quad F_{LS} \quad = \dfrac{0.22W}{\cos \theta}$

Again, use squared graph paper to produce an outline drawing to obtain the base angle θ - or calculate it by trigonometry. In this instance, use the values given in Fig.5.22, so

$$F_{LS} = \dfrac{0.22 \times 30}{\cos 28} = \dfrac{6.6}{0.8829} = 7.475$$

So the force in the lashing resisting sliding at the wheel end = 7.475 tonnef.

Combining the tipping and sliding forces: 18.874 + 12.877 + 7.475 equals 39.226 tonnef.

With mild steel chains the lashing load must not exceed 50% of the break-load; so the aggregate break-load of the lashings used must be 39.226 x 2 = 78.452 tonnef. This result is less stringent than the 3-times rule for weather-deck cargoes which, in this instance of a 30-tonne vehicle, would produce a break-load of 30 x 3 = 90 tonnef. It is also less stringent than the 114 tonnef arising from the use of the graphs. It is most probably because of these comparisons that the original M.Notice was withdrawn. So, if you are going to use this "Useful Alternative", and severe adverse weather conditions are likely to be encountered, I would suggest you double the value for sliding forces which, in this instance, would produce a lashing load of 59.578 tonnef, equating to a required break-load of 119.2 tonnef. And nothing in the above few pages should detract from the use of the excellent graphs for the various vehicle masses included in the ANNEX to the 1997Code and as exampled earlier herein, two more of which are reproduced on the following page.

9.5 TONNE LOAD LIMIT LINE

FOR: 6 LANE RO/RO SHIP; SEMI-TRAILER STOWED AT FORWARD END OF <u>OUTBOARD</u> <u>LANE; ROLL ANGLE 20 DEGREES; PITCH ANGLE 5 DEGREES.</u>

20 TONNE TRAILER

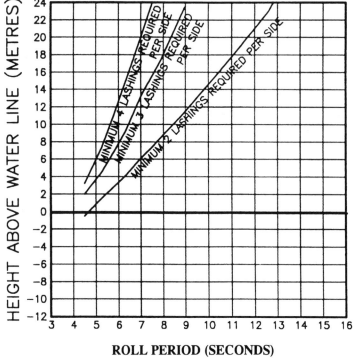

ROLL PERIOD (SECONDS)

+ + + + + + + + + + + + +1

32 TONNE TRAILER

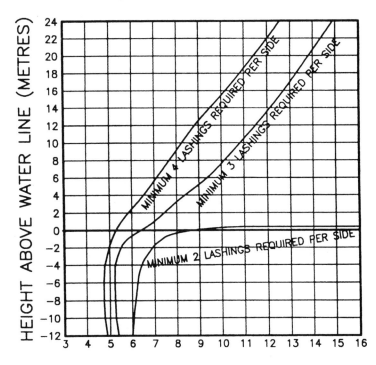

ROLL PERIOD (SECONDS)

Graphs: Courtesy The Stationery Office - Code of Safe Practice 1997.

CHAPTER 6

Cargo Containers On Non-Purpose Built Ships

20ft unit, a fully-enclosed and rigid rectangular box 20ft in length and , fitted with a pair of hinged doors at the rear end. In recent years containers of 8ft 6in height, a demand which has made this higher unit eated the problems of stowing containers in adjacent stacks of mixed nd 9ft 6in are becoming commonplace. The longitudinal extension 0ft and 40ft rectangular box. Containers of 35ft and 45ft length are nes. All these dimensions are external.

ructed:-

, ends, roof and floor: flat panels or corrugated sheets; (containers floor);

alloys in similar flats or profiles;

various thicknesses;

astic (GRP);

above materials.

ngs, bottom rails, under-bearers and sills are mainly of steel and erance and strength specifications as established by the International (ISO) and additionally by several of the ship classification societies. parts of a container.

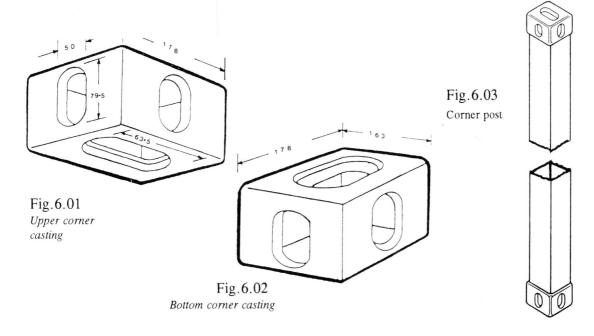

Fig.6.01
Upper corner casting

Fig.6.02
Bottom corner casting

Fig.6.03
Corner post

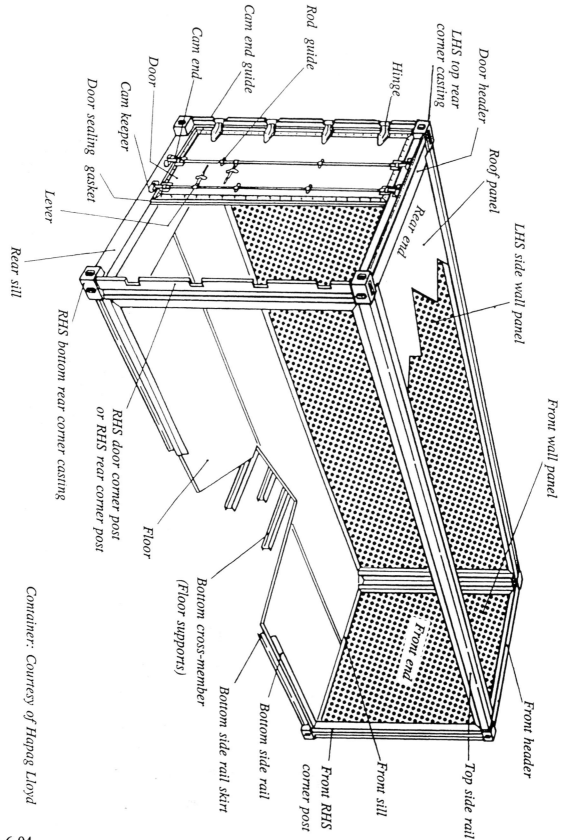

Door header

LHS top rear corner casting

Hinge

Rod guide

Cam end guide

Cam end

Door

Cam keeper

Door sealing gasket

Lever

Rear sill

RHS bottom rear corner casting

RHS door corner post or RHS rear corner post

Floor

Bottom cross-member (Floor supports)

Bottom side rail skirt

Bottom side rail

Front RHS corner post

Front sill

Top side rail

Front header

Front wall panel

Front end

LHS side wall panel

Rear end

Roof panel

Container: Courtesy of Hapag Lloyd

Fig 6.04

From this basic unit a multiplicity of variations has evolved, i.e. the open-top container, the tilt-sided container, flat rack, the various types of reefer units and bulk-liquid tanks of various shapes fitted with ISO structural frames. There are also variations in length and height. (See Figs.6.05 to 6.07, for instance.) Reference to JANE'S FREIGHT CONTAINERS and CONTAINERISATION INTERNATIONAL YEARBOOK gives some insight into the range of units available, any one of which may be presented for carriage as deck cargo.

Fig.6.05

Half-height duramin containers, double-stacked

Fig.6.06

20ft all-steel opening roof container

Fig.6.07

*20ft x 8ft x 8ft
tank container.
May contain highly
corrosive and/or
toxic liquids.*

SOURCE: Jane's Freight Containers

Another variation is the CUC cellular unit specially designed to carry two rows of 1.2m x 1m Europallets without wasted space. This has been achieved by increasing the external width dimension to 2.5m (8.2ft) and by recessing the corner posts (Fig.6.08).

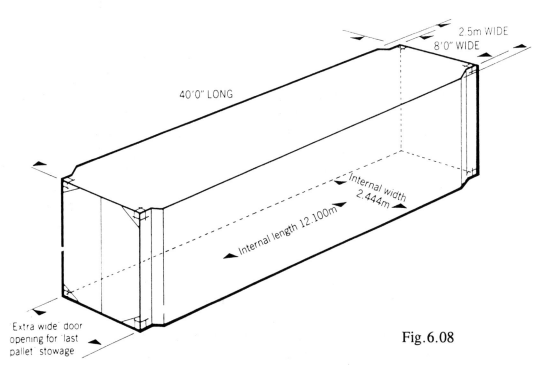

2.5m WIDE
8'0" WIDE

40'0" LONG

Internal width 2.444m

Internal length 12.100m

'Extra wide' door opening for 'last pallet' stowage

Fig.6.08

SOURCE: Cargo Unit Containers Ltd.

A normal 20ft unit has a tare weight of between 2 and 2½ tonnes, a cargo weight (payload) capacity of between 17½ tonnes and 18½ tonnes, with a maximum gross weight of about 22 tonnes. A 40ft unit has a tare weight of between 3½ tonnes and 4 tonnes, a cargo weight (payload) capacity of about 26 to 27 tonnes, with a maximum gross weight of 30 to 31 tonnes. Special 20ft units for carriage of steel coils, manufactured to much more stringent specifications, are able to carry cargoes of up to 27 tonnes weight. It is important that the relevant recommended gross weights are not exceeded.

The International Convention for Safe Containers - IMO 1992, lays down structural requirements for containers and requires countries who ratify it to establish effective procedures for testing, inspection, approval and maintenance. This Convention, which came into force in 1978, and its amendments which came into force in January 1993, requires that a Safety Approval Plate be affixed to every approved container. Amongst other things this plate should record the maximum operating gross weight, the allowable stacking weight and the transverse racking test load value.

Securing Containers - General

Currently there is little uniformity in the methods and systems utilised for securing containers to the ship's structure and to each other. One essential is that the securing gear used must be of the correct strength. A number of international companies produce and market container securing equipment and maintain their own consultancy services which provide advice on how to stow and lash containers safely in a particular ship. Where shipowners have sought the advice of such experienced manufacturers/consultants, the plans produced are generally effective and, when fully implemented, result in a very low incidence of loss or damage.

This Chapter, however, deals mainly with the idea that containers will not be part of a regular trade, but may be required to be carried as deck cargo at random intervals for which Class approval or naval architectural advice has not been sought, and where masters and mates may appreciate some guidance.

The wide variety of container securing fittings available on the market is matched by an equally wide range of technical terms used for the components involved. It would be of great assistance to shore-based personnel if ships' officers and surveyors, when referring to container securing devices, used only those words and terms appearing in the handbook of the manufacturer concerned, together with a photocopy (or photograph) of the type of component involved. Indeed, under the terms of the Cargo Securing Manual Regulations, and depending upon the trading pattern, such data may be required for the ship, even though not a purpose-built vessel. Manufacturers of securing equipment are usually willing to provide catalogues of components with detailed line drawings and pictures, and the appropriate handbooks should be kept on board the ships. The author extends his thanks to the manufacturers for allowing some of their drawings to be reproduced in this book.

Inter-layer stackers, twist-locks, turn-buckles, lashing rods, chains, deck connections, etc. are all subject to deterioration or physical damage of one kind or another and should always be inspected before use. Operational structural failure of components may result from them being weakened by rough handling. Hamburger turnbuckles should be closely inspected for acceptable manufacture; cheaply-made turnbuckles will display poor welding at U-bar-to-collar-nut attachments and should be rejected.

Although some minor and major failures of container stacks do occur in purpose-built ships, the greater number of such casualties involve containers carried above and below decks in non-cellular/non-purpose built ships, and there appears to be an increasing number of incidents arising from the weather-deck stowage of containers stacked two or more high without Class approval and without reference to competent naval architects and/or recognised container carriage consultants.

The author's own investigations into container casualties frequently reveal that, over a period of time, recommended measures which appear to be of minor importance are increasingly and successively left undone or overlooked without disaster; and then circumstances suddenly conspire to exert upon the container stack the maximum stresses which the full recommendations and full equipment had been designed to withstand. Damage and loss result. The frequent cry thereafter is: "But we have always carried the containers that way without any problems!" - a statement which, upon full investigation, seldom proves to be all the truth.

Containers As Deck Cargo

Firstly, a large number of vessels which have space on weather-decks and hatch covers are not provided with permanent fittings to restrain or lock the bottom corner castings of containers. This, of itself, is not a problem if the containers are carried in a single tier and are individually secured according to their deck cargo weight factors. For such vessels to carry containers in a second tier is a hazardous undertaking, even though the practice is widespread. (See the upper view on Colour Plate I between Chapters 4 and 5.)

Where containers on the weather-deck and hatch covers are adequately stowed and efficiently secured, they seldom, if ever, get washed overboard in heavy weather. In the absence of permanent foot-locks and similar approved restraint devices, transverse dunnage beneath the corner castings and the "3-times rule" for lashings strength will be found a safe guide. Where two tiers are carried, the base tier corner castings should be independently secured against movement, and the second tier units should be twist-locked to the base tier. So secured, the containers themselves may be extensively damaged by the impact of heavy seas coming aboard, but the securing arrangements, the container corner castings, and the corner posts should hold fast!

Containers are designed and constructed to stand on the four bottom corner castings alone. The bottom side rails and/or skirts, the front and rear sills and the under-floor cross-bearers should remain free of bottom contact at all times. **The skirts of bottom rails are not strength members, and will buckle and collapse if placed on dunnage timbers.** (See the two lower views in Colour Plate I and Figs.6.09 to 6.11.)

Fig.6.09

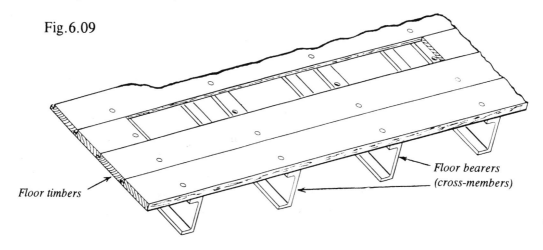

Floor timbers

Floor bearers
(cross-members)

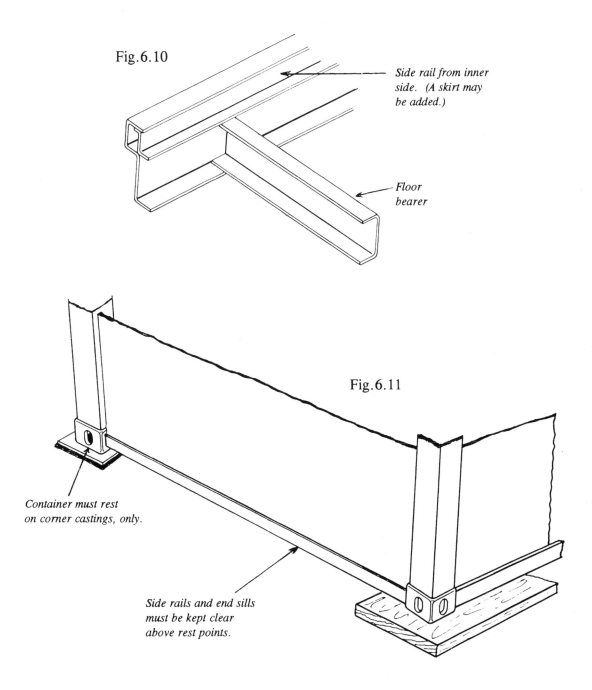

Fig.6.10

Side rail from inner side. (A skirt may be added.)

Floor bearer

Fig.6.11

Container must rest on corner castings, only.

Side rails and end sills must be kept clear above rest points.

If fittings are being welded to hatch covers, decks or tank-tops, full consideration must be given to the downward-acting forces which the ship's structure will be required to withstand when fully-laden containers are in position. A single stack of 2 x 20ft x 20-tonne units will exert a down-loading of 40 tonnes. Beneath each corner casting the point-loading will be about 345 tonnes/m². It is important to spread that load (see Chapter 1) and equally important to ensure that the plating and the structure beneath are sufficient to withstand such forces. Instances have occurred where hatch covers and deck plating have been pierced by the bottom corner castings of containers, resulting in ingress of water to cargo compartments and expensive repairs to the ship.

The United Kingdom Department of Trade Merchant Shipping Notice No.624 - October 1971 - (withdrawn in March 1985) stated, inter alia:-

> "3.   *Except where there is provision enabling a twist-lock, or other similar device, to be inserted in the bottom corner fittings of the container and into suitably designed recesses in the hatch covers or fabricated deck stools of appropriate strength, containers carried on deck should be stowed one high only. In such cases the containers should preferably be stowed fore and aft, prevented from sliding athwartships and securely lashed against tipping. Containers should be stowed on deck two or more high only on those ships which have securing arrangements specially provided. At no time should the deck loaded containers overstress the hatch cover or the hatchway structure; in cases of doubt details of stress limitations should be obtained from the classification society".*

Experience has shown that this advice is sound commonsense and good seamanship. Overloading of hatch covers may cause excessive deflection and loss of watertight integrity. The Merchant Shipping (Load Line) Regulations 1998, as amended by the Merchant Shipping (Load Line) (Amendment) Regulations 2000 state that, for mild steel hatch covers, any deflection must not exceed 0.0028 times the span under load; and for steel pontoon covers the deflections must not exceed 0.0022 times the span. Thus, in the case of a hatch panel of, say, 7.14m span the deflection must not exceed 20mm in the first instance, and not more than 15.7mm in the instance of pontoons. Schedule 2, Section 1, of the same LLR 1998/2000 says: *"weathertight" in relation to any part of a ship other than a door in a bulkhead means that water will not penetrate it and so enter the hull in the worst sea and weather conditions likely to be encountered by the ship in service.........."* so keeping hatch cover deflections to a minimum is of utmost importance, of which measures to spread the load evenly and with care should be followed.

Fig.6.12

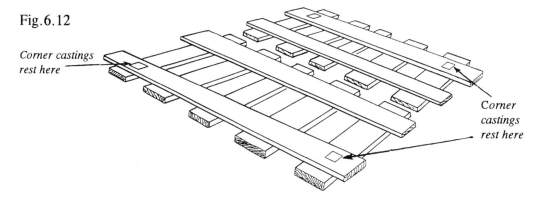

Corner castings rest here

Corner castings rest here

Points to consider when carrying containers on the weather-deck of a non-purpose built ship may be listed as follows:-

a.   Where permanent foot-locks and/or foot restraints are not welded to the ship structure, it is recommended that containers are not carried more than one tier in height and that the corner castings are placed on adequate timber dunnage laid in such a way as not to contact the sills and/or side frames. (See Figs.6.11 and 6.12.)

Spread the full load of the container over the area of the deck and/or hatch cover concerned. Fig.6.12 illustrates an example of acceptable dunnaging for 20ft units, from which it can be seen how the problem becomes compounded if 40ft units are involved. Containers so carried must be treated as "deck cargo", and secured in accordance with the deck cargo rules and recommendations. In other words, the total holding power of the lashing arrangements properly disposed and attached to appropriate terminal points, should be not less than three times the static gross weight of the container and contents. (See, also, Fig.6.29.)

b.   If containers are to be stacked two (or more) tiers high, the base tier should be provided with permanent foot-locks for the lower corner castings. The containers should be secured one above the other by means of twist-locks and/or lockable inter-layer stackers, and the upper corner castings of a block of units should be locked into each other transversely by means of screw-bridge fittings and/or tension clamps. (See Figs.6.13 to 6.19, for instance.)

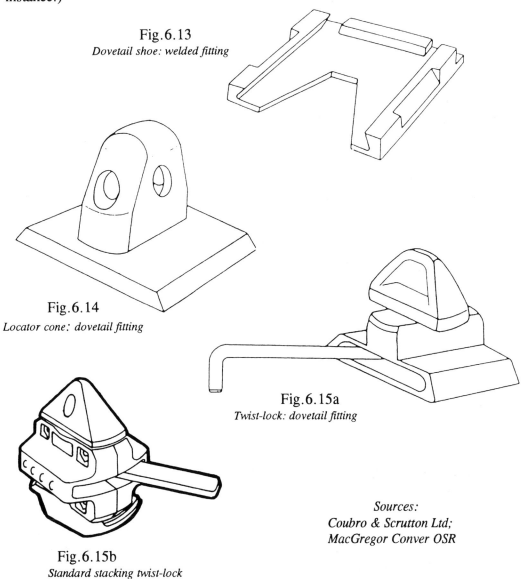

Fig.6.13
Dovetail shoe: welded fitting

Fig.6.14
Locator cone: dovetail fitting

Fig.6.15a
Twist-lock: dovetail fitting

Fig.6.15b
Standard stacking twist-lock

Sources:
Coubro & Scrutton Ltd;
MacGregor Conver OSR

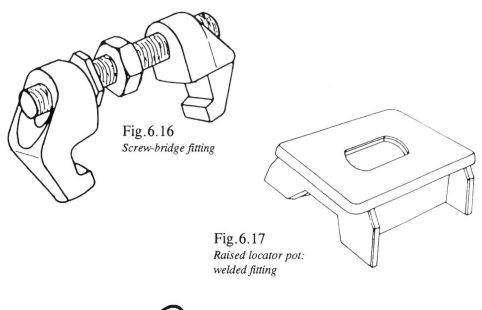

Fig.6.16
Screw-bridge fitting

Fig.6.17
*Raised locator pot:
welded fitting*

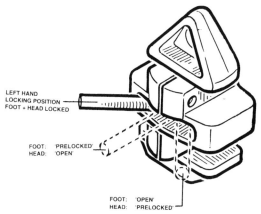

LEFT HAND
LOCKING POSITION
FOOT + HEAD LOCKED

FOOT: 'PRELOCKED'
HEAD: 'OPEN'

FOOT: 'OPEN'
HEAD: 'PRELOCKED'

Fig.6.18a
3-function twist-lock

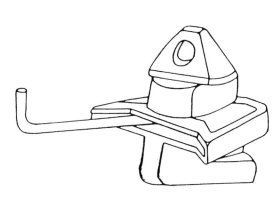

Fig.6.18b
Turnfoot twist-lock

*Sources:
Coubro & Scrutton Ltd;
MacGregor Conver OSR*

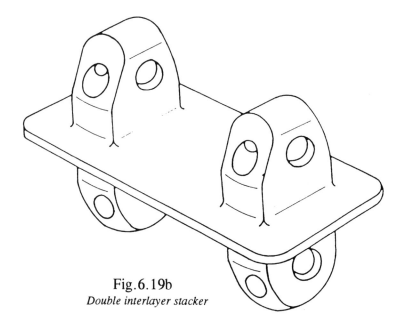

Fig.6.19a
Levelling type stacking cone

Fig.6.19b
Double interlayer stacker

c.   A variation on (b) allows for permanent welded restraints against transverse and longitudinal movement instead of foot-locks, and for non-lockable inter-layer stackers to be used between the units. However, lashing chains, lashing bars and/or lashing wires of appropriate strength and disposition must be utilised to secure the containers to the ship's structure. (See Figs.6.20 to 6.23, for instance.)

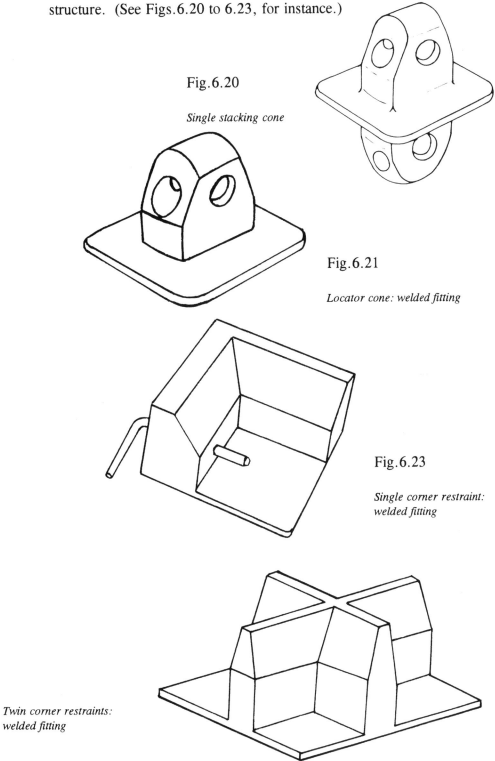

Fig.6.20

Single stacking cone

Fig.6.21

Locator cone: welded fitting

Fig.6.23

Single corner restraint: welded fitting

Twin corner restraints: welded fitting

Fig.6.22

d. If circumstances demand a twin-tier stack in the absence of foot-locks or welded restraints, then foot lashings (or foot chocks as a poor substitute) must be used and the units should be twist-locked together and provided with lashings adequate and in line with "deck cargo" requirements. (See Fig.6.24, for instance.)

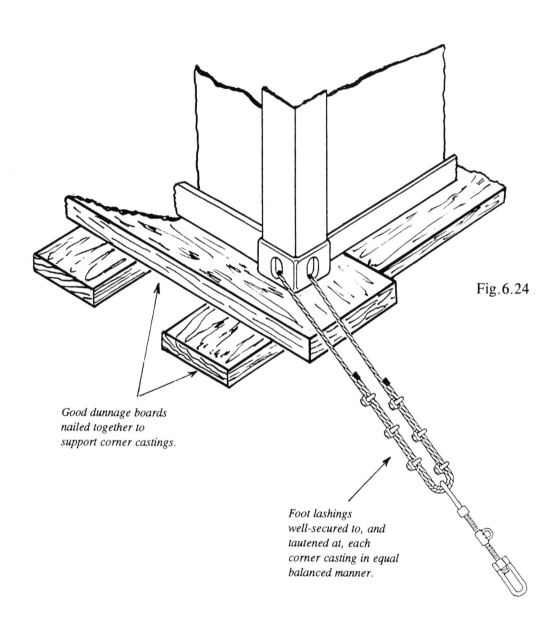

Fig.6.24

Good dunnage boards nailed together to support corner castings.

Foot lashings well-secured to, and tautened at, each corner casting in equal balanced manner.

It is appreciated that page 17 of the IMO CSS Code illustrates a simple system of foot chocks which may suffice in calm weather conditions. In adverse sea conditions, however, such chocks will be washed away and/or shocked loose leaving the bottom corner castings without restraint. Timber foot chocks require positive securing: they will not just stay put on their own. Figs.6.25 and 6.26 illustrate positive securing of timber foot chocks. Even that chocking will need daily attention in bad weather, and make you wish you had used secure foot lashings to start with.(See, also, the **INTRODUCTION** preceding Chapter 1.)

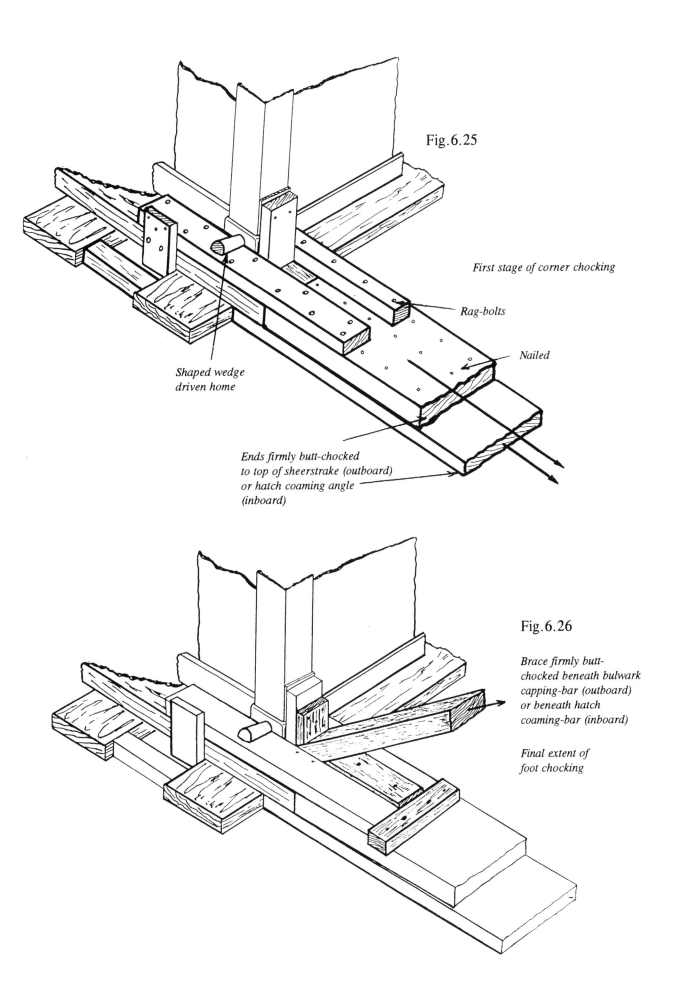

Fig.6.25

First stage of corner chocking

Rag-bolts

Nailed

*Shaped wedge
driven home*

*Ends firmly butt-chocked
to top of sheerstrake (outboard)
or hatch coaming angle
(inboard)*

Fig.6.26

*Brace firmly butt-
chocked beneath bulwark
capping-bar (outboard)
or beneath hatch
coaming-bar (inboard)*

*Final extent of
foot chocking*

e.	Where permanent foot-locks and bridging interlayer stackers are not used, it may prove essential to use screw-bridge fittings at upper and lower adjacent corner castings in transverse stow. In such instances, timber wedge-chocks should be driven between the corner castings and the screw-bridge fittings then fully tightened. This will assist in keeping the stowage rigid (see Fig.6.27). In the absence of wedge-chocks unacceptable working stresses may be engendered causing fracture of the screw-bridge fittings.

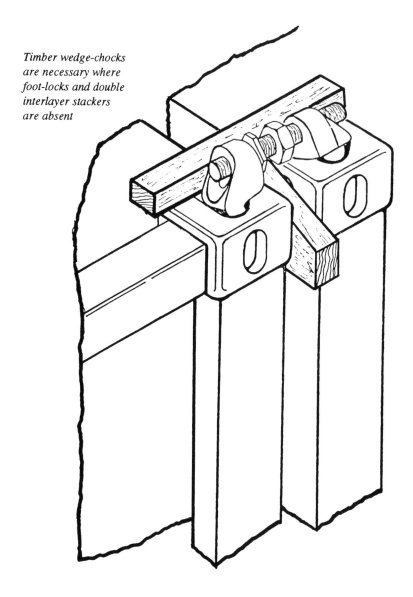

Timber wedge-chocks are necessary where foot-locks and double interlayer stackers are absent

Fig.6.27

f.	In the absence of foot-locks or permanent welded restraints, units in longitudinal row must be lashed and secured independently. They must not be loop-lashed as shown in Fig.6.28, 6.30 and 6.31. It is not sufficient to use only tension clamps or screw-bridge fittings in the longitudinal mode to secure together the abutting ends of each unit.

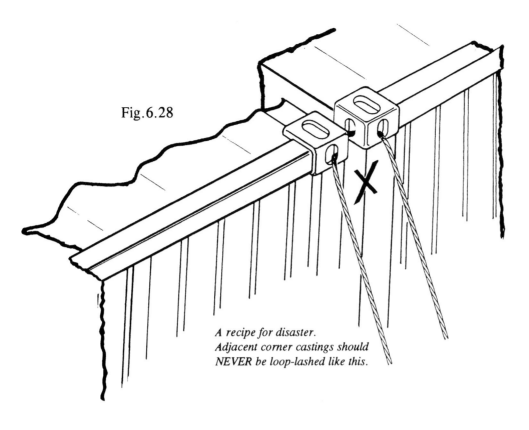

Fig.6.28

A recipe for disaster.
Adjacent corner castings should
NEVER be loop-lashed like this.

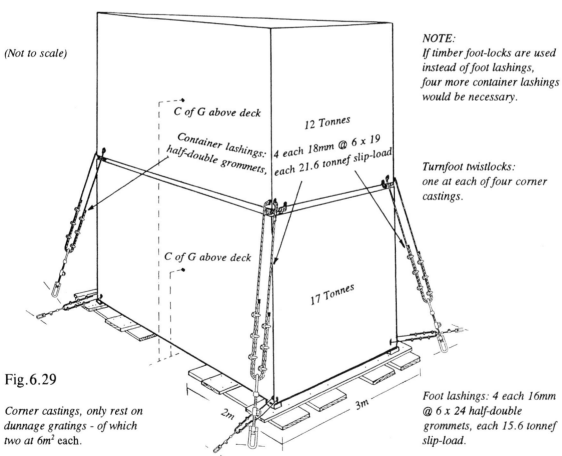

(Not to scale)

C of G above deck

Container lashings:
half-double grommets, 4 each 18mm @ 6 x 19
each 21.6 tonnef slip-load

12 Tonnes

C of G above deck

17 Tonnes

2m   3m

NOTE:
If timber foot-locks are used
instead of foot lashings,
four more container lashings
would be necessary.

Turnfoot twistlocks:
one at each of four corner
castings.

Foot lashings: 4 each 16mm
@ 6 x 24 half-double
grommets, each 15.6 tonnef
slip-load.

Fig.6.29

Corner castings, only rest on
dunnage gratings - of which
two at 6m² each.

Never use this bad lashing arrangement   Fig.6.30

When containers in stack are loop-lashed without rigid double interlayer stacking cones, the movement and vibration of the stack will cause wires to chafe and fracture as shown here.

Fig.6.31

g.   The individual gross weights of containers, or their precise position in the stowage, are seldom known before the stowage is complete, and the weights may not be confirmed until some time after the ship has left port. With this in mind, where precise weights are not known, ships' officers and surveyors should assume that all 20ft units have a gross weight of 20 tonnes on average, that all 40ft units have a gross weight of 26 tonnes on average, and that the centres of gravity lie at the geometrical centre of each container. The number, disposition, and breaking strain of the lashings should be calculated accordingly. Fig.6.29 is just one illustration of an effective method of securing containers on deck where the precise weights are known at time of loading.

Failure of the securing arrangements of deck-stowed containers has occurred, for example, where containers were mixed with break-bulk general cargo without careful planning and adequate securing. When circumstances require a mixture of general break-bulk cargo together with containers, whether above or below deck, great care must be taken with the stowage. Damage resulting from cargo shifting continues to occur in these situations and appears to result from an unrealistic reliance upon the containers acting as "restraining walls" instead of the cargo being secured in accordance with normal sound stowage practices. Reference should also be made to the IMO Code of Safe Practice for Cargo Stowage and Securing, 1992/(1994/1995 Amendments.)

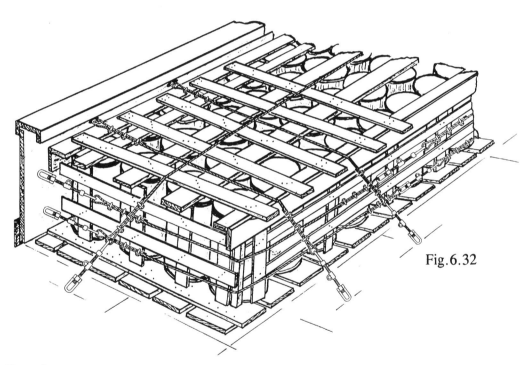

Fig.6.32

Other Containers

Containers of one sort or another have always been carried in ships. Today "containers" may include barrels, drums, bottles, large steel casings for delicate machinery, bags for liquids, etc. It would not be reasonable to attempt to cover the entire range of such containers, so what follows are no more than general guidelines, bearing in mind that the containers here under consideration are likely not to have any form of integral securing lugs. Drums of metal or plastic frequently require deck stowage, especially where IMDG (hazardous) commodities are involved. Drums in the range 40 to 45 gallons (180 to 200 litres) should be stowed in small blocks in single tier, be well-dunnaged, timber corralled, and lashed in such manner that the lashing wires do not contact the drums. Fig.6.32, above, illustrates sound practice.

Large steel containers holding integral machinery items are frequently offered for shipment with or without securing lugs. Such items must be dunnaged and chocked and provided with top-timbers so as to secure the container against transverse and longitudinal movement, and to lash down securely against vertical movement. Fig.6.33 provides a view of one method of stowing and securing such items on a weather-deck.

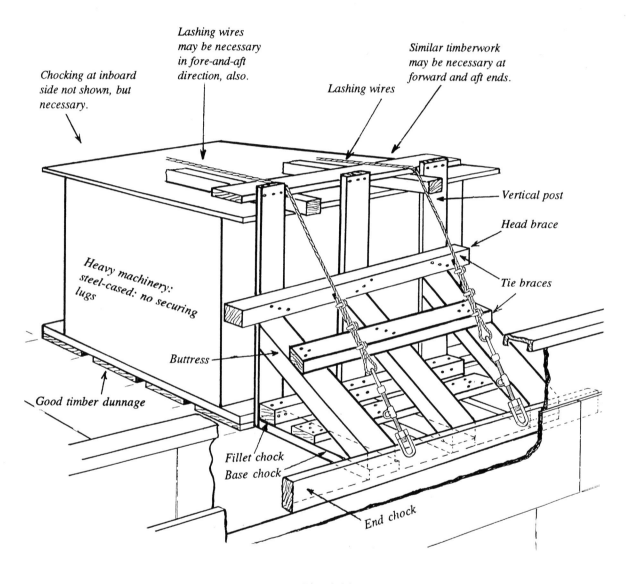

Fig.6.33

Where nearby structures are not available to chock against, "long drift" timber chocking can be used as illustrated in Figs.6.34 and 6.35, which are a 'plan' and 'elevation' extension of Fig.6.33. In each instance it is most important to cut and secure the buttresses to an angle somewhere between 45° and 60° from the horizontal, but no more and no less than that. Tie-braces are essential in any such securing arrangement, and their omission has frequently resulted in catastrophe both on-deck and below.

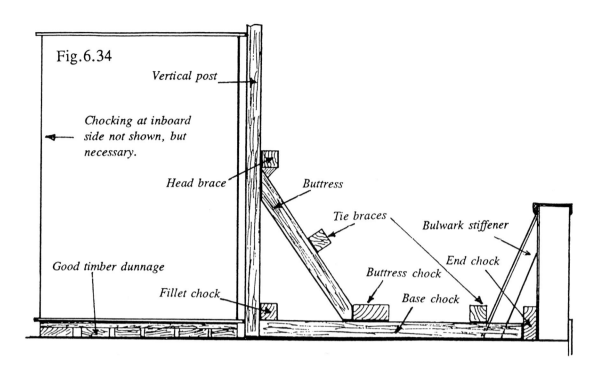

Fig.6.34

Vertical post

Chocking at inboard side not shown, but necessary.

Head brace

Buttress

Tie braces

Bulwark stiffener

End chock

Good timber dunnage

Buttress chock

Fillet chock

Base chock

This page for Figs 6.34 and 6.35.   Fig numbers are part of the drawings.

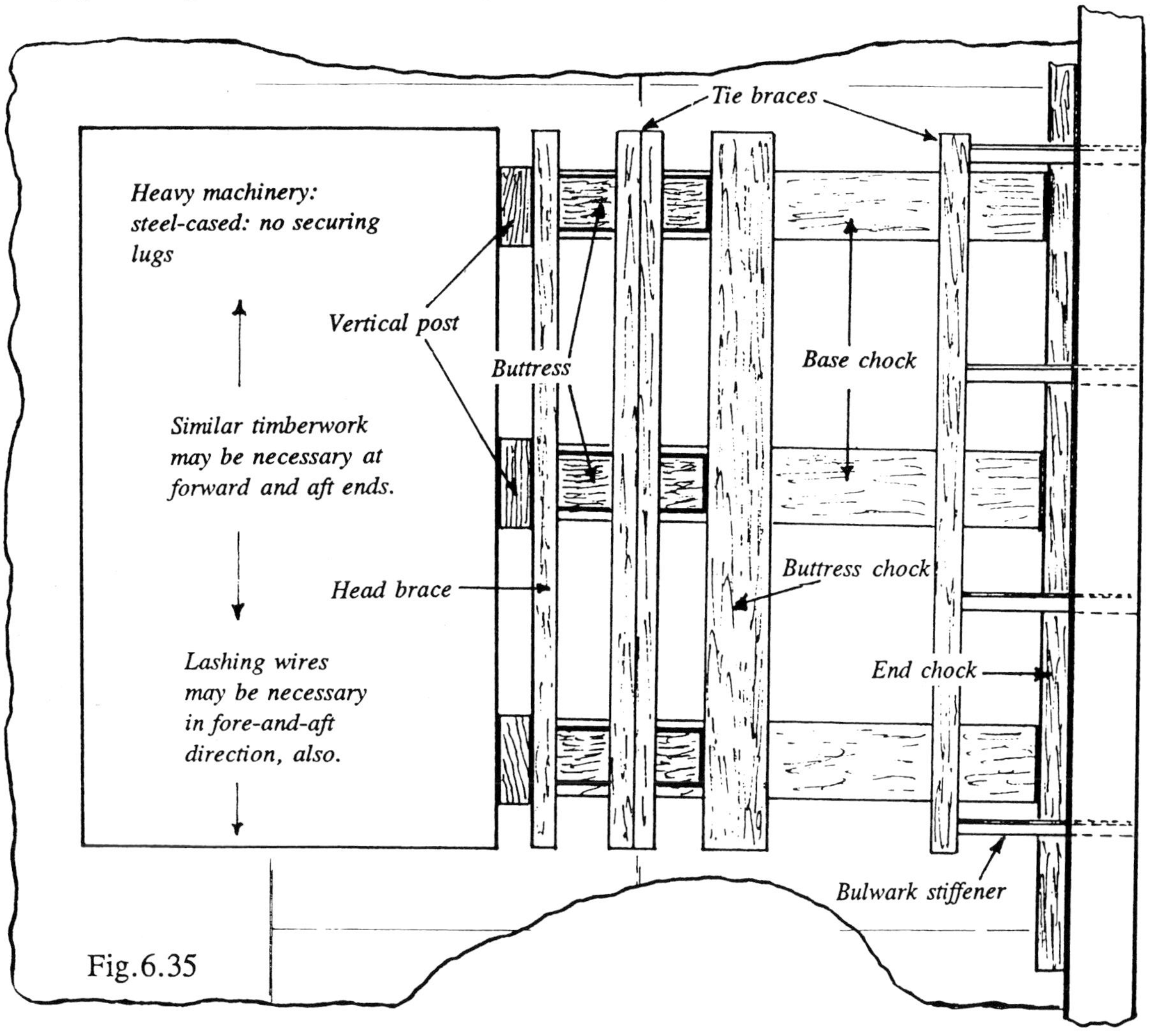

Tie braces

Heavy machinery: steel-cased: no securing lugs

Vertical post

Buttress

Base chock

Similar timberwork may be necessary at forward and aft ends.

Head brace

Buttress chock

Lashing wires may be necessary in fore-and-aft direction, also.

End chock

Bulwark stiffener

Fig.6.35

In all such stowage and securing arrangements, think of what needs to be done adequately to resist the effects of a large green North Atlantic breaking swell coming aboard just when the ship is rolling 20° into it. You won't get a second chance, so make it good before you leave port.

The Packing of ISO Containers

The stuffing of ISO containers is not just a ship operator's problem. Containers are often packed at places many miles and sometimes even several days' journey from the marine terminal. It is therefore important that everyone involved with containers, at whatever stage in transit, should be fully aware of the stresses that may be generated in the structure of the container itself and in and around the cargo within it, during transportation by road, rail or ship, and the extract from BS5073, reproduced at the end of this Chapter, may serve to indicate the magnitude of the acceleration and deceleration stresses exerted upon ISO freight containers and their contents. It is also, of course, essential that containers are in a sound condition each time they are put into service.

A number of shipping companies operating purpose-built container ships publish and supply concisely written pamphlets and handbooks which detail the stresses to which cargo and containers are subjected, with recommendations and instructions on the best methods of securing cargo against those stresses. Wherever containers are being packed, management and supervisory personnel should be supplied with copies of the relevant handbooks and be guided by them. There is little excuse for improper packing or inadequate securing of cargo within a container.

The great problem is that unlike break-bulk cargo, the ship's master and his officers do not sight, nor do they have any control over, the contents of containers or the methods by which they have been packed and secured. The duty of ship's personnel is to accept on board, secure and deliver safely, the containers as offered for shipment. If the contents of just one container are improperly packed or secured and, as a result, break adrift when the ship encounters heavy weather, the safety of many other containers and even the ship itself could be at risk.

Directional Movement

As indicated in the extract from BS5073 given earlier, when a container is on a road or rail vehicle it is subjected to forward, reverse and transverse movements. In normal circumstances these movements all take place in the horizontal plane. The acceleration engendered by a road or rail vehicle braking very suddenly can subject the contents of the container to stresses well in excess of those to be expected from the normal handling operations. If the cargo has room to move the acceleration/deceleration stresses could result in an insufficiently secured weight moving either forward or backward, imposing a sudden load equal to *twice* its own weight upon the front or back end of the container. When road vehicles are required to negotiate relatively small diameter roundabouts or to round bends at high speed, forces are generated which, if the cargo is not adequately secured or its centre of gravity is too high, may create transverse movement within the container, causing the collapse of the cargo followed by the overturning of the unit and vehicle. (See colour Plate J, for example.)

Aboard a ship the stresses are generated in all directions. Induced by the wave motion that the ship may encounter, a container and the goods inside it may be rolling through arcs of as much as 70°. The pitching of the ship will generate large vertical acceleration and deceleration stresses, all associated inseparably with a twisting, sliding motion and the ship's own headway velocity. It should therefore be realised that "packing" is only half the problem; the securing of the cargo within the container is of paramount importance. It is essential that the goods in the container are secured so as to prevent longitudinal movement, either forward or aft; to prevent transverse movement from one side to the other; and positively to prevent vertical movement. It is this last named measure which is most frequently overlooked. **Remember, from Chapter 1, that cargo will lift before it shifts!**

In most instances space in the container, longitudinally or transversely, will be taken up adequately by means of tomming or shoring, or chocks to the floor and sides of the unit. Often, however, where cargo has shifted within a container, it is found that precautions against vertical shifting had not been taken and the results were catastrophic. The following hints may be found of value, although they are not intended to supplement or replace the excellent handbooks and leaflets produced by many ship operators and which can be obtained on application to them.

The sides, ends, roof panel and floor of a container are not normally strength members. Under the floor there are floor bearers and it is normally these bearers and not the floor itself which provide the strength. Where relatively lightweight cartons or good timber cases can be afforded block stowage against all sides, ends, and up to the roof, there is little need for additional securing measures. But where cartons or cases do not occupy the full space of the container, then chocking and bracing with timbers or air "Cargo-Paks" (see Fig.6.36) should be adopted. This can be done in a variety of ways.

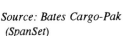

Source: Bates Cargo-Pak
(SpanSet)

Fig.6.36
Cargo-Paks used effectively to occupy free intermediate,
sides, and door end spaces.
Head space can be similarly dunnaged with Cargo-Paks floored above
with plywood panels to spread load across roof bows.

Where timbers are used, they can be nailed to the timber floor of the container to provide a foot-holding, but this in itself will not be sufficient. Some form of spread bracing will be required with the braces being taken to the corner posts or to cross-timbers which are supported at their ends by the corner posts. These bracings should not rely upon the end panels or side panels of the container for support. Where lightweight cargo is required to be secured only against vertical movement it may be necessary to do no more than tie the cargo to suitable blocks nailed into the floor of the container.

Where heavier items are involved, they should be securely lashed downwards to the D-rings which are fitted in some containers. If D-rings, or similar, are not available then the cargo must be tommed vertically downward from suitable cross-timbers supported at the heads of the corner posts or, alternatively, the head-space can be taken up with air "Cargo-Paks" floored above with plywood panels to spread the 'weight' (or pressure) across the roof bows. In other words, all tomming, chocking and bracing must be supported by the strength members of the internals of the containers themselves and never braced direct to the sides, ends or roof panels.

Suitable Containers

It is most important that containers which are manifestly unsuitable for their intended cargoes should be rejected. If medium height heavy weights are to be placed down the middle of the container in such a manner that commonsense demands they be lashed downwards by wire to the floor, then it is imperative that the container used has D-rings attached to the upper parts of the floor bearers as part of its structure. Alternatively, where lightweight cartons with frail contents are to be stowed to the full height of the container, it might be necessary to provide a mid-height flooring so that the lowermost cartons do not suffer compression. In such instances a container is required that has a mid-height rail down both sides, provided with pockets in which transverse support timbers may rest, so that a lightweight "second floor" may be created in the container as packing progresses from the extreme forward end to the after end.

The use of polythene or similar plastic bottles, barrels or jars for the carriage of liquid cargoes is increasing. Because of their non-rigid construction, they will flex and move and change their shape under quite moderate transport stresses. It is essential that they should be stowed in small blocks, corralled or fenced with flat board timber, block against block. The upper surface of the first tier must be fully floored with flat board dunnage before a second tier is stowed (or done progressively from the front end to the rear). The second tier should again be formed of small blocks, adequately corralled or fenced with timber, and similarly for additional tiers. The importance of not subjecting the lowest tier of plastic bottles to vertical pressures which they were not designed to withstand cannot be over-emphasised.

In summary, commonsense, together with an appreciation of the stresses and forces involved, will in most instances result in the cargo reaching its destination in sound condition. Do not do less with cargo inside a container than would be done with the same cargo if it was stowed in a conventional ship's hold.

The OSHA Requirements

MacGregor News No.134 reported that the July 1997 rules by the US Occupational Safety & Health Administration (OSHA) prohibiting stevedores and other employees from working on top of container stacks in US ports unless adequate safety precautions are in place, has effectively placed a ban on personnel climbing onto the top of containers. The use of conventional twistlocks will thus also be restricted.

MacGregor are of the view that semi-autmatic twistlocks, alone, may not solve the problem completely because such twistlocks can only be opened from above in the 76mm ISO-gap. MacGregor's solution is the combination of semi-automatic twistlocks along with the Company's Automatic Fixing Cone (AFC-1). Semi-automatic twistlocks such as the CV-20 (or alternatively the CV-14) solve the general application problem and the new AFC-1 solves the problem in the 76mm ISO-gap. (See Figs.3.37 and 3.38, below.)

Fig.3.38 - CV-20
Semi-automatic
Twistlock.

Fig.3.39 - AFC-1
Automatic
Fixing Cone

Source: MacGregor News No.134

BS5073: 1982 - Stowage of Goods In Freight Containers

Acceleration effects on freight containers in transit

A.1   *Acceleration effects. Acceleration effects, including vibration and shock effects, are the principal mechanical factors that affect a container and its contents. The order of magnitude of the accelerations that may be encountered under certain severe operating circumstances and that may last sufficiently long to be damaging when considered in relation to the principal axes of a container are as follows:-*

vertical   2g;

longitudinal   2g;

transverse   0.8g.

A.2   *Vertical acceleration: 2g. This order of magnitude of mean vertical acceleration will be felt by a container when it is set down hard on a virtually non-yielding surface such as paved ground, a ship's structure or another container which is already on such a surface.*

This lowering-to-ground effect is an impact or shock loading, lasting a few hundredths of a second in total. So far as the container structure is concerned, it may be regarded as a burst of high frequency oscillations involving accelerations measured in tens of g, but lasting less than a thousandth of a second. So far as the cargo is concerned, much of the shock effect is filtered out by the container structure.

For all but the most delicate of cargoes, an allowance of 2g deceleration, i.e. for each item of cargo to feel twice the pressure between itself and the container floor and twice the superimposed weight that it feels when the container is

stationary, will normally suffice. Fragile or delicate cargoes may require special treatment and should always be packed and stowed by specialists. Under severe conditions at sea, peaks of vertical acceleration of the order of 1.8g may be encountered. These are cyclical (approximately sinusoidal) accelerations, mainly associated with the pitch and heave motions of a ship and varying between 0.2g and 1.8g in total, i.e. including the normal gravitational effect over a period of 5s to 15s, depending on the size of the vessel concerned and the nature of the sea encountered. Accelerations of this order of magnitude are rarely encountered for more than a few hours (ship's Master can usually adjust course and speed to reduce the effect of severe seas), but of course lesser accelerations of this type can continue for many days.

Vertical accelerations of the vibrational and/or shock types will be encountered in both road and rail operations but although these may be more or less continuous, they are usually of such low order of magnitude that goods packed to withstand other types of shock loading will hardly feel them at all.

A3.   *Longitudinal accelerations: 2g. This order of magnitude of mean longitudinal acceleration or deceleration may be encountered in the more severe railway marshalling operations.*

If a container were to be carried on a wagon not having satisfactory shock absorbing features and the wagon were to be hump shunted at excessive speed, then decelerations of more than 2g could be encountered, but this is not the practice of responsible railway operators. On those railways which use close coupled wagons or specially designed block chains, i.e.

with bar couplings, for the carriage of containers, longitudinal decelerations will rarely exceed 1g.

The very fact that containers whose end walls have been tested to a load equivalent to 0.4 times the containers rated payload have proved perfectly satisfactory for all but the most extreme eventualities, which usually involve inadequately secured cargo with low friction factors, demonstrates that normal mean longitudinal deceleration levels will be significantly less than 2g.

Nevertheless, because some railway marshalling operations involve decelerations of a complex semi-shock nature, it is advisable to pack and secure cargo against a nominal 2g longitudinal deceleration. Again, specialist advice should be sought for packaging and stowage of fragile or delicate cargo.

The longitudinal decelerations encountered on road vehicles will normally be of a lower order of magnitude than those encountered on rail, and the longitudinal effects encountered at sea will be of a lower order still.

A4. *Transverse accelerations: 0.8g.* This order of magnitude of peak transverse acceleration can be encountered under the most severe conditions at sea. Such accelerations are mainly due to ship's rolling motions. They are cyclical accelerations (approximately sinusoidal) varying between ± 0.8g over a period of 10s to 20s depending upon the characteristics of the vessel, the state of the sea and the ability of the ship's Master to modify rolling effects by alteration of course and/or speed.

As with the longitudinal effect, the fact that containers whose side walls have been tested to a load equivalent to 0.6 times the container's rated payload have proved perfectly satisfactory in service, demonstrates that normal transverse

accelerations will be significantly less than 0.8g.

Nevertheless, it is prudent to allow for a transverse acceleration of this order, i.e. to assume that cargo could feel a deceleration similar to that felt by the driver of a modern road vehicle when braking hard.

It should also be remembered that while a container carrying vessel will very rarely roll as much as 30° to the vertical, larger rolls have been encountered in freak conditions.

The mean levels of the transverse effects encountered on road vehicles are of a lower order of magnitude than those encountered at sea, and those encountered on rail are of a lower order still.

The possibility of transverse vibration effects occurring either when a container is set down before all sideways motion has ceased, or when a rail wagon encounters discontinuity in rails at high speed, should not be ignored where the most delicate cargoes are concerned, but packaging which will protect such cargoes against the vertical and longitudinal shocks it may encounter should give more than adequate protection against transverse effects.

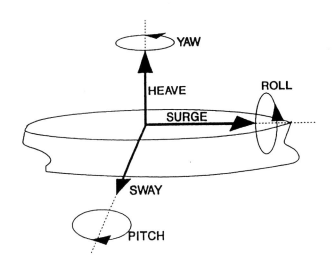

Vertical, transverse and longitudinal accelerations

Containers Adrift At Sea

When an ISO container is lost overboard at sea there are a number of principal and secondary aspects to consider. For instance, depending upon its contents and watertightness, the unit may float mainly visible above water in a number of positional attitudes of which 'A' and 'B', below, are just two of many.

 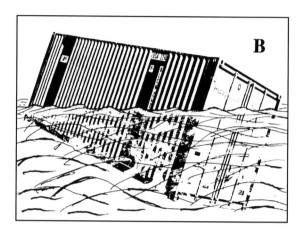

Cargo-Carrying Containers Adrift And Afloat

A standard 20'x 8'x 8' container, when totally submerged in oceanic sea water of sg.1.03, will displace roughly 34m³, or roughly 35 tonnes; so if a 20' unit of, say, 20 tonnes gross weight remains watertight and afloat it will only displace 4/7 (20/35) of its volume. Above water 3/7 (43%) of its volume will be visible in non-ice conditions. If the container is not quite watertight it will slowly fill with water and sink, of which 'C', 'D' and 'E' are just three of the many positional attitudes in the process of sinking in which the unit will become fully submerged and lost to view - again, depending upon the nature of its contents and the rate of water ingress:- slow ingress/slow sinkage; rapid ingress/rapid sinkage.

If the contents are not buoyant in nature the container will certainly sink to the sea bed at whatever rate the overall circumstances create. If the unit's contents are buoyant, the container may flood yet remain afloat in any one of an infinite number of positional attitudes from fully visible to not visible, and in which state the container will be a hazard to all ships; not so much in calm sea-state conditions where the vessel's bow-divergent pressure wave will most likely push the container aside; but, in rough and possibly confused sea/swell conditions, the vessel could roll/pitch heavily into an unseen and wildly moving unit with sufficient force to puncture the shell plating or damage the rudder or propeller. If a container, barely afloat at the surface, drifted downward a few feet and there met a layer of much denser water - there may be a tendency for the unit to assume neutral buoyancy - as shown in 'E', for instance - and to remain more-or-less in that state until some change in the water density brought about a change in the container's spatial disposition.

Containers full of cargo, adrift off the North African coast after a collision in which the container-carrying vessel capsized within minutes of the impact, remained afloat for many days and were eventually towed to and beached on the South coast of Spain. Not all the containers were recovered; it was assumed they had sunk in deep water, but there was a reasonable chance that they were still floating around somewhere, possibly in the positional attitudes illustrated in 'D' and 'E'.

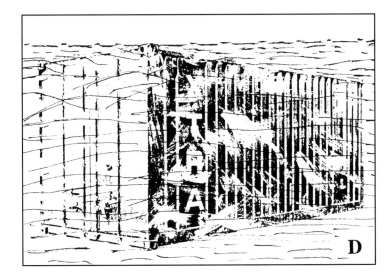

Container Fully Waterlogged And Submerged. May Remain Like This For Some Time Due To Nature Of Contents.

Containers in any of these dispositions will present a short-term or long-term hazard to ships in the vicinity. When containers are lost overboard, the ship's master has a statutory duty to inform the National Administration which controls the maritime area involved and to warn other vessels of the possibility of floating obstructions. I have no up-to-date statistics relating to the numbers of containers lost overboard, but in 1992 the Seatle-based oceanographer Curtiss Ebbersmeyer estimated that 1500 such units were

Neutral Buoyancy May Cause The Container To Remain Just Below The Surface

lost each year, and that almost all were not reported, apart from to the insurance companies who simply paid the claims!

The hazards to the environment may be more pronounced. Take, for instance, a container of drums deadly poison lost overboard in the Bay of Biscay due to the total inadequacy of its 'on-deck' securing arrangements. Quite apart from the financial loss of a valuable cargo and passing damage to transitory fish stocks, there was sufficient poison in that unit to destroy the more static crustaceous life of the Bay and its coastline for decades. The cost of locating and recovering that unit before the poison could get into the sea was enormous. A little extra money spent on lashing gear and the employment of a surveyor who understood the correct means of deploying it would have saved many people a lot of time and a lot of money. It's so much better to get the thing done correctly the first time around!

****

CHAPTER 7

Lashing Material Costs And Miscellaneous Information

Lashing Component Costs

The prices of lashing components, and the charges made by contractors for the labour involved in any given lashing/securing operation, vary widely throughout the world and from year to year. Dunnage boards and chocking timbers purchased in Vancouver will cost less than the same material bought in Saudi Arabia. One hundred 5-tonne SWL shackles ordered direct from the manufacturers in Birmingham for delivery to a ship in Liverpool will be much cheaper than the same 100 shackles required urgently by a ship in Tonga. On the other hand, labour charges in Tonga are likely to be much cheaper than in Liverpool. Overall, the end result may be very similar. High labour charges and cheap components in, say, New York, may very nearly balance with cheap labour charges and expensive components in some non-industrialised island in, say, the middle of the Pacific.

The component prices hereunder are averages in U.S. dollars which may apply in a sea port of, or near to, an industrial manufacturing community in 2002. For the most part, the firms who provided the information necessary to produce the following figures wish to remain anonymous for commercial reasons. Nevertheless, the author extends to them his sincere thanks for their co-operation.

Lashing Wire:
16mm 6 x 12 construction (NBL 7.75 tonnef) - $117 per 100 metres

16mm 6 x 19 construction (NBL 15.30 tonnef) - $147 per 100 metres
18mm 6 x 19 construction (NBL 19.30 tonnef) - $187 per 100 metres

18mm 6 x 24 construction (NBL 13.80 tonnef) - $211 per 100 metres

Rigging-Screws:

Hamburger - 30mm dia. screw thread (NBL 19.30 tonnef) $417 per 50.
type

Solid body - 25mm dia. screw thread (NBL 9.50 tonnef) $1041 per 50.
jaw & eye   32mm dia. screw thread (NBL 15.50 tonnef) $1702 per 50.
    35mm dia. screw thread (NBL 21.00 tonnef) $2013 per 50.
    39mm dia. screw thread (NBL 24.50 tonnef) $2758 per 50.

Solid body - 25mm dia. screw thread (NBL 9.50 tonnef) $789 per 50.
closed eyes 32mm dia. screw thread (NBL 15.00 tonnef) $1121 per 50.
    35mm dia. screw thread (NBL 19.00 tonnef) $1937 per 50.
    39mm dia. screw thread (NBL 24.00 tonnef) $1929 per 50.

Open body - 25mm dia. screw thread $2097 per 50.
hook each 32mm dia. screw thread $2976 per 50.
end

Bulldog-Grips:

For 16mm dia. wire - $48 per 100
For 18mm dia. wire - $57 per 100
For 19mm dia. wire - $61 per 100

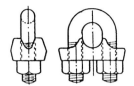

Shackles:

D-type - small 25mm dia. pin (SWL 3.50 tonnef) $ 683   per 100
D-type - small 29mm dia. pin (SWL 4.50 tonnef) $ 812   per 100
D-type - small 32mm dia. pin (SWL 5.50 tonnef) $1140 per 100
D-type - small 35mm dia. pin (SWL 7.00 tonnef) $2004 per 100

D-type - large 25mm dia. pin (SWL 3.00 tonnef) $ 615 per 100
D-type - large 29mm dia. pin (SWL 3.80 tonnef) $ 799 per 100
D-type - large 32mm dia. pin (SWL 5.00 tonnef) $1046 per 100
D-type - large 35mm dia. pin (SWL 6.00 tonnef) $1788 per 100

Bow-type - small 25mm dia. pin (SWL 3.00 tonnef) $ 677 per 100
Bow-type - small 29mm dia. pin (SWL 4.00 tonnef) $ 947 per 100
Bow-type - small 32mm dia. pin (SWL 5.00 tonnef) $1199 per 100
Bow-type - small 35mm dia. pin (SWL 6.30 tonnef) $2304 per 100

Bow-type - large 25mm dia. pin (SWL 2.80 tonnef) $ 697 per 100
Bow-type - large 29mm dia. pin (SWL 3.80 tonnef) $1038 per 100
Bow-type - large 32mm dia. pin (SWL 4.80 tonnef) $1166 per 100
Bow-type - large 35mm dia. pin (SWL 5.80 tonnef) $2104 per 100

Chains

Prices are for **lashing chains**, not for lifting purposes.

Long-Link -

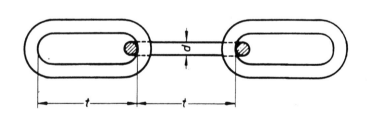

"d" = 9mm   -   break-load -   9 tonnef - $175 per 25m
"d" =11mm -   break-load - 15 tonnef - $400 per 25m
"d" = 13mm -   break load - 20 tonnef - $610 per 25m

NOTE: It is important to keep in mind that size-for-size, in relation to the diameter of the bar forming the link - "d", chain strengths vary depending upon the Standard to which they have been manufactured and the purposes for which they are intended. The break-loads and prices given here are those which may reasonably be expected of "lashing purpose" components.

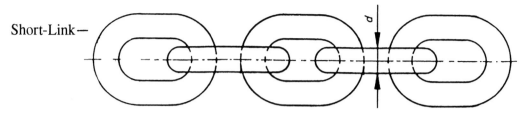

Short-Link—

"d" = 10mm - break load - 11 tonnef - $248 per 25m
"d" = 13mm - break load - 20 tonnef - $610 per 25m
"d" = 16mm - break load - 32 tonnef - £987 per 25m

Webbing - Prices hereunder are in US$ per metre for material bought in quantity.

NBL	WIDTH	PRICE
0.9 tonne	25mm	$0.60 per metre
1.7 tonne	50mm	$0.90 per metre
5.0 tonnes	50mm	$2.20 per metre
6.2 tonnes	50mm	$2.60 per metre
12.0 tonnes	75mm	$4.50 per metre
14.0 tonnes	75mm	On request

Ratchets - The first four prices hereunder are in US$ per unit, based on *Claw-Hook each end and 8m overall length of webbing with ratchet, and exclude "SuperLash" prices. Other end fittings are available on request. *(Source: SpanSet Ltd.)*

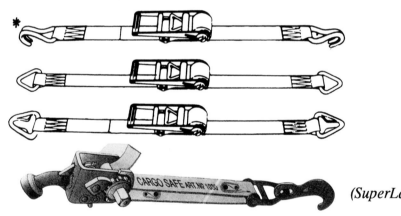

(SuperLash)

NBL	WIDTH	PRICE
0.5 tonne	25mm	$11.00 each
1.0 tonne	50mm	$15.00 each
5.0 tonnes	50mm	$24.00 each
10.0 tonnes	75mm	$80.00 each
14.0 tonnes	75mm	On request
20.0 tonnes	75mm	On request

NOTE; Webbing for lashing purposes is not colour coded or stitch-coded. It is therefore most important that breaking strength data is provided with any material supplied to the ship. As the CSS Code and CSM Regulations stand at the moment the MSL rating of webbing is 70% of breaking strength, but this may soon be reduced to 50% if the currently proposed amendment to Annex 13 is enacted, so remain alerted to this probability.

Timber:
Flatboard hardwood dunnage - random lengths - nominal thickness 25mm, widths 150 to 300mm - $97 per m³. (In rough terms, this equates to 80 boards each 3 metres long and 25 x 150mm cross-section.)

Rough-cut timber:

75 x 75mm (3" x 3")	$169 per 100 metres
75 x 100mm (3" x 4")	$228 per 100 metres
75 x 150mm (3" x 6")	$334 per 100 metres
75 x 225mm (3" x 9")	$495 per 100 metres
100 x 100mm (4" x 4")	$293 per 100 metres

Heavy timber baulks:

200 x 200mm (8" x 8")	$12.00/metre
225 x 225mm (9" x 9")	$18.00/metre
150 x 300mm (6" x 12")	$14.00/metre (Second-hand railway sleepers - $19 each)
300 x 300mm (12" x 12")	$31.00/metre

Mild Steel Flat-bar - standard sizes:

10mm thick

100mm wide	-	$6.00 per metre
150mm wide	-	$9.00 per metre

15mm thick

100mm wide	-	$9.00 per metre
150mm wide	-	$15.50 per metre

20mm thick

100mm wide	-	$12.00 per metre
150mm wide	-	$18.00 per metre

Handling and/or "middle men" charges can quickly inflate any or all of the prices here listed. On the other hand, cheaper prices for shackles and bottle-screws are available.

The nominal break-loads (NBL) given here for lashing wires and rigging-screws, and the safe working loads (SWL) given for shackles, are approximate values for marine lashing components.

When purchasing such components, or when longshoremen, stevedores, charterers and/or rigging contractors are supplying and using such components, it is good practice to ask for, and retain, copies of test certificates for all items. If such certificates cannot be produced, then attempt to have a small number - say 10 - of each item tested locally to the first yield point and record the results.

Where this cannot be achieved, assign to all components the lowest proof-load compatible with good seamanship. Bear in mind that safe working load factors and proof-load factors vary considerably depending upon the component, its application, and the statutory regulations which may apply. On the other hand, many cheaply-made, poor-quality components, made to no particular standard, are now widely available - their use must be treated with every caution herein.(See the Section on Breaking Strengths in the **INTRODUCTION** preceding Chapter 1.)

Under the terms of the CSS Code/CSM Regulations, manufacturers/suppliers have a mandatory duty to provide the end-using ship with details of breaking strengths (BS), test data, and maximum securing loads (MSL's) for all components intended for cargo lashing/securing purposes; so you have every right to insist on the provision of such data without any additional costs to the ship.

For cargo lashing purposes, and in the absence of specific data, the SWL of mild steel components is assumed to be half the proof-load (PL) and the PL (unless otherwise stated) is assumed to be 40% or 50% of the BS, ie, short of the first yield point. This means that if the SWL, only, is known, multiplying that SWL by 4 would provide an approximate BS erring on the side of safety; dividing that breaking strength by 2 will give the safe MSL value of all the materials assigned a 50% rating under Table 1 of the CSS Code/CSM Regulations. Working from the calculated BS, the MSL's for other components can be similarly approximated according to the percentage (%) rating given to them in Table 1. (See, also, Addendum No.5 at the end of this book.)

Hereunder, the 1:2:4 relationship (PL 50%) referred to above is shown schematically for ultimate breaking strength, proof-load and SWL. The MSL position on the line is in respect only of those items afforded a 50% rating in Table 1 of the CSS Code/CSM Regulations.

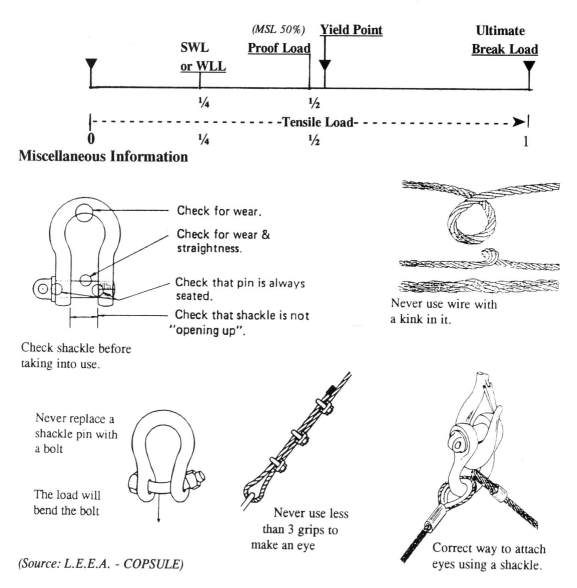

Miscellaneous Information

Check for wear.

Check for wear & straightness.

Check that pin is always seated.

Check that shackle is not "opening up".

Check shackle before taking into use.

Never use wire with a kink in it.

Never replace a shackle pin with a bolt

The load will bend the bolt

Never use less than 3 grips to make an eye

Correct way to attach eyes using a shackle.

(Source: L.E.E.A. - COPSULE)

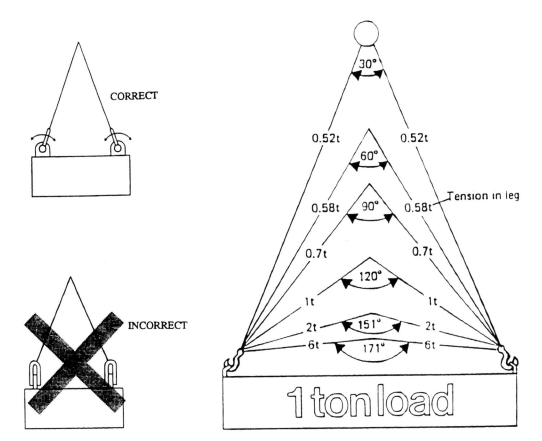

CORRECT

INCORRECT

30°

0.52t   0.52t

60°

0.58t   0.58t   Tension in leg

90°

0.7t   0.7t

120°

1t   1t

2t   151°   2t

6t   171°   6t

1 ton load

Correct & incorrect ways
to attach shackles to lugs.

Tension in angled legs.

(Source: L.E.E.A. COPSULE)

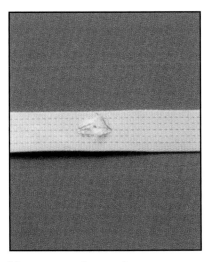

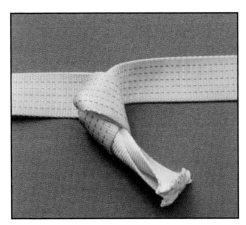

Never re-use damaged
or worn webbing.

Never use webbing
with a knot tied in it.

(Source: Spanset Ltd.)

***8

A container stowed with cargo with a high centre of gravity.
As the vehicle rounded a bend in the road the container and vehicle fell over.
Fortunately, no-one was injured.

Photograph: Courtesy of the "Yorkshire Post".

Plate J

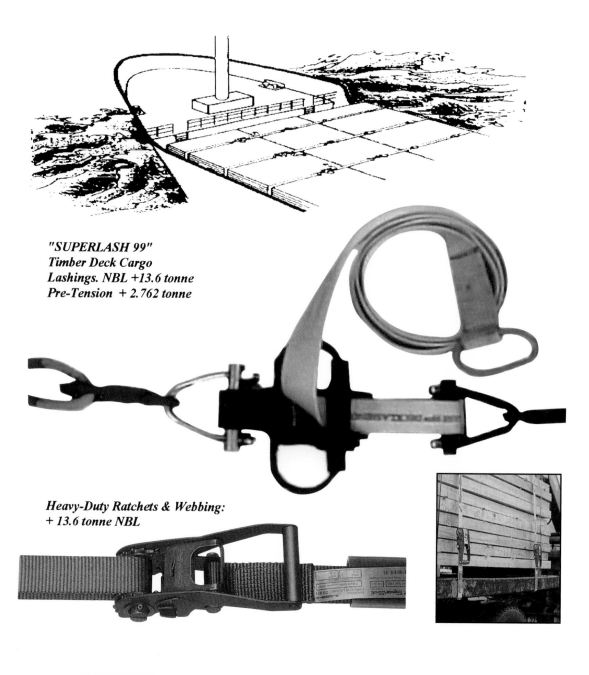

"SUPERLASH 99"
Timber Deck Cargo
Lashings. NBL +13.6 tonne
Pre-Tension + 2.762 tonne

Heavy-Duty Ratchets & Webbing:
+ 13.6 tonne NBL

Protective Sleeves

Numerous
Bolt-On Fittings:
10-tonne NBL

(Source: Cargo Safe SOE, Onsla & SpanSet, Cheshire)

Plate K

Entering port of refuge after loss of cargo from Nos. 2 & 3 Hatches.
Main deck plating torn open on port and starboard sides.
Correct and good-quality cross-lashings used at 3m pitch.
Uprights used instead of closing-down lashings to 1.5m pitch
where cargo height exceeded 4m.

(Photos: Maritech Services (Pty), Durban)

Plate L

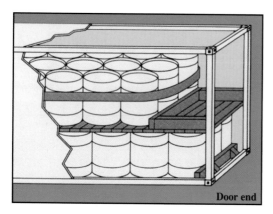

Drums, barrels, kegs, and the like, should be stowed upright, close together with a walkboard or ply-wood deck between each tier.

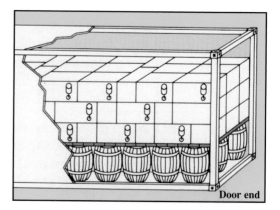

Wet goods should not be stowed with dry goods; but where this cannot be avoided the dry must be stowed above and separated by suitable decking.

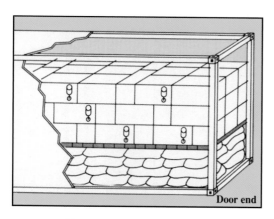

Heavy items must not be stowed on top of lightweight goods. The light-weight goods must overstow the heavy, with some form of suitable decking between.

Bagged cargo tends to shift during transport. Always take-up free door end space with adequate chocking braced off the strength member corner posts

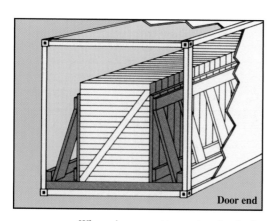

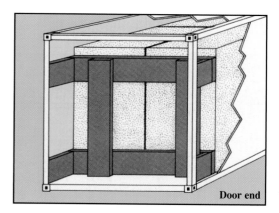

Where heavy units are involved, always ensure that side and/or end spaces are fully taken up with timber chocking and bracing. Don't leave things to chance.

(With acknowledgements and thanks to ScanDutch "STUFFING & STOWING")

Plate M

ADDENDUM No. 1

Conversion Factors

ADDENDUM No.1

CONVERSION FACTORS

LENGTH

To Convert	To	Multiply By
inches	millimetres	25.40
feet	millimetres	304.80
inches	centimetres	2.54
feet	centimetres	30.48
inches	metres	0.0254
feet	metres	0.3048* - Precisely - by definition.
feet	kilometres	0.0003048
miles (statute)	kilometres	1.609344
millimetres	inches	0.03937
millimetres	feet	0.00328084
centimetres	inches	0.3937
centimetres	feet	0.0328084
metres	inches	39.3701
metres	feet	3.28084
kilometres	feet	3280.84
kilometres	miles (statute)	0.6213712

(NOTE: The International Nautical Mile as accepted by the British Admiralty and most other nations is defined as 1852 metres (6076.12 feet). Hence, 1 knot - a unit of velocity - is defined as 1 nautical mile per hour, which equals 0.5144m/s (1.68781ft/s). A nautical mile in the traditional earlier British system was/is 6080 feet, but this converts to 1853.184m; so take care with these units if precision is required.)

12 inches	=	1 foot	10 millimetres	=	1 centimetre
3 feet	=	1 yard	10 centimetres	=	1 decimetre
6 feet	=	1 fathom	10 decimetres	=	1 metre
22 yards	=	1 chain	1000 millimetres	=	1 metre
10 chains	=	1 furlong	1000 metres	=	1 kilometre
8 furlongs	=	1 statute mile			

Multiplication Factors	Prefix	Symbol
1 000 000 000	giga	G
1 000 000	mega	M
1 000	kilo	k
100	hecto	h
10	deca	da
0.1	centi	c
0.001	milli	m
0.000 001	micro	μ
0.000 000 001	pico	p

AREA

To Convert	To	Multiply By
sq.inches (in^2)	sq.millimetres (mm^2)	645.1600
sq.feet (ft^2)	sq.millimetres (mm^2)	92903.0400
sq.inches (in^2)	sq.centimetres (cm^2)	6.4516
sq.feet (ft^2)	sq.centimetres (cm^2)	929.0304
sq.inches (in^2)	sq.metres (m^2)	6.4516 x 10^{-4}
sq.feet (ft^2)	sq.metres (m^2)	0.0929304 (1ft^2 = 144in^2)
sq.millimetres (mm^2)	sq.inches (in^2)	0.00155
sq.millimetres (mm^2)	sq.feet (ft^2)	1.076391 x 10^{-5}
sq.centimetres (cm^2)	sq.inches (in^2)	0.15500
sq.centimetres (cm^2)	sq.feet (ft^2)	0.0010764
sq.metres (m^2)	sq.inches (in^2)	1550.0031
sq.metres (m^2)	sq.feet (ft^2)	10.7639 (1m^2 = 1 000 000mm^2)

VOLUME

To Convert	To	Multiply By
cu.inches (in^3)	cu.millimetres (mm^3)	16387.064
cu.feet (ft^3)	cu.millimetres (mm^3)	28316846.59
cu.inches (in^3)	cu.centimetres (cm^3)	16.387064
cu.feet (ft^3)	cu.centimetres (cm^3)	28316.84659
cu.inches (in^3)	cu.metres (m^3)	1.638706 x 10^{-5}
cu.feet (ft^3)	cu.metres (m^3)	0.028317 (1ft^3 = 1728in^3)
cu.millimetres (mm^3)	cu.inches (in^3)	6.1024 x 10^{-5}
cu.millimetres (mm^3)	cu.feet (ft^3)	3.531467 x 10^{-8}
cu.centimetres (cm^3)	cu.inches (in^3)	0.06102337
cu.centimetres (cm^3)	cu.feet (ft^3)	3.5315 x 10^{-5}
cu.metres (m^3)	cu.inches (in^3)	61023.74409
cu.metres (m^3)	cu.feet (ft^3)	35.31467

(1m^3 = 1 000 000 000mm^3 - i.e. 10^{9}mm^3)

1 bushel (U.S.)	=	0.969 bushel (U.K.)
1 bushel (U.S.)	=	7.752 gallons (U.K.)
1 bushel (U.K.)	=	8 gallons (U.K.)
1 gallon (U.S.)	=	0.1337ft^3
1 gallon (U.S.)	=	0.8327 gallon (U.K.)
1 gallon (U.K.)	=	0.1605ft^3
*1 gallon (U.K.)	=	4.54609 litres = 0.00454609m^3

*(The U.K. gallon is defined precisely as 4.54609 cubic decimetres.)

WEIGHT

To Convert	To	Multiply By
pounds (lb)	kilograms (kg)	0.45359237* - Precisely - by definition.
pounds (lb)	tonnes (t)	$4.53359237 \times 10^{-4}$
tons	kilograms (kg)	0.0016047
tons	tonnes (t)	1.016047

(2240lb = 1 ton)
(2000lb = 1 short ton - U.S.)
(1 tonne (1000kg) = 0.9842 ton (U.K.) or 1.101 short ton - U.S.)

kilograms (kg) pounds (lb)		2.204623
tonnes (t) pounds (lb)		2204.623
kilograms (kg) tons		9.842065×10^{-4}
tonnes (t) tons		0.9842065

Weights & Volumes

$1cm^3$ = 10 x 10 x 10mm
$1cm^3$ of fresh water at sg 1.0 = 1 gram
$1000cm^3$ of fresh water at sg 1.0 = 1kg
$1m^3$ of fresh water at sg 1.0 = 1 tonne
$1m^3$ of salt water at sg 1.025 = 1.025 tonnes
1 tonne of salt water at sg 1.025 = $0.975m^3$

(NOTE: Although 1.025 is taken as the sg of salt water for general calculation purposes, it should be realised that oceanic water is more likely to be in the range 1.030 to 1.033 - try testing it for yourself!)

Force & Weight

Standard acceleration of gravity	g	=	$9.80665m/s^{-2}$ (9.807)
	g	=	$32.17405ft/s^{-2}$ (32.174)

1 Newton = 0.1019716 kgf
1 Newton = 0.22481 lbf

To Convert	To	Multiply By
kilograms force (kgf)	Newtons (N)	9.80665
Newtons (N)	kilograms force (kgf)	0.1019716
kilo Newtons (kN)	tonf	0.1003613
tons force (tonf)	kN	9.96402
tonnes force (tonnef)	kN	9.80665
kilo Newtons (kN)	tonnef	0.1019761
kilopondes (kp)	tonnef	0.001
tonnes force (tonnef)	kilopondes (kp)	1000.00

NOTE:　　　1 kiloponde (kp, overleaf) is the same as 1kgf, and 1kgf = 9.80665m/s^{-2}. Hence, 1000kp = 1 tonnef. For instance, 13600kp = 13.600 tonnef.

In some publications I have seen recently, the values given under the heading 'kp' are not 'kilo' pondes; rather, they are 'hecto' pondes, so take care. If the number shown does not produce a sensible number of tonnef, then the number shown may be short of a zero. For instance, a number given as 5432kp should equal 5.432 tonnef.

In some technical catalogues the symbol 'daN' is becoming more common in instances where the values would need to be shown with decimals if the more usual kN units were used. Just as kN means 1000's of newtons, so daN means 10's of newtons.

For quick approximate mental arithmetic:-

a.　　To convert kN to tonf - divide by 10.
b.　　To convert N to kgf - divide by 9.81.
c.　　To convert kp to tonnef - divide by 1000.
d.　　10 inches equals 254mm.
e.　　To convert m^3 to in^3 - multiply by 61000.
f.　　To convert m^2 to ft^2 - multiply by 10.8.
g.　　To convert ft^3 to m^3 - divide by 35.3.
h.　　To convert m^3 to ft^3 - multiply by 35.3.
i.　　To convert U.K. gallons to litres - multiply by 4.55.
j.　　To convert tons to tonnes - multiply by 1.016.
k.　　To convert kg to lb - multiply by 2.2.
l.　　One U.K. gallon equals 10 lb of fresh water.

Supplementary Units

The **radian** (rad) is the plane angle between two radii of a circle which cut off on the circumference an arc equal in length to the radius.

The **steradian** (sr) is the solid angle which, having its vertex in the centre of a sphere, cuts off an area of the surface of the sphere equal to that of a square with sides of equal length to the radius of the sphere.

Simple Hydraulic Testing

For every metre head of water standing in a double-bottom air pipe above the level of the tank-top plating the hydraulic pressure on the underside of the tank-top plating will be approximately 1 tonne/m², ie, if the vertical distance between the level of the tank-top plating and the overflow level of its air pipe at the weather-deck is 5 metres, then the hydraulic pressure on the underside of the tank-top plating will be 5 tonnes/m², approximately. (There is, of course, the matter of density and whether or not the water is fresh, brackish or salt, but the difference is not worth bothering about in this instance.)

****

ADDENDUM No. 2

Extract from L.E.E.A. Bulletin No.25
December 1991

ADDENDUM 2
L.E.E.A. BULLETIN No 25 - December 1991

Wire Rope Grip Terminations

The well publicised test programme into wire rope grips, undertaken by the HSE Research Laboratories, was completed in March of this year. This resulted in the immediate withdrawal of BS 462.

The long awaited report of the tests was introduced by Dr C Corden at a meeting held at BSI, London, in September. Several important points arise from the report and comments made by Dr Corden which must be considered and the following is a precis.

Initial Comments

In order to obtain a truly representative sample of grips, the HSE placed orders with various suppliers around the country specifying wire rope grips to BS 462: 1983. In fact none of the grips supplied complied with this standard and were generally found to be to the withdrawn 1958 version. As it was considered these represented the grips that were actually available, they were used for the tests.

The tests were mainly carried out on 16mm diameter wire rope with selective tests made on other sizes. The evidence is such that it can be concluded that similar results would be obtained for all sizes. Other patterns of wire rope grip, eg Crosby, Eureka etc, were tested to obtain comparative results. All tests were made on the same equipment and rigged by the same experienced, trained rigger to ensure consistent comparative results were obtained.

Details of the first series of tests, to establish when visible slip occurred are not given in the report as the results varied so much as to be meaningless. The subsequent, reported, tests were made using measuring equipment to determine microslip.

Torque

Although BS 462 did not give any recommendations for torque settings DIN 1142 and most manufacturers of proprietary grips do. It was found that, with the exception of DIN 1142 grips, it was either impossible or impracticable to tighten the nuts sufficiently in normal conditions. Indeed with some grips the recommended torque could not be attained with the grips clamped in a vice and an extended lever fitted to the spanner.

Efficiency

At the average practical torque the efficiency of BS 462 grips was found to be in the order of 20%-30%. When the torque was increased by restraining the grips in a vice the efficiency was improved to 40%-50%. These figures could be further improved by fitting 4 instead of the recommended 3 grips, but at a practical torque still only achieved efficiencies in the 30%-40% range. Of the other types of grip tested only the DIN 1142 attained an expected efficiency of approximately 80%.

Loss of Torque

It was found that when the grips are first fitted some loss of torque occurs. Although this is unexplained, bedding down of the wire and core is no doubt a factor. The tests show that in the early stages this loss is rapid but tends to stabilise after several days. Even so some loss still occurs after many weeks and seems to be ongoing. Grips fitted one day and left with no load applied were found to loosen overnight, when checked the following day a 50% loss of torque was measured in some cases.

Slip

The tests show that once slip occurs it is ongoing and, as with loss of torque, slip in the initial period is at a faster rate. After a period of time the rate of slip slows considerably, but never stops.

Fitting Method

The same experienced rigger was used throughout the test programme but to obtain some comparative results a few eyes were made by other riggers, all of whom were experienced and trained in fitting grips. The method of fitting and equipment used in the tests were the same and the torque settings checked so that for all practical purposes the eyes were identical. It was found that the eyes made by the rigger who was used for the main test programme had a far higher efficiency than the others. This surprising result implies that some latent variation in the fitting technique affects the result and that simply relying on the torque setting is not a reliable means of establishing if the fitting is satisfactory.

The DIN 1142 standard recommends that the thread of the clamp and nut should be greased prior to fitting. When this practice was applied to the BS 462 grips better results were achieved. This is probably explained as the applied torque acting on the gripping of the rope rather than being wasted in overcoming friction in the threads.

BS 462 recommended that grips should be spaced at six times the diameter of the rope. This was found to be correct. At this spacing the rope recovers its full diameter between each grip. If the grips are placed closer together the rope remains flattened to some degree as the result of the clamping action.

Rope Construction
The construction of the rope used has a considerable effect on the results. Eyes made with wire cored ropes gave far better results than those made with fibre cored ropes. Unfortunately the tests did not study this aspect in depth but the results also imply that ordinary lay ropes give better results than Lang's Lay. Better results were achieved when the tail end of the rope was served with soft wire. PVC tape and other means of binding the tail allow the rope to unlay, this also implies that preformed ropes would maintain their shape better than non-preformed ropes.

Galvanising
It was found that self colour (ie ungalvanised) grips gave better results than galvanised. Similarly if the rope was bright rather than galvanised the results improved.

Product Quality
It was generally considered that BS 462 grips were of poor quality. The threaded legs of the clamp were not parallel, holes in saddles were often such that the nuts pulled into them. The saddles on one of the proprietary grips were consistently radiused so that the nuts only made point contact. The threaded body and bolt arrangement of another proprietary grip was such that threads were readily stripped. The DIN 1142 grip was generally found to be of good quality, the clamp was well formed, holes were of an appropriate size and nuts with combined washer base ensure even tightening.

It was found that grips with grooved saddles performed less well than those with plain saddles. In no case did the rope sit in the grooves and as movement occurred there was a tendency for the grooves to wear, leading to some loss of torque and further slip.

Conclusions
The results of the tests heavily favour the DIN 1142 grip which consistently achieved the 80% efficiency expected for this type of termination. None of the other grips tested performed as expected.

The HSE report draws certain conclusions and makes recommendations on the use of wire rope grips. It recommends that only DIN 1142 should be used but points out that in Germany the standard prohibits their use in lifting applications. The report also points out that the cost of the termination is negligible to the overall cost of the assembly or value of the load. Whilst the initial cost of alternatives may seem higher the efficiency and subsequent maintenance cost savings far outweigh this as a consideration.

Combining the recommendations contained in the report with earlier LEEA advice it is recommended that the following should be observed:

(a)   Use of Grips
(1)   An alternative method of terminating the rope should always be sought. There are few, if any, lifting situations where other methods of forming eyes or terminating ropes cannot be used, eg ferrule secured, wedge sockets etc.

(2)   Where the use of wire rope grips cannot be avoided, use only DIN 1142 grips in conjunction with heart shaped thimbles. A lower grade DIN standard grip exists, care must therefore be taken to ensure only DIN 1142 grips are specified and used.

(3)   Do not use galvanised grips or galvanised wire rope; other plated finishes are acceptable.

(4)   Where possible use ordinary lay IWRC preformed ropes; avoid Lang's Lay.

(5)   Always serve the tail end of the rope with soft wire.

(6)   Follow the DIN 1142 recommendations with regard to the number of grips and torque values, eg in the case of 16mm diameter this is 4 grips with nuts torqued to 49Nm (36 1bf.ft).

(7)   Grease all threads and nut bearing surfaces before fitting.

(8)   Space the grips at centres of at least 6 times the diameter of the rope placing the first grip as close to the thimble as possible. The saddle of the grip should be in contact with the live part of the rope and the clamp bolt should sit on the free side of the rope.

(9)   Tighten the nuts in small increments alternating from nut to nut until the required torque is achieved. A record of the torque setting should be made for reference purposes.

(10)   Allow the rope and eye to settle for a period prior to service, overnight seems reasonable. Retorque to the original setting once the service load is hung on the rope. The nuts must then be retorqued after (i) 24 hours (ii) 7 days (iii) 1 month and (iv) at 6 monthly intervals thereafter. A record of each retorquing should be kept with the relevant certificates.

(b)   Existing Assemblies Which Utilise Grips
(1)   The overall condition of the termination should be checked to ensure the correct number of grips have been used and that they are correctly fitted and spaced. Examine the rope for broken wire paying particular attention to the area adjacent to the grips and ensure the free end of the tail is correctly served and maintains its shape and size.

(2)   Look for any visual signs of movement of the rope through the grips, ie slip. Check and if necessary reset the torque of all nuts. In this respect look for evidence of periodic retorquing by reference to records.

(3)   Users should be advised that the use of wire rope grips must be given careful consideration and inform them of the report from the HSE. Advise the user of alternative methods of terminating the rope which are suitable for the particular application. Where the circumstances are such that no alternative is possible, advise the user of the HSE reports recommendation that only grips to DIN 1142 should be used.

(c)   General

The above details have been included in this year's Correspondence Course, however all interested parties should be made aware of the report and the recommendations.

****

ADDENDUM No.3

Notice No.M.1264 of January 1987 - Navigation Bridge Visibility

NAVIGATION BRIDGE VISIBILITY

Notice to Merchant Ship Designers, Builders, Owners and Masters

1.   The Maritime Safety Committee of the International Maritime Organisation (IMO), at its Fifty-first Session, approved guidelines on navigation bridge visibility. The Department of Transport recommends that the guidelines, reproduced in the Annex to this Notice, should be followed within the Industry.

2.   Scope and Application

2.1   The guidelines have been developed to ensure that ships are designed with adequate visibility from those navigation bridges where bridge watches will be regularly maintained. Builders and designers of ships are urged to use the guidelines during the design process.

2.2   When ships of unusual design cannot comply with the guidelines, arrangements should be such that they provide a level of visibility as near as possible to the level recommended in the guidelines.

2.3   In existing ships, whilst structural alteration or addition of equipment will not be required, the application of paras 1.2 and 1.3 of the Annex is recommended as far as is practicable.

Department of Transport
Marine Directorate
Sunley House
90/93 High Holborn
London WC1V 6LP
January 1987

© Crown copyright 1987

GUIDELINES ON NAVIGATION BRIDGE VISIBILITY

1. Field of Vision

1.1   Every effort should be made to place the bridge above all other decked structures, not including funnels, which are on or above the freeboard deck.

1.2   The view of the sea surface from the conning position should not be obscured by more than two ship lengths, or 500 metres, whichever is less, forward of the bow to 10° on either side irrespective of the ship's draught, trim and deck cargo.

1.3   Blind sectors caused by cargo, cargo gear and other obstructions forward of the beam obstructing the view of the sea surface as seen from the conning position, should not exceed 10° each. The total arc of blind sectors should not exceed 20°. The clear sectors between blind sectors should be not less than 5°. However, in the view described in 1.2, each individual blind sector should not exceed 5°.

1.4   The height of the lower edge of the front windows above the deck should be kept as low as possible. In no case should the lower edge present an obstruction to the forward view as described in these guidelines.

1.5   The upper edge of the front windows should allow a forward view of the horizon, for a person with an eye height of 1800 mm, at the conning position when the ship is pitching in heaving seas.

1.6   The horizontal field of vision from the conning position should extend over an arc from more than 22·5° abaft the beam on one side, through forward, to more than 22·5° abaft the beam on the other side.

1.7   From each bridge wing the field of vision should extend over an arc from at least 45° on the opposite bow through dead ahead and then aft to 180° from dead ahead.

1.8   From the main steering position the field of vision should extend over an arc from dead ahead to at least 60° on each side.

1.9   The ship's side should be visible from the bridge wing.

2. Windows

2.1   Framing between windows should be kept to a minimum and not be installed immediately forward of any work station.

2.2   To help avoid reflections, the bridge front windows should be inclined from the vertical plane top out, at an angle of not less than 10° and not more than 25°.

2.3   Polarized and tinted windows should not be fitted.

2.4   A clear view through at least two of the front windows and, depending on the bridge configuration, an additional number of clear view windows, should be provided at all times regardless of weather conditions.

ADDENDUM No.4

**Department of Transport Merchant Shipping Notice No.M.1167
"Carriage Of Containers And Flats In Ships Not Designed Or
Modified For The Purpose"**

CARRIAGE OF CONTAINERS AND FLATS IN SHIPS NOT DESIGNED OR MODIFIED FOR THE PURPOSE

Notice to Shipowners, Masters and Deck Officers, Stevedores, Shippers and Packers of Containers and Flats

This Notice supersedes Notice No. M.624

1.   Shippers, Shipowners and Masters should be aware of the inherent dangers when containers and flats are carried in ships not specially constructed or effectively modified for the carriage of such cargo units, if they are not adequately secured against movement. Masters should satisfy themselves in this regard for all containers and flats, whether stowed on or below deck, before the ship leaves her berth. They should not accept units for loading which, from external inspection, they consider to be structurally unsafe, or large units which, if stowed athwartships, would result in an overhang of the ship's side.

2.   Containers carried on deck should be stowed one high only, preferably fore and aft, prevented from sliding athwartships and securely lashed against tipping. At no time should deck-loaded containers overstress the hatch covers or the hatchway structure. In cases of doubt details of stress limitations should be obtained from the Classification Society.

3.   Securing of containers and flats should be by means of chains, wires or other equally effective arrangements, in each case provided with means of tensioning. Deck fittings should be so located that there will always be a good lead for securing arrangements. It is not sufficient, however to ensure the security of the unit itself in the ship; particular regard should also be paid to the security of the cargo stowed on flats. Heavy metal products, vehicles and farm implements are some of the more difficult cargoes and there are particular problems with bulky cargoes stowed in polythene bags. It cannot be emphasised enough that it should never be assumed that cargo which has been loaded on flats at inland depots, and which may arrive at the port covered by tarpaulins, is adequately secured for a sea passage.

4.   It is particularly important that Masters obtain an accurate Cargo Stowage Plan showing the distribution of weights and in addition, details of the contents of any cargo units containing dangerous goods. It is also important that due regard be paid to prevailing, forecast, and anticipated weather conditions during the voyage.

5.   Further to paragraph 3, the attention of Shippers and Packers of containers and flats is drawn to the importance of ensuring that containers and flats are suitably packed for the type of voyage to be undertaken, and

if they contain dangerous goods that they are marked with the appropriate identification label. Guidance on packing is given in the IMO/ILO Guidelines for Packing of Cargo in Freight Containers and Vehicles. (MSC Circular 383)*

6. Satisfactory means in the form of guard rails, life lines, walkways or gangways, etc should be provided for the protection of the crew in getting to and from their quarters, the machinery space, and all other parts used in the necessary work of the ship. If fore and aft access cannot be gained on the deck because of inadequate width to the side of containers, safe and efficient access should be arranged over the top of the cargo.

7. The Merchant Shipping (Load Lines) (Deck Cargo) Regulations 1968 relate to the safe stowage of deck cargoes and the provision of safe access for the crew. Failure to observe the requirements under these Regulations renders a master liable to proceedings under the Merchant Shipping (Load Lines) Act 1967.

8. General guidance on the carriage of containers on deck is also given in Chapter 28 of the Code of Safe Working Practices for Merchant Seamen.

* Expected to be published in Spring 1985 and will be available from the International Maritime Organisation, 4 Albert Embankment, London SE1 7SR.

Department of Transport
Marine Directorate
London WC1V 6LP
March 1985

Dd 8820586 C14 4/85 Ed(224453)

ADDENDUM NO. 5

Tables of Break Loads, Proof Loads, SWL's & MSL's
For
Shackles, Soft Eyes, Etc.

ADDENDUM NO. 5

Tables Of Break Loads, Proof Loads, SWL's and MSL's
For Shackles, Chains, Soft Eyes In Wire, Etc.

D-Shackles - Small - Grade Scale 1: 2: 5, ie, Minimum Break Load = 100%

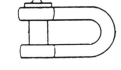

Proof Load = 40%
SWL = 20%
(MSL = 50%)

d = diameter of shackle pin.   w = inside width across jaw.

Size				Break Load		Proof Load		*SWL (WLL)	*MSL (50%)
inch		mm		kN	Tonnef	kN	Tonnef	Tonnef	
d	w	d	w						
¾	1	19.1	25.4	87	8.89	17.45	3.56	1.78	4.45
⅞	1¼	22.3	31.8	125	12.70	50.00	5.08	2.54	6.35
1	1⅜	25.4	35.0	175	17.80	70.00	7.12	3.56	8.90
1⅛	1½	28.6	38.0	224	22.85	89.63	9.14	4.57	11.43
1¼	1¾	31.8	44.5	288	29.40	115.33	11.76	5.88	14.70
1⅜	1⅞	35.0	47.6	349	35.55	139.45	14.22	7.11	17.77
1½	2⅛	38.0	54.0	369	40.65	159.46	16.26	8.13	20.32

D-Shackles - Large

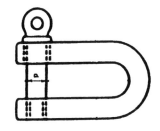

d = diameter of shackle pin.   w = inside width across jaw.

Size				Break Load		Proof Load		*SWL (WLL)	*MSL (50%)
inch		mm		kN	Tonnef	kN	Tonnef	Tonnef	
d	w	d	w						
¾	1¼	19.1	31.8		7.60		3.04	1.52	3.80
⅞	1½	22.3	38.0		10.15		4.06	2.03	5.08
1	1¾	25.4	44.5	Multiply tonnef by 9.80665	15.25	Multiply tonnef by 9.80665	6.10	3.05	7.62
1⅛	2	28.6	51.0		19.05		7.62	3.81	9.58
1¼	2⅛	31.8	54.1		25.40		10.16	5.08	12.70
1⅜	2⅜	35.0	60.3		30.50		12.20	6.10	15.25
1½	2⅝	38.0	66.7		35.55		14.22	7.11	17.78

Note: All values and conversions are approximate. If the SWL is not marked on the shackle, the Break Load and MSL shown above should be reduced by 20% i.e. multiply by 0.8.

Bow-Shackles - Small   - Grade Scale 1: 2: 5, ie, Minimum Break Load = 100%

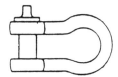

Proof Load = 40%
SWL = 20%
(MSL = 50%)

d = diameter of shackle pin.   w = inside width across jaw.

Size				Break Load		Proof Load		*SWL (WLL)	*MSL (50%)
inch		mm		kN	Tonnef	kN	Tonnef	Tonnef	
d	w	d	w						
⅝	⅞	15.9	22.3	Multiply tonnef by 9.80665	5.10	Multiply tonnef by 9.80665	2.04	1.02	2.55
¾	1⅛	19.1	28.6		7.60		3.04	1.52	3.80
⅞	1⅜	22.3	35.0		11.60		4.64	2.32	5.80
1	1½	25.4	38.0		15.25		6.10	3.05	7.63
1⅛	1¾	28.6	44.5		20.30		8.12	4.06	10.15
1¼	2	31.8	50.8		25.40		10.16	5.08	12.70
1⅜	2¼	35.0	57.0		31.75		12.70	6.35	15.88

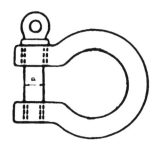

Bow-Shackles - Large

d = diameter of shackle pin.   w = inside width across jaw.

Size				Break Load		Proof Load		*SWL (WLL)	*MSL (50%)
inch		mm		kN	Tonnef	kN	Tonnef	Tonnef	
d	w	d	w						
¾	1⅛	19.1	28.6	Multiply tonnef by 9.80665	6.35	Multiply tonnef by 9.80665	2.54	1.27	3.18
⅞	1⅜	22.3	35.0		10.16		4.06	2.03	5.08
1	1⅝	25.4	41.3		13.40		5.58	2.79	6.70
1⅛	1¾	28.6	44.5		19.05		7.62	3.81	9.53
1¼	2	31.8	50.8		24.15		9.66	4.83	12.08
1⅜	2¼	35.0	57.0		29.20		11.68	5.84	14.60
1½	2½	38.0	63.5		36.85		14.74	7.37	18.43

Note: All values and conversions are approximate. If the SWL is not marked on the shackle, the Break Load and MSL shown above should be reduced by 20% i.e, multiply by 0.8.

Chain - Grade Scale 1:2:4 ie, Minimum Break Load = 100%, Proof Load = 50%,
SWL = 25%, (MSL = 50%)

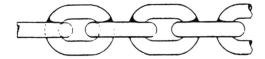

d = diameter of the bar forming the chain link

Nominal Size				Break Load		Proof Load		*SWL (WLL)	*MSL (50%)
inch		mm		kN	Tonnef	kN	Tonnef	Tonnef	
d	w	d	w						
		6.0		35.8	Multiply kN by 0.101976	17.9	Multiply kN by 0.101976	0.9	Multiply kN by 0.101976
		8.7		75		37.5		1.9	
		10.3		106		53.0		2.6	
		12.0		144		72.0		3.6	
		13.0		168		84.0		4.2	
		19.0		358		179		9.1	
		25.4		640		320		16.2	

Note: All values and conversions are approximate. Where SWL's are not known, take SWL for chain size, multiply by 4 for approximate break load, then divide by 2 to obtain MSL.

Small Wire Ropes *(Courtesy of Wood & Clark Ltd)*

	Nominal Diameter mm	Approximate Equivalent Diameter in	Approximate Weight kg/100m	Minimum Breaking Load/Force at 1770N/mm2	
				t	kN
6 x 7 (6/1) Fibre Core	2	5/64	1.38	0.24	2.35
	3	1/8	3.11	0.54	5.29
	4	5/32	5.54	0.96	9.40
	5	3/16	8.65	1.50	14.70
	6	1/4	12.50	2.16	21.20
	7	9/32	17.00	2.94	28.80
6 x 12 (12/F) Fibre Core	3	1/8	2.26	0.34	3.33
	4	5/32	4.02	0.60	5.92
	5	3/16	6.28	0.94	9.25
	6	1/4	9.04	1.36	13.30
	7	9/32	12.30	1.85	18.10
6 x 19 (12/6/1) Fibre Core	3	1/8	3.11	0.50	4.89
	4	5/32	5.54	0.89	8.69
	5	3/16	8.65	1.39	13.60
	6	1/4	12.50	2.00	19.60
	7	9/32	17.00	2.92	28.60
7 x 7 (6/1) Wire Strand Core	2	5/64	1.52	0.26	2.54
	3	1/8	3.43	0.58	5.72
	4	5/32	6.10	1.04	10.20
	5	3/16	9.53	1.62	15.90
	6	1/4	13.70	2.33	22.90
	7	9/32	18.70	3.17	31.10
7 x 19 (12/6/1) Wire Strand Core	3	1/8	3.43	0.58	5.77
	4	5/32	6.10	1.04	10.20
	5	3/16	9.52	1.63	16.00
	6	1/4	13.70	2.35	23.10
	7	9/32	18.70	3.20	31.40

Suggested Working Values for Soft Eyes in Wires made up properly with three (3) bulldog grips as shown.

Diameter (mm)	Construction Strands x Wires	NBL of Wire Tonnef	Slip Load (NBL) of Eye - Tonnef	MSL of Eye (50%)
8	6 x 12	1.94	1.36	0.60
8	6 x 24	2.60	1.82	0.91
12	6 x 19	6.42	4.49	2.25
16	6 x 12	7.75	5.43	2.72
16	6 x 19	11.40	7.98	3.99
16	6 x 24	10.40	7.28	3.64
18	6 x 12	9.80	6.86	3.43
18	6 x 24	13.20	9.24	4.62
20	6 x 19	17.80	12.46	6.23
20	6 x 24	16.20	11.34	5.67
22	6 x 19	21.60	15.12	7.56
22	6 x 24	19.70	13.79	6.90

(1 tonnef = 9.80665kN - see Addendum 1 - Conversion Factors)

****

Suggested Working Values for Half-Double Grommets in Wires made up properly with six (6) bulldog grips as shown.

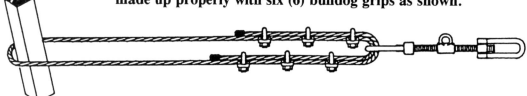

Diameter (mm)	Construction Strands x Wires	NBL of Wire Tonnef	Slip Load (NBL) of Grommet Tonnef	MSL of Grommet (50%) Tonnef
8	6 x 12	1.94	2.91	1.46
8	6 x 24	2.60	3.90	1.95
12	6 x 19	6.42	9.63	4.82
16	6 x 12	7.75	11.63	5.82
16	6 x 19	11.40	17.10	8.55
16	6 x 24	10.40	15.60	7.80
18	6 x 12	9.80	14.70	7.35
18	6 x 24	13.20	19.80	9.90
20	6 x 19	17.80	26.70	13.35
20	6 x 24	16.20	24.30	12.15
22	6 x 19	21.60	32.40	16.20
22	6 x 24	19.70	29.55	14.78

Suggested Working Values for Single Loops in Wires made up properly with six (6) bulldog grips as shown.

Diameter (mm)	Construction Strands x Wires	NBL of Wire Tonnef	Slip Load (NBL) Single Loop - Tonnef	MSL of Single Loop (50%) Tonnef
8	6 x 12	1.94	2.72	1.36
8	6 x 24	2.60	3.64	1.82
12	6 x 19	6.42	8.99	4.80
16	6 x 12	7.75	10.85	5.43
16	6 x 19	11.40	15.96	7.98
16	6 x 24	10.40	14.56	7.28
18	6 x 12	9.80	13.72	6.86
18	6 x 24	13.20	18.48	9.24
20	6 x 19	17.80	24.92	12.46
20	6 x 24	16.20	22.68	26.34
22	6 x 19	21.60	30.24	42.34
22	6 x 24	19.70	27.58	38.61

(1 tonnef = 9.80665kN - see Addendum 1 - Conversion Factors)

****

Weights Per Unit Volume For A Range Of Materials

Material	Weight in kilograms per cubic metre	Weight in pounds per cubic foot
Aluminium	2700	170
Brass	8500	530
Brick	2100	130
Coal	1450	90
Copper	8800	550
Concrete	2400	150
Earth	1600	100
Iron-steel	7700	480
Lead	11200	700
Magnesium	1750	110
Oil	800	50
Paper	1120	70
Water	1000	62
Wood	800	50

(Weights - Courtesy of L.E.E.A. COPSULE)

Rigging Screws, Straining Screws & Turnbuckles
(Courtesy of Wood & Clark Ltd.)

The data shown hereunder relate to Pattern No.25, of which the Rigging Screws on the facing page 193 are examples. To estimate the MSL:- starting from the far left screw dia. column, move to the right and take the lower of the numbers in the second column in from the right-hand side along the line of **the preferred** screw diameter. Divide that number by 1000, multiply by 4 and divide by 2 = MSL; this in keeping with the methods set out elsewhere herein. (However, for the same end result you can simply multiply by 2 the value in the kg column.)

For example: *Find the approximate MSL of a type No.25 rigging screw of which the screw diameter is 32mm.* The value in the kg column is 3810. Divide that by 1000, multiply by 4 and divide by 2 = 7.62 tonnes. (Alternatively, multiply 3810 by 2 = 7.62 tonnes.) The answers thus obtained are not necessarily precise, but they are near enough for cargo lashing purposes and they are a damn sight better than guessing!

SCREWS
Rigging Screws No.25 Pattern

IMPERIAL DIMENSIONS IN INCHES
METRIC DIMENSIONS IN MILLIMETRES

Dia. Screw A	B	C	D	E	F	G	H	I	J	K	Circ. Wire X	kg	Wt. Tons kg	SWL Cwts
1/4	4	5/16	1 1/2	7/8	3/16	3/16	7/8	3/8	11	8	3/4			2
6	102	8	38	22	4	4	22	10	280	203	19	.14	102	
5/16	5	5/16	1 1/2	7/8	1/4	1/4	1	1/2	12 7/8	9	3/4			3
8	127	8	38	22	6	6	25	12	327	229	19	.3	153	
3/8	6	3/8	1 3/4	1 1/4	5/16	5/16	19/16	5/8	15 1/8	10 5/8	7/8			7 1/2
10	153	10	45	33	8	8	39	16	384	270	22	.45	381	
1/2	9	9/16	2 1/2	1 5/8	3/8	3/8	1 5/8	3/4	22 3/8	15 1/4	1 1/8			10
12	229	15	64	41	10	10	42	19	568	387	28	1	508	
5/8	9	9/16	2 1/2	1 5/8	1/2	1/2	2 1/8	7/8	23 3/4	17 1/8	1 1/4			15
16	229	15	64	41	12	12	53	22	603	435	32	1.7	762	
3/4	9	3/4	2 3/4	2 1/8	5/8	5/8	2 5/8	7/8	23 7/8	17 1/2	1 1/2		1	2 1/2
20	229	19	69	53	16	16	66	22	606	445	38	2.7	1143	
7/8	12	7/8	3 1/4	2 3/8	5/8	3/4	3	1	30 3/8	21 1/2	1 3/4		1	12 1/2
22	305	22	82	60	16	19	75	25	771	546	44	4.5	1651	
1	14	7/8	3 3/4	2 3/4	3/4	7/8	3 1/8	1 1/4	35 3/4	25	2		2	2 1/2
26	356	22	95	70	19	22	80	32	908	635	51	5.9	2159	
1 1/8	14	1 1/8	3 7/8	2 15/16	3/4	7/8	3 3/16	1 1/4	35 1/8	25 1/4	2 1/4		2	15
28	356	28	100	75	19	22	81	32	892	641	57	7.3	2794	
1 1/4	15	1 1/8	4 5/8	3 3/8	7/8	1	3 5/8	1 3/8	38 1/8	27 1/2	2 1/2		3	15
32	381	28	118	85	22	26	92	35	968	699	63	9.6	3810	
1 3/8	15	1 5/16	5 1/2	4 1/8	1	1 1/8	4	1 1/2	38 1/4	28	2 3/4		4	5
35	381	33	141	105	25	28	100	38	971	711	70	12.3	4318	
1 1/2	16	1 5/16	5 1/2	4 1/8	1 1/8	1 1/4	4 1/4	1 5/8	41 7/8	31	3		5	2 1/2
39	406	33	141	105	28	33	108	41	1063	788	75	17.3	5207	
1 3/4	16	1 3/4	6 1/2	4 7/8	1 1/4	1 3/8	4 5/8	1 3/4	42 1/2	32 1/2	3 1/2		7	0
44	406	44	165	124	32	36	118	44	1080	826	90	24.1	7112	
2	16	2	7 1/4	5 1/2	1 1/2	1 5/8	5 7/8	2 1/4	45 1/8	35 3/8	4 1/2		9	5
51	406	51	184	141	38	42	149	57	1146	898	114	33.6	9398	
2 1/4	16	2 1/2	10 1/4	7 1/2	1 3/4	1 7/8	6 7/8	2 1/2	47 3/8	39	5 1/2		11	10
56	406	63	260	190	44	48	175	64	1201	991	141	51	11684	
2 1/2	16	2 7/8	10 3/8	6 1/2	1 7/8	2	7 5/8	2 3/4	46 7/8	39 1/4	6		15	0
64	406	72	263	165	48	51	194	70	1190	997	153	64	15240	
2 3/4	18	3 3/8	11 1/2	8 1/4	2 1/8	2 1/4	7	3 3/16	52 1/4	43 1/2	6 1/2		20	0
72	458	86	292	206	54	57	178	80	1327	1105	167	98	20320	
3	20	4	15 1/2	11 3/4	2 1/4	2 1/2	8 1/2	3 5/8	61 1/2	51 1/2	7 1/4		25	0
76	510	100	393	298	57	64	216	93	1563	1309	184	146	25400	
3 1/4	20	4	15 1/2	11 3/4	2 1/2	2 3/4	10 1/4	3 1/2	61 3/8	52 1/4	7 1/2		27	10
82	510	100	393	298	63	70	260	90	1557	1327	191	149	27940	
3 1/2	20	4	15 1/2	11 3/4	2 3/4	3	10 3/4	3 3/4	65 1/4	55	7 1/2		32	10
85	510	100	393	298	70	76	273	95	1657	1397	191	205	33020	
4	20	SIZES OF SHACKLES AND THIMBLES FOR THIS SIZE ARE											40	00
100	510	AVAILABLE UPON REQUEST											40640	

NOTE: Larger Sizes available on request   Screw threads, BSW, UNC, Metric or Acme

RIGGING SCREWS

(Courtesy Wood & Clark Ltd)

The rigging screws here illustrated relate mainly to Pattern No.25, the dimensions and data for which can be found on the facing page 192.

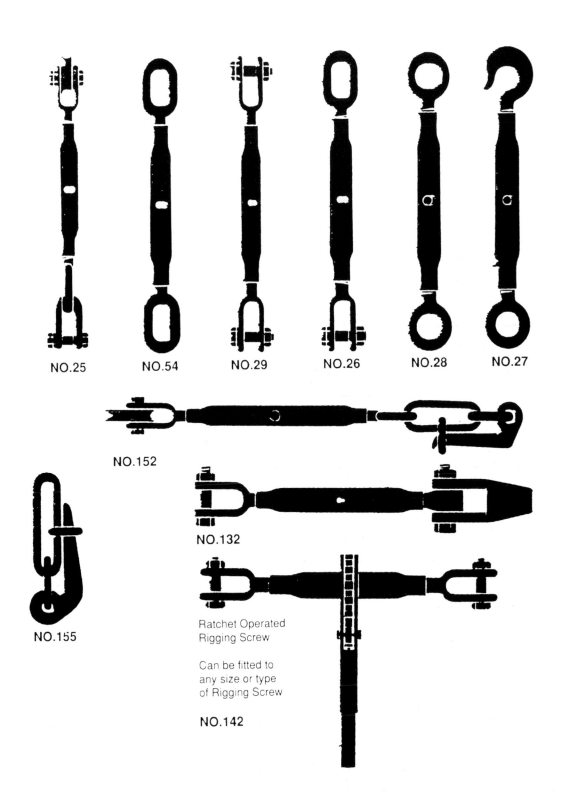

NO.25   NO.54   NO.29   NO.26   NO.28   NO.27

NO.152

NO.132

NO.155

Ratchet Operated
Rigging Screw

Can be fitted to
any size or type
of Rigging Screw

NO.142

Turnbuckles

(Courtesy Wood & Clark Ltd.)

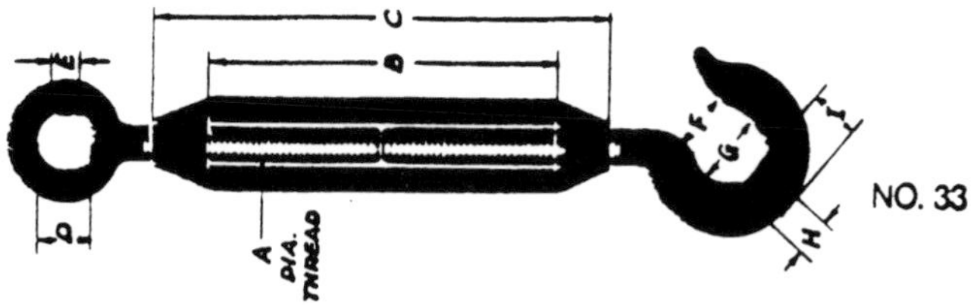

IMPERIAL DIMENSIONS IN INCHES
METRIC DIMENSIOINS IN MILLIMETRES

Dia. A	B	C	B	C	B	C	B	C	B	C	B	C	D	E	F	G	H	I	SWL Tons kg	Cwt
1/4	3	4											5/16	1/4	5/16	1/4	1/4	5/16		2
6	76	102											8	6	8	6	6	6	5	102
5/16	4	5											1/2	5/16	3/8	9/32	3/8	9/32		3
8	102	127											13	8	9	7	9	7	152	
3/8	4 1/2	5 7/8	6	7 1/4									9/16	3/8	19/32	5/8	13/32	3/4		7 1/2
10	115	150	152	185									14	9	14	16	11	19	381	
1/2	6	7 7/8	6 3/8	7 7/8	7 1/2	9	12	14					3/4	1/2	11/16	7/8	1/2	7/8		10
12	152	201	162	201	192	229	305	356					19	13	18	22	13	2	508	
5/8	6	8	8	10	9 1/2	12	12	14	13 1/4	15 1/2			15/16	9/16	1	1 1/8	5/8	1		15
16	152	203	203	254	242	305	305	356	336	394			24	14	25	28	16	25	762	
3/4	6	8 1/2	6 1/2	9	9 1/2	12	11 1/2	14 3/4	13 1/4	15 1/2	15	18	1 1/8	5/8	1	1 3/8	3/4	1 1/4	1	2 1/2
20	152	216	165	230	242	305	292	365	336	394	381	457	28	16	25	34	19	31	1143	
7/8	6	8 3/4	9	12	11 1/4	14	12 3/4	16	15	18	18	21	1 1/4	7/8	1 1/4	1 3/4	20/32	1 1/2	1	12 1/2
22	152	223	229	305	285	356	325	406	381	457	533	32	22	32	44	24	38	1651		
1	6	9	9	13	11 1/4	14	12 3/4	16	15	18	18	21	1 9/16	7/8	1 3/8	1 3/4	1 1/16	1 13/16	2	2 1/2
24	152	229	229	305	285	356	325	406	381	457	457	533	39	22	34	44	26	46	2159	
1 1/8	6	9 7/8	9	13 3/8	11 1/4	15	18	21 7/16					1 13/16	20/32	1 3/4	2 1/4	1 1/2	2 3/8	2	15
27	152	252	229	339	285	381	457	545					46	24	44	57	38	60	2794	
1 1/4	6	9 7/8	9	13 3/8	11 1/4	15	18	21 7/16					2	7/8	1 3/4	2 1/4	1 1/2	2 3/4	3	15
33	152	252	229	339	285	381	457	545					51	22	44	57	38	60	3810	

Straining Screws - BS 4429: 1987

NO. 183
Eye-to-eye type

No.185
Fork-to-fork type

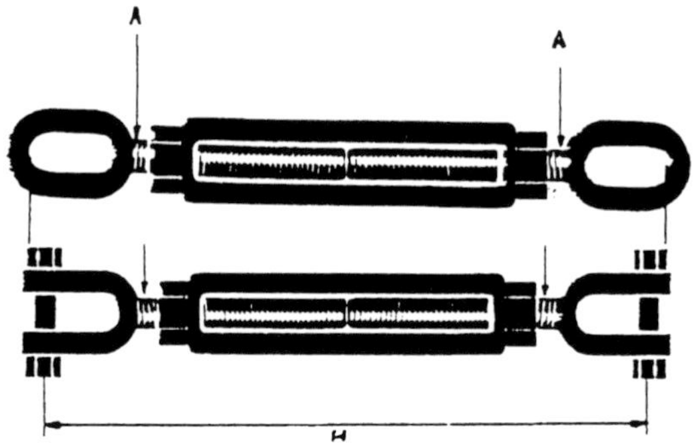

Size screw A	Open and closed dimensions (H) and safe working loads for turnbuckles												
	Dimension H												safe working load SWL
	Eye-to-eye (see figure 183)				Eye-to-fork (see figure 185)				Fork-to-fork (see figure 185)				
	Series no.1		Series no.2		Series no.1		Series no.2		Series no.1		Series no.2		Lifting purposes
	Closed	Open	Closed	Open	Closed	Open	Closed	Open	Closed	Open	Closed	Open	
mm	mm	mm	mm	mm	mm	mm	mm	mm	mm	mm	mm	mm	
8						Not available							-
10	252	370	284	434	241	359	273	423	230	348	262	412	300 kg
12	334	525	298	448	332	523	296	448	330	521	294	444	500 kg
16	372	550	342	492	371	549	341	491	370	548	340	490	750 kg
20	384	550	366	516	382	548	364	514	380	546	362	512	1.25 t
22	460	689	384	534	462	691	386	536	464	693	388	538	2t
24						Not available							-
27	534	807	412	562	532	806	410	560	530	803	408	558	3t
30	544	828	420	570	562	846	438	588	580	864	456	606	4t
33	596	870	472	622	602	876	478	628	608	882	484	634	5t

ADDENDUM NO. 6

Short Form For Draught/Cargo Weight Calculation

Short Form For Draught/ Cargo Weight Calculation

This "Short Form" does away with the need to measure "BUNKERS" (approximate values for known consumption and weights taken can be used) and does away with the need to assign any value to "CONSTANT". The Form will provide a relatively quick method of calculating the weight of cargo loaded/discharged at any stage during loading/discharging operations. It will not provide the data usually required of a full deadweight survey by charterers and/or shippers This Form was designed some years ago and is derived from work done by the author and others in the field too numerous to mention but fully acknowledged nonetheless.

Displacement

Ballast

Before   Before

After _____   After _____

                               Change _____   tonnes

_____ → +/-   tonnes

F. Water

Before

After _____

_____ → +/-   tonnes

Bunkers

F.O. Cons

D.O. Cons _____

_____ → -   tonnes

F.O. Taken

D.O. Taken _____

_____ → +   tonnes

**Algebraic Sum   +/- _____ →   _____   tonnes

Cargo Loaded/Discharged =   _____   tonnes

**NOTE: For Algebraic Sum - Follow the sign where cargo has been discharged.
                  Reverse the sign where cargo has been loaded.

---

*Displacement - from draughts and water densities read accurately - should be calculated by using the ship's plans, tables and hydrostatic data, and by whatever method with which the user is familiar and confident, including the relevant computer software for the ship, if available. In other circumstances the following lay-out is considered to be sufficiently accurate for the purposes here intended, **but it is not a short form.**

Much of the problem related to obtaining reasonably accurate draught survey/deadweight results arises from the difficulties often experienced in ascertaining reliable values for ballast - in a large vessel with a steep trim and ballast in tanks all over the place, for instance. The lay-out given here assumes that the vessel will not be in a steep trim, but will be in a trim adequately covered by the corrective tabular data available on board, and that accurate tank soundings will be taken and converted with care to the appropriate weights.

DRAUGHT/DISPLACEMENT/DEADWEIGHT LAY-OUT

Forward Draughts:

Port		metres
Starboard	_____	metres
Mean		metres
Perp. Correction	_____	metres
True Mean Forward	_____	metres

After Draughts:

Port		metres
Starboard	_____	metres
Mean		metres
Perp. Correction	_____	metres
True Mean Aft	_____	metres

Amidships Draughts:

Port		metres
Starboard	_____	metres
Mean		metres
Perp. Correction	_____	metres
True Mean Amidships	_____	metres

Apparent Trim at Perpendiculars   =   metres by (head) or (stern)

Mean of Means Draught   = $\dfrac{\text{FORWARD} + \text{AFT} + (6' \times \text{AMIDSHIPS})}{8}$

(Fine lined vessel)'

= $\dfrac{\underline{\quad\quad} + \underline{\quad\quad} + (6' \times \underline{\quad\quad})}{8}$

Mean of Means Draught   =   metres

Mean of Means Draught

(Full-form & box-shaped vessels)''   = $\dfrac{\text{FORWARD} + \text{AFT} + (4'' \times \text{AMIDSHIPS})}{6}$

See NOTE hereunder.

Note: Use formula ' for fine-lined vessels. Use formula '' for full-form and box-shaped vessels.

From Hydrostatic Tables:

Displacement at   metres draught =   tonnes **(1)**

Trim Correction:

       Trim =   metres (cms) by (head) or (stern)

       LCF =   metres aft of amidships

       MCT =   tonnes metres

       TPC =   tonnes

* MCT (1) at draught metres =   tonnes metres

                 ~

\+ MCT (2) at draught metres =   _____ tonnes metres

           Dm/DZ =   _____ (difference between * and +)

[* MCT (1) at draught 0.5m greater than mean of mean]

[+ MCT (2) at draught 0.5m less than mean of mean]

Correction for Trim   = [*Trim (cms) x LCF x TPC] + [**(Trim (m))^2 x 50 x Dm/DZ]

                         LBP   LBP

         = [____ x ____] + [____ ^{2} x 50 x ____]

         =   [   ]   +   [   ]

         =   tonnes **(2)**

If LCF is same direction from amidships as deepest draught, then add*.

If LCF is opposite direction from amidships, then subtract*.

Portion of equation marked ** is always added.

List Correction:

** TPC at port draught ** (DP)   (metres)   =   tonnes

* TPC at starboard draught * (DS)   (_____ metres)   =   _____ tonnes

      Difference   _____ metres   =   _____ tonnes

      Correction for List   = 6 x (TPC* ~ TPC**) x (DP ~ DS)

                   = 6 x (~   ) x (~)

                   =   tonnes **(3)**   -   always added - if any.

Corrected Displacement:

(1)   Displacement at mean of means draught =   tonnes

(2)   Trim correction   =   tonnes

(3)   List correction + (if any)   =   _____ tonnes

                  Corrected Displacement   =   _____ tonnes

Density Correction:

Confirmed Dock Water Density =   kg/m^3

Dock Water Displacement

$$= \frac{\text{Corrected Displacement x Dock Water Density}}{1025}$$

$$= \frac{\underline{\hspace{3cm}} \; x \; \underline{\hspace{3cm}}}{1025}$$

∴ Dock Water Displacement   =   _____ tonnes

Dock Water Displacement   tonnes

Lightship   _____ tonnes

Deadweight   _____ tonnes (dw) - See below

###

If, from here onwards, you wish to complete a full "Cargo" survey, you can follow the route hereunder:-

Known Weights:

     Heavy Fuel Oil   tonnes

     Diesel Oil   tonnes

     Fresh Water   tonnes

     Water Ballast   _____ tonnes

     Total Known Weights   _____ tonnes

     Deadweight (dw)   tonnes

     Known Weights   _____ tonnes

     Constant (plus Cargo) _____ tonnes (a)

NOTE: If survey is commencing before any cargo is loaded, or after all cargo has been discharged, the answer at (a), above, will be the "Constant" (i.e. "other non-cargo"), and the value for "Constant" may be applied to the subsequent "Cargo" calculation with some reasonable measure of acceptable reality, ie -----

```
-----    Cargo Plus Constant    =        W + w

                 Constant    =            - w

                    Cargo    =          W
```

If the survey is commencing before any cargo is discharged, or after all cargo has been loaded, the answer at (a), on the previous page, will be "Constant plus Cargo". In such event, the "Cargo" part cannot be separated accurately until the "Constant" is known. If the "Constant" has been ascertained before cargo loading commenced, then there is no problem in separating "Constant" from "Cargo", as indicated in the specimen layout shown immediately above.

If the vessel is newly-arrived and loaded, the "Constant" cannot be ascertained accurately until the cargo has been discharged. However, if everyone is pressing for some idea of the "Cargo" weight before discharge commences (as they will), then use a "Constant (about)" figure taken from (i) the load-port survey (hopefully); (ii) the ship's previous documents; or (iii) the master's best guess, ie:-

```
Cargo Plus Constant    =        W + w (?)
    Constant (about)    =            - w (?)
       Cargo (about)    =          W (?)
```

Additionally, there may be instances where other items require some aspect of separation, such as deck cargo, timber deck cargo, containers on deck, and/or general items, so as to arrive at a weight for bulk cargo or steel slabs, or some such. In which event you can do no more than assess the individual weights and apply them, i.e:-

```
        Constant (about)        =               tonnes
        Containers (manifested) =               tonnes

        Timber (manifested)     =               tonnes

        Generals (manifested)   =               tonnes
                                   _____
                  Total         =               tonnes

Cargo plus Constant (a)         =    -          tonnes
                                   _____
Wt. Of Other Cargo (about)      =               tonnes
```

****

Don't allow any of the full Lay-out in the previous pages discourage you from using the Short Form. The Short Form, however, does require you to obtain an accurate Displacement value, and if you can do that the Short Form may well produce a more accurate "CARGO" weight result, providing no-one is interested in the true weight of Bunkers on board (so the Chief Engineer wont need to try and hide those 163 tonnes of fuel oil he's "got up his sleeve") and no-one is interested in ascertaining the true weight of that elusive Constant.

GOOD LUCK & BON VOYAGE

****

INDEX

- o -